Louis

The Louis Armstrong Story
1900-1971

Max Jones & John Chilton

A DA CAPO PAPERBACK

W9-CYG-636

Library of Congress Cataloging in Publication Data

Jones, Max.
  Louis, the Louis Armstrong story, 1900-1971.

  Reprint. Originally published: London,
1971. With new pref.
  Includes index.
  1. Armstrong, Louis, 1900-1971. 2. Jazz
musicians — United States — Biography.
I. Chilton, John, 1931 or 2-   . II. Title.
ML419.A75J625   1988   785.42′092′4 [B]   88-1195
ISBN 0-306-80322-6 (pbk.)

This Da Capo Press paperback edition of *Louis: The Louis Armstrong Story
1900-1971* is an unabridged republication of the edition published in London
in 1971, here supplemented with a new preface by Dan Morgenstern. It is
reprinted by arrangement with the authors.

Published by Da Capo Press, Inc.
A Subsidiary of Plenum Publishing Corporation
233 Spring Street, New York, N.Y. 10013

Louis

The Louis Armstrong Story
1900-1971

The authors, MAX JONES and JOHN
CHILTON, are both highly regarded in jazz
circles. Max Jones is well-known through
his work for *Melody Maker* and his frequent
radio broadcasts since 1944. John Chilton
is himself a distinguished trumpeter, the
author of *Who's Who of Jazz* and *Billie's
Blues*, a new biography of Billie Holiday.
Together they have recently completed a ten-
week series of hour-long radio programmes
under the title 'Satchmo – the story of
Louis Armstrong'.

This biography, though the product of hard
research over a twenty-year period, is in
essence a labour of love. It owes a
considerable debt to the enthusiastic
assistance of Louis Armstrong himself who
contributed dozens of tape recordings and
numerous letters written in his inimitable
style.

PREFACE TO THE DA CAPO EDITION

Max Jones and John Chilton got to Louis Armstrong just in time. Though he did not live to see this warm and illuminating tribute, the co-authors enjoyed his full and active collaboration, and it's no slight to them to note that the lengthy passages in Louis' own words are highlights of the book.

At this late point in his life, Louis was willing to discuss things for the record that he'd previously kept to himself and a few close friends and associates, as he does so charmingly in the chapter called "Days of the Vipers." It's not only revelatory, but also beautifully told, proving once again that this remarkable man, who hadn't finished fifth grade, was a writer to the manner born.

Of course he didn't tell it all. Like all public men, he had a keen sense of discretion. But some day we may learn more: Louis once told me that he hadn't stopped work on his autobiography with the first volume (*Satchmo: My Life in New Orleans,* recently reprinted by Da Capo Press, and required reading). "I've been writing it all down, and I mean *all,*" he said, adding that he well knew it could not be published during his lifetime. Now that a Louis Armstrong Archive, based on the treasure trove of materials that had been resting (undisturbed, one hopes) at his landmarked house in Corona, has been established at Queens College, we shall learn if his manuscript has survived.

Meanwhile, there is a lot to learn from this book, which has its origin in a much shorter work, *Salute to Satchmo,* published in 1970 as a birthday present to its subject by the *Melody Maker,* the pioneering British music periodical that had played an important role in Louis' first visit to Europe in 1932. For this project, Jones and Chilton collaborated with Leonard Feather. It's sad that Louis didn't get to see the finished portrait, but he clearly liked the sketch.

Jones, a veteran British jazz writer with a talent for making friends with the artists he met and interviewed, had Louis' trust, and Chilton, who'd already established himself as a first-rate researcher with his *Who's Who in Jazz: From Storyville to Swing Street* (the fourth, expanded edition is published by Da Capo), is a fine trumpeter—the best credential anyone could present to Satchmo. No wonder he was inspired to take some riveting choruses himself along the way, augmented by letters and quotes from interviews that are much more than decorative riffs.

Chilton's survey of the Armstrong legacy on records is a first-rate job, not least because it is free from any dichotomy between "artistic" and "commercial," a peculiar prejudice that has afflicted even some of Louis' greatest admirers. Tellingly, Jones falls victim to it when he summarizes a list of tunes including classic Harold Arlen and Hoagy Carmichael works as "among the innocuous Tin Pan Alley creations" recorded by Armstrong. In this post-rock era, most sensible people have come around to recognize that the oft-maligned Alley produced much gold and silver as well as disposable alloys. The fact that Armstrong was the first jazz artist to demonstrate what a great player and singer could do with a great song (in the process launching many an "evergreen") is but another of the countless contributions he made to the growth of jazz.

It is sobering to realize that we have arrived at a point in jazz history when many among us, ranging from young adults to little kids, have never seen Louis Armstrong in the flesh, and may not even be instantly able to identify that voice, that face, that smile. Our time consumes images and sounds, live and recorded, at such a pace that Louis' presence is no longer a given. Yet our audio-visual technology does insure some aspects of immortality, and Louis is still very much with us.

It's been said that those who only know the Armstrong seen and heard in his later years could form no clear conception of the revolutionary and revelatory impact he'd made on jazz. But if they had ears, couldn't they hear what that horn and that voice still had to say: that Louis Armstrong and jazz are synonymous?

And if the full implications of that truth aren't always evident to newcomers, they can listen to what the musicians have to say. Miles Davis will tell them that nothing can be played on a horn that Louis hasn't already played. Wynton Marsalis, who has already listened, tells them to listen too, pointing out that "study is the only protection against folly." (Those who think Wynton doesn't mean what he says because, to them, he doesn't sound like Louis when he plays, haven't understood that one of the key lessons in the Armstrong Book of Jazz is that knowledge leads to freedom.)

Or let them listen to Gil Evans, in 1987: "The first record I ever bought was Armstrong's "No One Else But You." After that I bought every Armstrong record that came out — every one — from 1927 to 1935.... I really learned music from Louis Armstrong. As far as how to handle a song and how to love music. I learned from him."

And here's Bud Freeman, who also was there from the start, listening to a 1942 Jimmie Lunceford record on a blindfold test for *Down Beat* in 1986: "It was all Louis. That arrangement was all taken from Louis Armstrong phrases. Louis created every bar in that thing."

Amen. The plain truth is that Louis Armstrong created the language of jazz. It is a marvelously flexible and expandable language that can be spoken in ever so many accents, and as long as it is spoken as a living tongue, it will refer back to its creator.

We can learn about the man who did all that from this book, the man who at the end of his life could say: "I never want to be anything more than I am; what I don't have I don't need. I'm satisfied with my work — I play music. You call it what you want to; I don't try to prove nothing."

Not trying to prove anything, Louis Armstrong proved all, and no one could aspire to be anything more than he was.

Read the book, then go to the music. As the old song has it, it's right here for you — and for always.

— DAN MORGENSTERN

New York City, December, 1987

(Dan Morgenstern is Director of the Institute of Jazz Studies at Rutgers University.)

Contents

Letter from Louis   15

Ambassador of Jazz   21

Playing That Lead   34

Creole Brothers   42

Everybody from New Orleans Can Do That Thing   64

Miss Lil   76

Big Apple and Back   92

Just Glad to Play   106

Days of the Vipers   125

Sweet Sunny South   139

Louis in Britain   157

Louis the European   172

Swing That Music   188

Going Back Home   199

Arkansas and Africa   203

'Louisiana' – 1: The Man   213

'Louisiana' – 2: The Legends   224

Satchmo Says   232

Louis on Record   247

Travellin' Man   287

Film List   294

Index   297

For
Lucille Armstrong

This book would never have been attempted without the helping hand of the genius, Louis Armstrong. Besides being the greatest of all jazz musicians he was also a remarkably warm-hearted and unaffected man.

It is because of Louis Armstrong, more than any other single musician, that jazz has been accepted throughout the world, yet fame and fortune never diminished his honesty. During our researches he seldom shunned a question; nor did he tailor his answers to fit an image.

We will always treasure his friendliness, and be ever grateful for his priceless co-operation.

London, 1971

Since Louis Armstrong's Death several of his friends have provided us with new information which has been included in this edition.

MAX JONES and JOHN CHILTON

London, 1975

Acknowledgements

The Authors would like to express their gratitude to the following for their advice and guidance: Jeff Aldam, Steve Allen (and the British Broadcasting Corporation), Walter C. Allen, Ernie Anderson, Lillian Armstrong, Lucille Armstrong, Jeff Atterton, Yannick Bruynoghe, Beryl Bryden, Joe Bushkin, Lionel Crane (of the *Sunday Mirror*), Doug Dobell, Leonard Feather, Charles Fox, Nat Gonella, Sidney Gross, Geoffrey Haydon (and the British Broadcasting Corporation), Jack Hutton, Dan Ingman, Eric Keartland, John Kendall, Albert McCarthy, Ira Mangel, Dan Morgenstern, Hugues Panassié, Brian and Linda Peerless, Denis Preston, Johnny Simmen, Ernest R. Smith, Keith Smith, Sinclair Traill, Alan Walsh, Valerie Wilmer, Laurie Wright, and Ray Coleman for allowing the authors complete freedom to consult the *Melody Maker* files.

Publications consulted: *Melody Maker, Down Beat, Metronome, Record Changer, Jazz Review, The Jazz Record, Bulletin du Hot Club de France, Coda, Life, International Times, Crescendo, Storyville, Jazz Journal.*

Books: *Swing That Music* by Louis Armstrong (Longmans, Green, 1937); *Satchmo – My Life In New Orleans* by Louis Armstrong (Peter Davies, 1955); *King Joe Oliver* by Walter C. Allen and Brian Rust (Sidgwick & Jackson, 1958); *Horn Of Plenty* by Robert Goffin (Allen, Towne & Heath, 1947); *Jazz: New Orleans, 1885–1963* by Samuel B. Charters (Oak Publications, 1963); *New Orleans Jazz, A Family Album* by Al Rose and Edmond Souchon (Louisiana State University Press, 1967); *Jazz Masters Of New*

11

Orleans by Martin Williams (Macmillan, 1967); *Jazz Masters Of The 20's* by Richard Hadlock (Macmillan, 1965); *Louis Armstrong* by Albert J. McCarthy (Cassell, 1960); *Second Chorus* by Humphrey Lyttelton (MacGibbon & Kee, 1958); *Early Jazz* by Gunther Schuller (Oxford University Press, 1968); *Louis Armstrong* by Hugues Panassié (Nouvelles Editions Latines, 1969); *This Is Jazz* by Ken Williamson (Newnes, 1960); *Jazzmen* by F. Ramsey and C. E. Smith (Sidgwick & Jackson, 1957); *Really The Blues* by Mezz Mezzrow (Random House, 1946); *Music In A New Found Land* by Wilfrid Mellers (Barrie & Rockliff, 1964); *Serious Music – And All That Jazz* by Henry Pleasants (Gollancz, 1961); *Jazz from the Congo to the Metropolitan* by Robert Goffin (Doubleday, New York, 1944).

List of Illustrations

The street in which Louis was born (*Edmond Souchon collection, courtesy Sinclair Traill*)
Lulu White's Mahogany Hall (*Max Jones collection*)
Family group in New Orleans, 1919 or 1920 (*courtesy Louis Armstrong*)
Satchmo, as he looked on his 1932 visit to Britain (*Melody Maker files*)
Fate Marable and his Riverboat Orchestra (*Melody Maker files*)
The Original Dixieland Jazz Band in London (*courtesy the Record Changer*)
Louis with Jack Hylton and orchestra (*Max Jones collection*)
Creole Jazz Band
Ory's Original Creole Jazz Band (*courtesy US Information Service*)
Erskine Tate's Vendome Orchestra
Armstrong's Hot Five in 1926
Louis with Johnny Collins and bandleader Henry Hall (*Melody Maker files*)
Freddie Keppard, an early photograph
Pianist–arranger–bandleader Fletcher Henderson
Les Hite's band, Hollywood 1930
On Parade: Kid Shots Madison and Bunk Johnson (*courtesy Bill Russell*)
Preston Jackson (*courtesy John Steiner*)
Henry Red Allen (*photo: Teresa Chilton*)
Louis Armstrong and his orchestra, 1936/7 (*courtesy Joe Glaser*)
The Armstrong–Russell band's rhythm section (*courtesy Joe Glaser*)
Melody Maker get-together with American bandleader–arranger Benny Carter in London, 1936

Coleman Hawkins in London, 1934
Albert Nicholas, New Orleans-born clarinettist (*photo: Hans Harzheim*)
Hines, Teagarden, Cozy Cole, Barney Bigard, Arvell Shaw (*Melody Maker files*)
Louis at the piano (*Melody Maker files*)
Louis in London – between chores (*photo: Valerie Wilmer*)
Louis in London – at work
Louis (*photo: Bill Francis*)
John Chilton with altoman Bruce Turner and visiting celebrity Bill Coleman (*photo: Harry Diamond*)
Max Jones greeting Louis at Victoria Station during early 60s
Louis and his second wife, Lil (*photo: courtesy Melody Maker*)
Ghana welcomes the All Stars in 1956 (*courtesy Volta River Project Publicity*)
'Rocking Chair' . . . sung by Louis and Trummy Young (*photo: Bengt Malmqvist, courtesy Melody Maker*)
Joe Glaser, Louis' manager (*Melody Maker files*)
Louis sings at a Humphrey Lyttelton Club party (*photo: Gilbert Gaster, courtesy Melody Maker*)
Warming up (*photo: Bengt Malmqvist, courtesy Melody Maker*)
Louis sings in concert
Louis in pensive mood (*photo: Jan Persson*)
Louis with Bing Crosby, recording 'Pennies from Heaven', 1936 (*Max Jones collection*)
Mr and Mrs (Lucille) Armstrong, on tour, arrive in Sweden (*photo: Bengt Malmqvist, courtesy Melody Maker*)
Trombone team: Kid Ory and Dicky Wells (*photo: Terry Cryer, courtesy Melody Maker*)
Pops off-stage (*photo: Valerie Wilmer*)
Louis disciples: Nat Gonella and Humphrey Lyttelton
Ernie Anderson and Artie Shaw
Louis' funeral, 9 July 1971 (*photo: David Redfern*)
Autographed photo of Louis

Letter from Louis

Dear Max,

I was glad to hear about the book and hope to enjoy it, the same as anything that you should write. I am feeling very good these days and so is Lucille. I am gradually going back to work, doing little odd jobs, and warming up – few hours per day – so everything is shaping up real beautiful. No rush. Just like the title of my new recording, *We Have All The Time In The World*.

You speak of my home town, New Orleans, and I don't want ever to forget those days. Just imagine me in those wonderful times (around 1915) when I was just a kid listening to Joe (King) Oliver, my idol, and Emmanuel Perez, a fine trumpet man, and old Bunk Johnson who was very good also.

Now I must tell you that my whole life has been happiness. Through all of the misfortunes, etc, I did not plan anything. Life was there for me and I accepted it. And life, what ever came out, has been beautiful to me, and I love everybody.

Even in the jails, in the old days in New Orleans, I had loads of fans. One morning, on my way to court, the prisoners raked pans on their cell bars and applauded so thunderously, saying 'Louie ... Louie Armstrong,' until the guy who was taking me to court said: 'Who are you, anyway?' I said to him, 'Oh, just one of the cats.' And that's how it has always been.

I am now playing the album of the Town Hall concert on to my tape recorder, just as I tape all of my old recordings. So's I can have them for my Grand Children to listen to. I

15

am not taking any chances on these records lasting, because somebody might sit on them, and all they will say (in excuse) is 'Oh I am sorry.' Humm. I know within myself that if I record them on tape and index them (my system) they will be here for ever. Even after I am dead and buried. 'Ya dig?'

Speaking of Storyville, well, I was born in what they called the poor man's Storyville. Of course it was later on they changed the name to that, after a man called Story. But it was always the Red Light District, or just District, to me. And will be in my memory the rest of my life. It knocked me out when you mentioned Freddie Keppard, Baby Dodds, Fate Marable, all fine cats in the early days of music.

Now I am listening to the Concert we recorded at the Symphony Hall in Boston, thinking about my All Stars band. Billy Berg['s] in Hollywood was the club where that was formed. Big Sid, Arvell Shaw, Barney Bigard and that white boy [that] plays trumpet but was on piano with me. That's before Earl Hines came in. This piano player is very good. He's on that Symphony Hall album. And then Jack Teagarden joined me there, and of course Velma came right along with us as vocalist. What a smile that big gal had. And then there was me there. Great band. They were really something 'else'. I'll never forget it. We were making the picture, *A Song Is Born* with Danny Kaye, when that band happened.

Now to London and my first visit which I shall also remember the whole of my life. All of those fine English cats gave a big party for me my first day in. T'was a bitch wasn't it? Yes, Johnny Collins was my manager at that time. I don't know where he is now. You must understand I did not get real happy until I got with my man – my dearest friend – Joe Glaser (yea man). Nobody will ever touch that man in my books. I can go all night and all day talking about that man.

When I left New Orleans to go up north in 1922 the toughest Negro down there – his name is Slippers – he gave me a pep talk (in his way) expressing it from his heart. Tough character – feared nobody, but he also had a soul for my music which he heard every night in the honky tonk where he worked when I was about 17. He loved the way I played those Blues. He was the bouncer of the joint, and whenever something went wrong, which was often, you had Slippers shooting them in their asses every time they'd get out of line.

But tough as he was he always looked after me, and he was very fast with his gun. When he found out that I was leaving to go to Chicago, he was the first one to congratulate me. And while he shook my hand, here are the words that he said, which I shall remember 'til the day I die. As he shook my hand he said 'I love the way that you blow that Quail.' Of course he meant the cornet. Of course I dugged him because I was interested in him, and I knew he would have said cornet if he knew to call it by that name. He always called it a Quail.

By my being raised up in that place at that time I spent all my young days around those whores and pimps and gambling fellers and some of the baddest people that was ever born. And there were some bad cats came from what we called the Swamp, known to carry a big Forty Five under their jacket and will shoot it at the drop of the hat. Slippers was a bad M-F (Mother for you) but dropped everything when he learned I was leaving them and the Honky Tonk. He came right over to me and said 'When you go up north, Dipper, be sure and get yourself a white man that will put his hand on your shoulder and say "This is my nigger".' Those were his exact words.

He was a crude sonofabitch but he loved me and my music. And he was right then because the white man was Joe Glaser. Dig, Gate? Those people down there when I was a youngster, they didn't have too much education. But they were sincere! Those are the kind of people whom I was raised around and came up without a scratch, and I am so proud until nothing else matters.

With me it's to each his own. People can have what they

want – do what they want in life – that's their business. But those people in my neighbourhood instilled in me one thing: that I will run into a lot of phony and dog-ass people in this world, which I did. That is why I shall always remember them and, in my mind, rate them tops over every other ass. Yea.

Now about the questions that you asked me about. Of course there is a whole lots I probably have forgotten. But for you, Daddy, I will do my damdest (my best). You are my boy. So here goes. Anything that I have no recollections of . . . just forget it and throw it out of your cotton-pickin' mind. P.S. Just a cute little expression of ours over here 'Tee Hee'. Maybe some of the questions are not so important anyway. As for me, if I tell you that a Hen Dip Snuff, you just look under her wings and you'll find a whole can full. Meaning that I don't waste words either. Wow.

Yes, Max, you can use any material that you wish pertaining to me and the things that I foresaid, etc, it is OK. I don't remember it of course, but my mama told me the first two words that I said were 'Oh Yeah!' I still use them right to this day when I am singing and it seems as though they have rubbed off on the world.

Now those *carving* contests with Buddy Petit, Keppard, Johnny Dunn and Jabo Smith, etc, you seek information about. Buddy Petit – Kid Rena – all of us youngsters used to meet on the corners in the advertising wagons and do some carving. Of course we all had our moments, because we were all good at blowing on our cornets. So if Buddy carved me once it's OK by me. I liked the way he blew very much indeed. And I was the pallbearer at Buddy's funeral. That was 1931 and I was playing at the time at the Suburban Gardens out there by the Protection Levee. Yes, I made old Buddy's Funeral and it was a sad day for all of us. He was well liked by everybody.

You must understand that in my days blowing in New Orleans cutting contests were considered having *fun*. No malice! Jabo Smith was *good* also on his horn. It has been

18

so long ago that I don't remember cutting him. But if so you can bet your bottom dollar that it was all fun. Johnny Dunn was also tops in his days. Keppard was a little bit fancy but good too.

Yes, all those years that you mention were jumping. Chicago was really jumping too in those Twenties. I am not sure whether I met Emmett Hardy in person or heard him. He didn't live long enough for anyone to pick up on him. Me especially. Shots Madison and I were raised up around Liberty and Perdido street together, and he was also Daisy's boy friend. Lee Collins was a youngster also blowing fine horn with us. Poor boy – we lost him too. Yes, the story about King Oliver and I recording at the Gennett studio are true [this refers to Louis being placed ten or twenty paces behind Oliver, away from the recording horn, so as not to overpower the older man – M.J.]. As for Dodds and others in the Oliver band striking because of me: King Oliver's men were always talking about striking for something or other. I was a young member and didn't 'dig' their personal grievances much. So your guess as good as mine about that.

Well, Max, I hope that I helped you out and that you can now get on with your book. Lucille sends regards. Hope we will see you all soon.

'S'all',
From Satch,
Louis Armstrong

Ambassador of J(

It is fitting that the first bugle and the first cornet mastered by Louis Armstrong should repose in a music museum; and that the museum should be situated in New Orleans, Louisiana. That is the birthplace of jazz – in legend if not in provable historical fact – and the birthplace of Louis Armstrong. Louis was the city's greatest music master, and probably the foremost genius of American jazz.

As music goes, jazz is neither very old nor complicated. But in a span of 70 years or so it has managed to generate as much controversy as any of its elders and betters. One reason is that jazz has always been pushy, in a hurry to get places. In growing up quickly, almost violently, it has tried to compress a huge mass of musical material and experience into too small an idiom in too short a time. Already its evolution begins to take on the character of a telescoped history of European and Afro-American music, with a late chapter added on the sounds of the Orient. No wonder onlookers sometimes feel bewildered or hostile.

Early in life jazz broke most of the musical rules. Its origins in the black ghettos and its development in low-class dance halls and saloons meant there was never a hope of its winning a good-conduct medal from respectable society. Jazz audiences, since the music became international, have made unnecessary confusion by arguing endlessly about integrity, social implications, style and topicality. Too often, criticism has been little more than a matter of dates. Jazz appeals to youth; the most hotly creative examples of it have been made by youngish people; and youth inclines to intolerance. We have been saddened to see the cruel neglect of established talent that has taken place with each stylistic 'revolution'. At the same time, writers with a different point of view complain of the way most truly original young instrumentalists are misunderstood and, for a while, ignored. On all sides waste and frustration is caused by partisanship.

There is also a semantic cloud fogging the whole subject. 'Jazz is probably the world's most recognized musical term in every language,' says Clay Watson, chief relic collector at the New Orleans Jazz Museum. 'And it is equally the world's most misunderstood word. Really, we don't know what the word means.' That is true. No satisfactory definitions exist for jazz or Dixieland or bop or mainstream; or for qualities in the music such as swing and soul. What are the limits of what can properly be called jazz? Many undecided battles have been fought over that territory. Nevertheless we are hoping readers of this book know more than enough to recognize the sound of jazz, or most of it anyway. Questioners asking 'What is jazz?' will simply be passed on Louis' answer: 'If you still have to ask ... shame on you.'

Notwithstanding the arguments and smoke screens, we can recognize the figure who towered over the first half-century or so of jazz's existence – Louis Armstrong. He was not a pioneer from the music's pre-history, nor one of the ragtime heroes or early trumpet kings. There can be no aural testimony now of the musical stature of those semi-legendary players that preceded him in the New Orleans story; not from their heyday, anyhow. It may be impossible to prove him the best trumpeter the city ever reared, though the majority of his contemporaries believed so; but it is easy to lay out evidence supporting the contention that he was the first great jazz soloist to make gramophone records, and that he became the finest of them all – and much more.

There is also evidence for saying that he contributed more than any other person to what jazz became in Chicago in the middle '20s, and that he was blessed with a creative musical talent so remarkable that it profoundly influenced not only jazz but almost the whole field of Western popular music. It would be hard to over-estimate his importance in twentieth-century music.

Not being given to pomposity, Louis regarded his career chiefly as a lifetime's job of making people happy through his music. He took the reverence of a generation of musicians, and the applause of three generations of ordinary listeners, very much in his stride. Not for Louis the role of grand old man or solemn jazz immortal. 'You understand I'm doing my day's work, pleasing the people and enjoying my horn.'

In *New Orleans Jazz, A Family Album* – a comprehensive directory of down-home jazz names – the Armstrong story is thus encapsulated: 'Louis Armstrong (t,c) b. N.O., July 4, 1900. Most famous of all jazzmen. Has led band since mid-twenties. Protégé of King Oliver. Began in Waif's Home Band.' There are a couple more lines but that is the substance of it, and it tells the initiated that Louis played both trumpet and cornet, was born in what one of his forerunners talked fondly of as 'the city of dear old New Orleans', and was coached by the boss cornetist of the period, Joe Oliver, after a stay in reform school.

'Most famous of all jazzmen' is fair comment. Nearly everyone who has listened to the music, intentionally or otherwise, is familiar with his name – or his nickname, Satchmo. Record-buyers and cinema-goers of all ages, in all parts of the globe, know his work. He was truly a world figure, recognized by millions of people as a symbol of jazz. Perhaps only Duke Ellington and Benny Goodman rivalled him in the latter respect, and neither is quite the international household name that Louis Armstrong became. In any event, neither personifies the birth and growth of jazz, and its movement along the Mississippi River, as he did.

The breadth of Louis' appeal gives him a few lengths start in any popularity race. One winter, some sixteen years ago and before Louis had started his regular visits to Britain with the All Stars, the writer–musician Benny Green conducted a poll informally among ten strangers on the

London to Portsmouth Road. It came about as the result of an argument on the band 'bus, and its object was to prove Satchmo's popularity with the lay public. The conditions were that the pedestrians, random choices, were to be asked, 'Who is Louis Armstrong?' Green recalled:

> Ten times we stopped the coach and shot our question. One victim took one look at us and ran for his life. Another thought that Louis Armstrong was a boxing champion. But the other eight came through with flying colours ... The eight people who had some idea who Louis was all gave different replies. One said he was a trumpeter, another a bandleader, an actor, a singer, a comedian, a film star. Each one of those answers was correct.

To them could have been added 'unofficial ambassador', for many people thought of Louis as an emissary on an American friendship mission. What he had to offer won him the admiration and affection of masses of ordinary people in the five continents. In the last twenty years or so of his life he led his All Stars through most countries – though never Russia – and was spontaneously and thunderously welcomed everywhere. He was jazz music's champion world traveller.

In retrospect these foreign tours can be seen as triumphant successes which brought him increased fame and fortune, as well as all sorts of official recognition, but they didn't look like that in the beginning. Apart from the Nice Jazz Festival of 1948, an engagement far from typical of those offered to touring jazz groups from the United States, the overseas saga of Armstrong's All Stars started with the trip to Europe in September 1949. At that time Joe Glaser (Louis' manager) had serious doubts about Europe as a commercial proposition, and the majority of European promoters had little more faith than Glaser. Britain was not on the agenda then, because of a long-standing dispute between the British and American musicians' unions. The band, accompanied by Louis' wife, Lucille, and its normal retinue, set out for Scandinavia with a few firm bookings,

24

no promotion and a lot of expectations, Ernie Anderson, who represented the Glaser office, had hopes of success in Europe. He'd been there on and off since the early '30s, and knew the effect Satchmo had on European jazz fans, but he remembers that Louis was the one who had real confidence in the trip from the start.

That confidence was vindicated before the plane even touched down in Copenhagen, where it stopped on the way to Stockholm. The flight was ahead of time and the pilot wondered if Louis wished to spend the extra hour or two in Copenhagen or arrive at Stockholm early. He reported that a crowd was gathering at the airport there. It was decided to wait in Copenhagen and land at Stockholm on time. Said Anderson:

> When we came in I couldn't see any crowd at first, just twenty or thirty men waiting for us – publishers, promoters, agents and maybe some officials. I didn't know them but I could see they were important people from the way they were dressed. But pretty soon we saw the crowd. And what a crowd. They hadn't been allowed near the tarmac, and most of them were behind some kind of a fence.

A first-hand account from Sweden of this hero's welcome says that Louis was serenaded at the airport by trumpeter Gosta Torner playing *Sleepy Time Down South*, Armstrong's theme tune, and other appropriate songs in Louis-inspired style. Three thousand people strained the airport's facilities to the limit, and many more were held back by police outside the gates. When the Americans left they were accompanied by a parade of cars and bicycles and assorted transport – including a lavish float carrying a jazz band – stretching for nearly a mile. The procession made its noisy way to a city park where a further 40,000 people, mostly young, were waiting to greet Louis.

Anderson, Lucille and Louis got into the back of a large limousine, with three of the 'important people', and drove out with difficulty past the floats and bands and fans along a road lined with crowds of people shouting and waving little American flags.

> The three men [said Anderson] had no English, but there was so much going on that it made little difference. I was worried about Louis, who needed rest, but what could I do? When the car stopped near a wood and the driver indicated we should get out, I tried to refuse but Louis said we'd go and see what they had waiting. So we got out and walked to the park and there was a kind of amphitheatre full of people who couldn't get to the airport. They told me there were 40,000. It seems that a local paper had printed details of Louis' arrival, and it looked as though the whole of Stockholm had turned out. As we neared the Hotel Carlton we ran into an enormous crowd and another band. We had a hell of a time getting through, and inside we were confronted by a big table filled with glasses of aquavit. As I say, Louis was tired. But I could see there was no hope. As a matter of fact we had started on that aquavit while waiting in Copenhagen, so we thought what the hell? I'd seldom seen Louis take a drink, but he drank that day.

Naturally enough the concerts sold out, as they did in the rest of Scandinavia, in Italy, France, Switzerland, Finland and the other countries the band visited. As Anderson recalled:

> Pretty soon all available dates were filled. We went back into Scandinavia four times that trip and must have crossed Europe five times, making jumps like Helsinki to Naples. Louis, of course, scored a tremendous personal success. Just before we left New York, Joe Glaser had said, 'I hope it won't bug you, Louis, but these promoters have asked you not to sing over there.' He said audiences wouldn't understand the language, and promoters were afraid the tour would flop. Well, you know Pops ... he took no notice, went out there and sang *Black And Blue* to start with and was a riot. The same thing everywhere: houses packed out for two shows, staggering ticket sales and thousands of people standing in the streets to see him. In Rome he had a job to leave and enter the theatre, and every place he played

there were queues of people outside the dressing-room – and a good many inside with him. Anna Magnani, I remember, was in his dressing-room in Rome, talking to Louis who was in his shorts with the usual knotted handkerchief on his head. The next day he had an audience with the Pope. But that's another story.

Every night there was a reception of some kind somewhere, often two. Armstrong's stomach was bothering him and he began to be sick. As he remembered later, in a letter to *Down Beat*, 'One morning I went to get out of bed and fell flat on my face.' He went back to what he called his baby diet, a regime featuring discouraging amounts of milk, cream, malted milk and beaten eggs. The letter was signed 'Am Ulceratedly Yours, Louis Armstrong'.

Ulcers or no, Satch was soon 'back on the mound', though he had a lay-off that August with severe gastric inflammation. He barn-stormed the United States and Canada and, in 1952 and 1955, Europe again. Australia and Japan were visited too, and in 1956 he embarked on the most comprehensive journey he had so far undertaken – one which introduced him to what was then the Gold Coast. After that, one tour followed another: Europe, Africa once more, the West Indies and South America, Australia, New Zealand, the Hawaiian Islands and the Orient. It was capacity business as usual. In Helsinki the band broke an attendance record established by Sibelius; in Kingston, Jamaica, they were greeted by 10,000 fans; and late in 1957 they received a 'wildest welcome to date' in Brazil.

Ernie Anderson mentioned the emotional response to Armstrong of the extrovert audiences in Rio's Opera House, and the generous extent of the entertaining there. The impact of Armstrong on South America was, it seems, an eye-opener even to the much-travelled Ernie. 'It was a fantastic thing, my boy,' he assured one of us recently. The memory was vivid still.

Like in Buenos Aires, where thousands overran the airfield

27

when we came in. We couldn't get out of the place of course, the crush was indescribable; and in the middle of it all our clarinettist, Edmond Hall, had his pocket picked. I remember that. It needed two fire trucks, big ones you know, and the hoses and everything to rescue Louis and get him in the car. Even then they had to take him to the office and lock him in. Something happened every place we went ... The Argentine, Chile, Brazil, Uruguay. We did a concert for the dictator in Caracas a few nights before the revolution.

So the international excursions continued. Each country was captivated by Louis' music and personal magnetism; each country's reception committee tried to stage something special. Whether they succeeded or not, Louis managed to look pleased. He disliked disappointing anybody, and his patience was almost matched by his stamina. He learned to say 'no' to a badly timed meal, and after his experience with the schnapps he began to 'nix on the nips'.

In Australia, where schnapps is not one of the major risks, no indispositions were reported, and the enormous grosses made even Joe Glaser's eyebrows go up in delight. In November 1954, shortly after that visit, he said:

This thing Louis did in Australia was more successful than anything he'd done in all the thirty-two years I've known him. He did twenty concerts in ten days, a double each day, and every one a complete sell-out. The smallest audience was 12,000, the biggest 26,000 for a single concert.

Counting heads and dealing in percentages was Glaser's business. He did it well and helped to make Armstrong a rich man. Popularity, though not a true criterion of music, remains a vital fact of life for the professional musician. Although we have the gramophone record and the tape recording to enable us to verify real artistry, the financial and other measurable aspects tell us how successful he is, or was, as a public performer.

Frank Holzfiend, owner of the Blue Note at Madison and Dearborn in Chicago, where Louis often worked, said of him in the '50s:

A current runs through our place on an opening night for Louis, the kind of electricity you don't pay Commonwealth Edison for. The sparks come from Louis' horn and the starched white handkerchief always in his hand ... and mostly from the audience who try to comprehend that this is what it is like to be listening to the purest that man has yet made in jazz.

Plenty of witnesses say that his presence made a similarly powerful impact when he played second cornet to Papa Joe at the Lincoln Gardens, Chicago, in 1922.

Britain took to Satch from the start and he responded like the proverbial duck. Preparing to return there in 1956, after an absence of twenty-two years, he said in so many words that he felt he was coming home. Lucille, needless to say, had heard much of this special relationship over the years, and most of his company knew about it before the Pan-Am plane brought them into London on Thursday, 3 May. A sizeable delegation of friends and devotees had assembled at the airport. Benn Rayes, the impresario who had booked the band into London's Empress Hall, was there; so were the Marquis of Donegall, who had been campaigning for Armstrong's return, bandleaders Humphrey Lyttelton, Vic Lewis, Freddy Randall and Cy Laurie, and a variety of jazz instrumentalists and journalists. Freddy Randall's band was to visit the United States on the exchange plan agreed between the musicians' unions, but Randall was still in England then, and playing his part in the blowing-in ceremony. Louis explained happily:

As soon as we flew into the airport, Lucille and Velma and the guys could see what I'd been beatin' my gums about. There was old Humphrey and a whole gang of cats wailing like crazy out there on that field. And I spied many an old friend waiting to give me the hello. Felt great to be back.

That afternoon Louis dealt with a Savoy Hotel press conference in his own highly informal fashion. In the evening he was interviewed on TV, and next day he made ready to appear at two evening performances at the Empress Hall. Those were enjoyable days; in addition to the music, there were abundant official and unofficial parties and sundry eating, drinking and talking sessions, which featured Armstrong and perhaps some of his musicians. An unexpected bonus was an invitation to Humphrey Lyttelton's club in Oxford Street. There, after doing two tough concerts, Louis and trombonist Trummy Young played a few numbers with rhythm section and stood in with Humph and his clarinettist Wally Fawkes. They listened to the Lyttelton band and sat around chewing the fat.

Louis was everlastingly being given things: personal objects, small mementoes, rare recordings, uncommon instruments, cakes, bottles, books, handkerchiefs by the dozen, photographs, music and hats – especially hats. All of these, of course, were in addition to the awards and trophies, often valuable, handed over to him ceremonially. One article was certainly kept, because of its significance: the Lyttelton crown. 'Humph' – whose band had been added to the Empress Hall bill after opening night – constructed the head-dress out of cardboard and such during the run. Its turrets were surmounted by 'jewels' which were in fact ping-pong balls, and it bore the title 'King Louis'. At the close of the final show, Lyttelton produced the crown and pronounced the great man King of Jazz 'on behalf of all British musicians'. He could have included all those connoisseurs out in the arena.

The extensive tours of 1955 and 1956 were what started the change of popular image from King of Jazz to Ambassador Satch. Audience reaction in Western Europe had been so intense that it led to world-wide publicity, an American TV documentary, *I Can See It Now*, and some on-the-spot recordings released under the 'Ambassador Satch' title. It can be said that Armstrong turned Europe's pressmen on to Jazz Power, and that this directly influenced the US Government, which had not been breaking its neck to promote or subsidize the foreign travels of its best-known jazz groups. A correspondent of the *New York*

Times summed up the situation almost poetically. 'America's secret weapon is a blue note in a minor key. Right now, its most effective ambassador is Louis (Satchmo) Armstrong,' wrote Felix Belair. 'American jazz has now become a universal language. It knows no national boundaries, but everyone knows where it comes from and where to look for more.'

Louis, enthusiastic about his front-page coverage, supplied a postscript:

> We played in West Berlin on the last tour, and people sneaked over from the East Zone to hear us. They wouldn't dare do that for food or anything else. Man, there were even Russians who came over. Hardly any of them could speak any English, but that didn't bother them or us. The music did all the talking for both sides.

If these events had an effect on him, it was nothing to what he felt when the band travelled to West Africa in May 1956. In his own way Louis was always a 'race' man, and he explained that summer that something in his heart attracted him to the Gold Coast. He believed his ancestors came from that region, that he would find reminders of his family – as indeed he did.

Ed Murrow, the TV commentator, and producer Fred Friendly and his sound and camera crews were filming scenes from the international tours for the Columbia Broadcasting System. Their efforts helped to pay for the African adventure and pave the way for Louis and his band. Some of the happenings were instigated by them, no doubt, for story interest. Even so, the size of the crowds which came to enjoy Louis, or support him, and the turbulent warmth of their welcome deeply impressed him.

At Accra airport – where Louis landed with wife, twelve pieces of personal baggage, his band and singer, valet–companion Doc Pugh, physician Doctor Schiff, and the ubiquitous Anderson – the Americans were met by a platoon of Gold Coast musicians and, of course, the CBS team. Notable among the musicians was a number of African 'trumpeteers', instruments at the ready. Armstrong's was soon ready, too, and with it he led the squad – augmented by Trummy Young and Edmond Hall from his All Stars – round the airfield in a parade. It was not radically different from those he had played in or followed in his youth. A faint flavour of this joyous reception can be caught on the LP 'Satchmo The Great', and the shindig can be seen as well as heard in Murrow's documentary film of that name, released by United Artists. The tune played in Armstrong's honour was a traditional song, *Sly Mongoose*, re-titled *All For You, Louis* as a tribute to the brother from across the sea.

Later that day the band mounted a rostrum in the Old Polo Ground to give an open-air concert. The attendance, said by police to be a record for the Gold Coast, was reported locally to be more than 100,000 strong. *Life* estimated it at over half a million. When the people started surging forward, on hearing the theme *Sleepy Time*, something had to give. First down were the improvised towers holding the speakers. With those removed, the crowds at the back (almost out of the musicians' sight) pressed towards the platform in an attempt to follow the source of the sound. Police in front of the bandstand felt obliged to take a hand in what promised to become a very unruly situation. Since there were clubs in their hands, it was not long before violence started. As soon as he learned of it, Louis put down his horn and refused to go on. The band had not quite completed its second tune, a drum solo having inspired what turned out to be the crucial forward pressure. Woodstock it was not, but this huge gathering can be regarded as the daddy of the mammoth outdoor pop festival. There's a saying that Louis did it all first.

Other performances, formal and informal, were not marred by over-crowding or violence. Most were recorded by CBS. A highspot for the band, and the film-makers, was the 'Satchmo At The Opera' concert – 'a wonderful show', in Armstrong's words – presented by the Arts Council at the Opera Cinema to an invited, non-segregated, audience.

Kwame Nkrumah heard Louis announcing, 'We'd like to lay this next one on the Prime Minister ... *Black and Blue*.' History hasn't recorded what Nkrumah thought of the words, but as a jazz fan from his student days he should have been familiar with the old Fats Waller song.

For once, Louis and Lucille had time for social engagements. They watched traditional dancing and sometimes joined in. Lucille and the band's vocalist, Velma Middleton, led a kind of tribal jitterbug set. At the open-air Paramount night-club Louis walked through dancers, playing trumpet while an African boy danced on a nearby roof. Through it all, the cameras rolled for CBS. The Armstrongs visited a boys' school; they lunched with the master and fellows of the University College, and were entertained by Dr Nkrumah at his official guest-house. At the Achimota Durbar, a festival of traditional West African dance and drum music, Louis met a woman dancer who reminded him irresistibly of his mother Mayann. The meeting, like much else in Ghana, remained in his mind. He felt sure that the beginnings of jazz, as well as his family roots, were to be found in that region. So Africa became another spiritual home. When he left for New York – to the expected big send-off complete with choruses of *All For You, Louis* – he claimed that the experience had been the second most exciting of his life (the first was when he joined King Oliver's band). 'From now on I want to come home at least once a year,' he said as he departed.

Playing That Lead

The almost non-stop touring of the '50s may have made Armstrong an internationally renowned and highly paid entertainer, but it had no bearing on his reputation as a major jazz innovator and influence. That was established many years before, and if he had played nothing since the Oliver, Henderson, Clarence Williams, Bessie Smith and Hot Five and Seven recordings of the '20s his place in jazz, and in music as a whole, would have been assured. Louis was a big noise among musicians almost from the start of his career in Chicago. His inventive flair was as staggering as his technical skill. It must be next to impossible for anyone unacquainted with that period to grasp the extent of his originality, because what he originated has been borrowed, built upon, reproduced over and over again. His music could not be copyrighted since he seldom composed on paper. Every idea he produced – and they ran into thousands – quickly went into the public domain. The effect of this over the years was summed up by Humphrey Lyttelton: 'Now that the mode of expression which he founded has become common – and often hackneyed – currency, it takes energetic mental gymnastics to appreciate in full his contribution to jazz.'

A comparison of records featuring Louis with those that do not should convince the most sceptical listener of Armstrong's surpassing qualities, but he would need a keen imagination to feel the jolt experienced by people who heard Louis' music when it was comparatively new. I [M.J.] don't say that I heard it new. I first remember meeting it on a record made in 1929. It worked again in 1932 when he preached in person at the London Palladium. Records had not prepared me for the blistering tone and attack when experienced 'live'. I had read what musicians said about Louis in the '20s, but I shall never know just how he sounded in those Chicago days. I do know that he changed the course of jazz, as significantly as one man can change any music. He accomplished this with curiously little opposition, extending the boundaries of jazz naturally and unselfconsciously, apparently admired and applauded by all who witnessed him at work. The fact that jazz was entertainment music, and ultimately the province of black people, is one explanation for the lack of fuss. There was no art-for-art's sake faction then, no press to comment on the implications of what he was doing. More important, he was progressing within a tradition, retaining valuable characteristics of New Orleans jazz while carrying it to hitherto unimagined peaks of virtuosity. He respected the style which gave him his musical grounding, and love of New Orleans music and its insistence on a clearly stated melody line was inherent in everything he played.

This boundless talent, however, could not be confined forever within a style as closely organized as that of New Orleans; for it must be remembered that Louis played pure New Orleans jazz (or ragtime, as it was often called then) from his middle teens until his mid-twenties. Then, whenever he cut loose on cornet, he dented the tradition a bit. Finally he broke through to emerge with a lead-and-solo style so powerful and brilliant that it unavoidably left most of the conventions of ensemble jazz behind. It may be that the old tradition was dying out in Chicago anyhow; and it is certain that other musicians – the clarinettist and saxophonist Sidney Bechet is a notable example – had developed virtuoso techniques which no longer fitted the New Orleans pattern of music-making. Someone or some group would have revolutionized the parent style sooner or later. As it happened, Armstrong's was the hand that did most of the reshaping. His effect on music reached far beyond

Chicago and the classic jazz style. He inspired whole schools of trumpet-players, and other instrumentalists too, and altered the way in which jazz was felt and expressed rhythmically. His rhythmic awareness, more than anything else, pushed jazz forward dramatically after about 1925. He changed the nature of jazz singing, perhaps of all popular singing (in the Western sense), and he changed the way people composed and arranged jazz. It has often been claimed that Louis' ideas on beat and phrasing, and his gift as a melodist, led to the development of true big band swing music. Much accepted jazz language started as his personal idiom.

Louis' influence was not restricted to the United States for long; in Europe, after his early recordings had circulated, trumpet-playing was never the same as it had been before. After he had been seen in the vibrant flesh the consequences were even more striking. Every trumpeter's sights were raised. Range no longer had the same limits; tonal possibilities had expanded; most of the theories about technical command and physical endurance had gone. Musicians outside jazz had their eyes and ears opened; also, as Martin Williams says, 'No composer of any category writes for brass the way his predecessors did, simply because Louis Armstrong played things on trumpet that no one had played before him.'

These innovations helped to set new standards for jazz improvisation. Armstrong built up the extended instrumental solo to become the most significant element in a jazz performance, but he never forgot the more fundamental art of playing melody. Better than anyone else in jazz, he knew the secret of interpreting a theme straight – more or less as its composer intended – while investing it with distinctive and ardent qualities that enchant or disturb a listener. This penchant for playing the tune, at the root of his musical philosophy, linked him with the Creole fathers and the whole Louisiana tradition. He was never a 'sweet' player, by jazz definition, but much of his music had a taste of sweetness. His heart was always in music which pleased the senses. Talking of some modern trumpet men 'who tear out from the first note', he told Barry Ulanov: 'You ask yourself, "What the hell's he playing?" ... I wouldn't play that kinda horn if I played a hundred years.' And he repeated King Oliver's advice of years earlier: 'You got to play that lead sometimes. Play the melody, play the lead, and learn.' This remained a corner-stone of Satch's thinking. It is a tenet of jazz criticism that any New Orleans trumpet man worth his place in a band must be capable of driving out a solid lead in an improvised ensemble. Though Louis spent the best part of twenty years of his career demonstrating other techniques, he never lost that ability. His lead in the All Stars' performances, since the end of 1947, proved that. His trumpet statements are not perhaps those of conventional New Orleans or Dixieland, but they were hardly that in 1925. They are models of poise, swing and authority.

To Louis everything was simple enough. He followed Oliver's dictum: 'If a cat can swing a lead and play a melody, that's what counts.' He once told Leonard Feather, 'A straight lead is better than any jazz solo you know of.' Feather's reaction was that what seemed to Louis like a straight lead might be 'an exquisite jazz solo by the standards of others'. During his late twenties Louis reached a pinnacle of creative artistry when masterworks poured from the trumpet in amazing succession. In the early '30s displays of unrivalled technical facility left a question mark in the minds of his admirers. The records of that time cannot be ranked alongside *Potato Head Blues, Wild Man* or *Tight Like This* as artistic entities, but they include many passages of superlative trumpet, put down when Armstrong was glorying in his ever-increasing range and command. Most of his solo variations, even the grandiose ones, were logical developments of the theme. The exuberance overflowed in dazzling embellishments now and then, but it was not often that lyricism and legitimate jazzcraft gave way to empty virtuosity. Every single solo was illuminated by his full-blooded, burnished tone.

On the subject of the often-debated big band recordings of 1932 and 1933, certain points need to be emphasized. The standard of the orchestras accompanying Louis was uneven, to put it kindly. This lessened the impact of some performances, although his playing can hardly be faulted after all these years, except on the shifting grounds of taste, which he never bothered about. He had the taste and transcendent talent to create the magnificent *West End Blues* and beautifully timed and contoured improvisations on countless other records; yet he regarded himself as a skilled musical labourer with a flair for comedy, who was justifiably expected to amuse audiences with weak but catchy tunes and diverting forms of presentation. *Laughin' Louie*, described by one writer as 'a novelty tune of dubious distinction', was composed to showcase his comic ability. In his 1933 recording (Armstrong would not have dreamed of refusing to record the song because of its banality) he sets out to milk the situation for laughs. His singing swings, as it always did, and he later delivers a little trumpet lesson, unaccompanied except by shouts and laughter, in which the playing reveals a considerable range of mood. *Hobo, You Can't Ride This Train*, made four months earlier, features talking and train effects. This time the tune itself was moderately good, and in the event it provided a vehicle for admirably lusty singing and a trumpet solo remarkable for its restrained force. In fact, many of these titles are better than they have been painted. Although the same band could sound dreary in one number and very spirited in the next, all the performances of that era, played end-to-end, tell one story – the same as that told by Louis' entire recorded output – that the man responsible was among the natural wonders of this world.

At the core of his genius lay the vocal approach to playing – the application of a singer's feeling and nuances, his special sonority and sense of phrasing, to instrumental interpretation. It was not a technique peculiar to Armstrong, for vocalized tone is the basis of the jazz sound, but he exemplified this process as he did so many aspects of jazz.

Every owner of a handful of his recordings can confirm that Louis' singing resembles his playing, though historically the singing came first. Henry Pleasants claims it would be more accurate to say that Louis 'plays the way he sings, that his trumpet is an instrumental extension of his voice'.

Louis' vocal style is a markedly individual compound of kidding, creative paraphrasing, showmanship, blues inflections and unerring swing. One facet of it deserves separate attention. His scatting – wordless singing – was an utter novelty when he introduced it in the mid-'20s, and it made a vivid impression on record-buyers. Sometimes it was used for humorous effect; sometimes meaningless syllables were mixed with the words of a song to intensify the mood; at other times, as in *Song Of The Islands*, the scat vocal was intended simply to convey a feeling that ordinary lyrics could not carry.

Louis' singing turned upside down the generally accepted ideas about singing popular music. Jazz singing hardly existed outside the blues field in the earlier '20s, and a case could be made for Louis as pioneer of the idiom. Singers as disparate as Jack Teagarden and Billie Holiday came under his spell, and he was a germinal influence on three out of every four jazz trumpeters who ever stepped to a microphone to ad lib a vocal chorus. From Wingy Manone, Cootie Williams, Lips Page, Louis Prima and Jonah Jones in the United States to Humphrey Lyttelton, Kenny Ball and Nat Gonella in Britain, the guttural singing trumpet stars bear hoarse witness to the pervasive admiration felt for Satchmo by his fellow valve-men.

His effect on popular artists may be less obvious but it is equally real. Bing Crosby, a long-term friend of Armstrong, was more affected by jazz than by anything else in his youth. He credits two trumpet-players, Bix Beiderbecke and Louis, with firing his imagination.

Just as Bix himself found inspiration in Armstrong out on the South Side of Chicago in the late '20s, so did I. Yes, I'm proud to acknowledge my debt to the Rev. Satchelmouth. He is the beginning and the end of music in America.

Billy Eckstine, a singer who plays trumpet and valve trombone from time to time, once said

> Of course I got something from Louis. Everybody singing got something from him because he puts it down basically, gives you that feeling. It's right there; you don't have to look for it. Louis I love and have always loved. You don't go any higher. Any son-of-a-bitch who picks up a trumpet and blows a few notes is going to play a phrase that belongs to Louis. And most of them today don't realize it. What he did for the instrument is too much to portray in words, yet so many of them don't have any idea of it. The reason a lot of trumpet players today are walking is because that man taught 'em to crawl.

Albert Nicholas, the American clarinettist who lived in Europe for many years, was born in New Orleans about five weeks before Armstrong. He grew up listening to the same music as Louis and often played alongside him. He rated Armstrong the finest of all the musicians he ever worked with. One remark he made crystallizes our own feelings, which many must share, when confronted by Armstrong's genius. 'It's amazing how he came up from the ghettos and turned out to be the world's greatest.' A number of great men have been born poor, and it is easy to imagine that the poverty can be a spur to ambition. A majority of New Orleans' black musicians of the first jazz age came from a slum environment of one kind or another, and all suffered racial oppression. As music-making was one of the few avenues of escape from drudgery or near-slave labour open to black Louisianians, it is hardly surprising that much of their creative energy was directed into music. New Orleans and its surrounding neighbourhoods produced something like a thousand jazz-players during the decades around the turn of the century. Many went out into the world and found fame, and a few – King Oliver, Sidney

Bechet, Jelly Roll Morton, Johnny Dodds, Henry Allen and George Lewis – achieved jazz immortality. Armstrong, poorer than most at the outset, started with more obstacles to overcome, but he went further and lasted longer than anybody else.

Creole Brothers

The origins of Armstrong's family are obscure, and it is therefore useless to guess what influence his forebears may have had on his genius. Louis' great-grandmother was born into slavery; she spoke of her mother who had been born while Louisiana was still a French colony, that is to say before the early 1760s, when the huge Louisiana Territory was turned over to Spain. Louis also said that his great-grandfather and his grandmother had been slaves. In slave days, the recording of births and deaths among blacks was casual, to say the least. Families were broken up and moved in haphazard fashion, and the pattern of slave imports to the Americas was far from simple. During the French and Spanish colonial periods, large numbers of Africans were brought into the Louisiana region from the French and Spanish lands as well as from the slave coast of Africa. These divers influences, which affected the music and dance of Louisiana, had a powerful bearing on the nature of jazz. As we have seen, Armstrong believed his ancestors reached America from the Gold Coast. He felt that he was a 'pure-blooded' black. We know his family had none of the French or Spanish associations discernible in so many New Orleans jazz families.

As a seaport New Orleans inevitably became a city of conflicting cultures and races. It was known as much for its crime and violence, its gambling and prostitution, as for its architecture, commerce, music and annual Mardi Gras parades. It was a place where anything in the way of drugs, sex, food, drink or other amusement could be bought; a place where, in Jelly Roll Morton's phrase, 'everything in the line of hilarity' was on tap for those with money to pay. The sailors and tourists, pimps and gamblers, thieves and successful upright citizens came up with cash to keep it thriving. The poor people who lived there, or a large proportion of them, earned what they could get by catering for the pleasure-seekers' needs. Jazz musicians and Creole girls of colour alike were kept busy in the District. It was into an impoverished family living in one of the most squalid sections of town that Armstrong was born in 1900. By common consent the date was 4 July, though once, long ago, a researcher suggested 7 April. No record of the birth exists, though Louis is said to have been christened in a local church, but he was satisfied that it was 'a blasting fourth of July, my mother called it, that I came into the world and they named me the firecracker baby'.

The details of Armstrong's early life are hard to come by, or wrapped in the air of doubt and mystery that surrounds so much early jazz history. His full name was always in doubt; the time he began to learn cornet is disputed; the date of his entry to the reform school is uncertain; even the name of the street where he was born is difficult to verify. In truth, the reference books have been more often wrong than right. Louis insisted, in books, articles and conversation, that he was born in James Alley – not Jane Alley, 'as some people call it'. About half the jazz books refer to James Alley, the other half to Jane. While preparing this story I [M.J.] asked him, 'Louis, were you born at number 719 James Alley in New Orleans?' He replied, 'Yes, well, I didn't know the address. All I can say for sure is James Alley. But I'm glad to know that's the number on the plate.' Was that the house where he and his mother lived for a time? 'Yes.' The Alley, whatever its title, was a small and overcrowded lane – 'about a good block long', according to Louis – which ran between Gravier Street and Perdido Street in the back o' town district.

From every account the street was dingy and dangerous, the whole area peopled with an abnormally high percentage

43

of toughs, drunks, robbers and women 'walking the streets for tricks'. The house he was born in was a wooden, one-roomed, backyard building, approached by a side alleyway. In the yard was what Louis used to call 'a big old China-ball tree'. A photograph taken much later shows clapboard tenements still occupied on the corner of the alley and Perdido. To increase the confusion, the street sign on a telegraph pole reads 'Jane Al'. Here, for a short while, Louis lived with his parents and grandmother. Soon, his father and mother quarrelled and separated, and he was left with grandmother Josephine Armstrong. The comings and goings of Louis, his father Willie and his mother Mayann (real name Mary Ann), are more tangled than anything else in the Armstrong story. The parents were together long enough for a girl, Beatrice, known as Mama Lucy, to be born some two years after Louis. Louis said in *Swing That Music* that Mayann took him and his sister to live with a great-grandmother 'right in the city in what is called the Third Ward'.

In his second autobiography, *Satchmo – My Life in New Orleans*, the details were different. He said he was with his grandmother when Beatrice was born and didn't see his sister until he was five. Obviously he could not remember much of his first years, but he was sure that after his parents split up he didn't see Willie Armstrong again until he had grown 'to a pretty good size'. Willie, who worked for most of his life in a turpentine factory near James Alley, died in 1933. Mayann came from Butte, Louisiana, and moved to New Orleans as a child. She was a servant to a white family whose children she helped to bring up, and she married at fifteen. Armstrong's father may have been a resolute man with some exceptional traits. The only hint we get is from Louis' reference to his long stay at the turpentine plant, where 'he could hire and fire the coloured guys who worked under him'. It suggests some sort of quality in that hard, hostile milieu. Nowhere, however, is there a clue to Louis' musical inheritance.

Louis was blessed with good health, a robust constitution

and, of course, the germ of tremendous artistic talent. Fate was on his side in the matter of date and place of birth, but not in much else. Many of his contemporaries had the advantage of being raised by musical families, with instruments in the home and advice next door. Albert Nicholas, one of a large family of musicians, was presented with his first clarinet before he was twelve, and was soon sitting on the kerbs practising alongside Sidney Bechet. Edmond Hall's father, a member of the Onward Brass Band, would pass out clarinets to each of his five children as they reached a certain age. Louis had none of these benefits. His formal education was rudimentary, and his parents were barely literate. There was no money for instruments or other luxuries, and very little for food. Often there were no parents, either, and much of his childhood was spent with his grandmother (or on the streets) or in a reformatory. Louis survived the emotional upsets, domestic crises and other deprivations with a marvellous resilience. He came to think of the early struggles as the origin of his self-reliance and determination to succeed. Louis wrote to us in 1970, 'concerning my father writing, really I never saw him write at all. In fact I didn't see him do *anything* much. Because he left my mother when Mama Lucy and I were real babies. Mother could read and write a little.'

During the years the Armstrongs lived there, James Alley was 'the lowest Negro slum in New Orleans', according to Robert Goffin. But music was around you even in the slums. So little Louis, playing games on empty sites or dancing and singing in the streets, began while he was still with his grandmother to absorb the marches and folk tunes in the air. There was religious music, too. This was a city of many churches and religions, besides voodoo, and the poor and ignorant were, as ever, the most devout churchgoers in the community. From his earliest years Louis attended church; his grandmother and great-grandmother saw to that. 'That, I guess, is how I acquired my singing tactics. Yes, I learned that good music right there in the church. All that music that's got a beat, it comes from the same place, from the old sanctified churches. It's the same old soup warmed over.' He was always grateful for that sacred soup, and astonished at the respect those apparently godless citizens had for 'the little church that was in the block'. Speaking of the time when Mayann had moved to a new home in the Liberty and Perdido area, Satch stressed that everyone from church people to roughnecks had the greatest respect for his mother, despite her move to a neighbourhood 'filled with cheap prostitutes who did not make as much money for their time as the whores in Storyville'. He added, with customary frankness, that whether she 'did any hustling I cannot say. If she did, she kept it out of my sight.'

Louis loved and admired Mayann, and took her advice when he could. She warned him not to fight or steal and he did his best to avoid both temptations, although the company he found himself in was excessively wild. He was very young – 'four or five, still wearing dresses' – when he was taken to see her and allowed to stay in the house in Brick Row, near the intersection of Liberty and Perdido and some 18 blocks from where he was born. Though he had been fond of his grandmother, and made comfortable by her, he recalled that nothing could take his mother's place. James Alley was getting even more dilapidated, and although Louis likened Brick Row to a motel, 'a lot of cement, rented rooms', it was afterwards noted by Goffin that they were mansions compared with the James Alley 'hovels', which were demolished as they fell vacant. Number 719 was finally pulled down in 1964, and if there isn't a plaque in the new development the city fathers should be ashamed of themselves.

It was only by bad luck, it seems, that Louis' birthplace was not preserved. The shack – 'at 2723 Jane Alley, off South Broad Street', said a report at the time – was discovered by an enthusiast just before the wreckers levelled the site. He bought the shack for $50 and told the New Orleans Jazz Museum, which arranged to move it. Unfortunately they could not meet the demolition firm's deadline and the building was burned down. Louis' home measured about 26 ft by 24 ft, and comprised one large room, divided by upright boards into two or three sections. It was described as 'in terrible condition'.

The new home was a strange universe to Louis, tough in a different way and containing saloons with pianists and dance halls with inspiring ragtime bands. It was the place where his imagination was really stirred by music, where it all happened in his heart and mind, perhaps because he was reunited with Mayann. 'I was so thrilled to see her,' he could say fifty years later. 'When she said she was actually going to keep me with her, it was the news I'd been hoping for when I left my grandmother.'

In the Third Ward Louis began to pick up on jazz, following parades, looking in from outside at the Masonic (or 'Funky Butt') Hall, listening to funeral music or singing on the dockside with friends from his local gang.

In those days it was called ragtime music. And whenever there was a dance or a lawn party the band of six men would stand in front of the place on the side walk and play a half hour of good ragtime music. And us kids would stand or dance on the other side of the street until they went inside. That was the only way that the young kids could get the chance to hear those great musicians such as Buddy Bolden, Joe Cornet Oliver, my idol, Bunk Cornet Johnson, Freddy Cornet Keppard...

In this manner, Louis filled himself with music. Jazz was beginning to flower at that time, and he fell in love with it and seemed to sense where his future lay. He felt music in him and, as he recounted in 'Satchmo Says', further steeped himself in it by singing tenor parts in a street quartet from about the age of ten.

Meanwhile he was doing various odd jobs, such as selling newspapers, to help his mother 'make both ends meet', as well as going to Fisk School where he was said to be bright. There were no family crafts for him to be apprenticed to, and he had no fancy for the turpentine factory where, later, his half-brother worked. He sold papers from the age of

47

seven in St Charles Street and a year or two later was employed in the Konowski family's coal business, where his task was to fill up the buckets on the wagon and try to sell them with cries of 'Stone coal, ladies, five cents a water bucket'. It was about this time that he formed the quartet with Little Mack, Redhead Happy Bolton and Big Nose Sidney. He used to go out with them after supper and sing sweet, ragtime and comedy songs along Rampart Street, past Gravier towards Canal Street. 'When someone would call to us, we'd sing a few songs and then pass our hats round. At the end of the evening we would divi up, and we made a nice little taste there most nights.' Louis, proud to be earning, would rush home to Mayann with his 'taste'.

By now he had acquired some nicknames. Gatemouth was one, Dippermouth another. The latter was usually shortened to Dipper or, on account of his small stature, Little Dipper. And there was Little Louis. In letters, he used to spell it Louie to distinguish it from the popular American pronunciation 'Lewis'. Later, he added Satchelmouth. A long-standing confusion exists over his given names. Compilers of critical and reference works have plumped more or less equally for Louis Daniel (Martin Williams, Panassié, the Danish *Jazzens Who's Who*, etc.), Daniel Louis (Schleman, *Esquire Jazz Book*, Feather, etc.) or just plain Louis Armstrong. Louis himself said:

I was born Louis Armstrong. The Daniel came later from somewheres 'down the line'. It came out of clear skies, I guess, I don't remember Mayann (Mary Ann) ever calling me by Daniel. It's not important anyway. Since I met Percy Brooks, the day that I landed in Plymouth, England, that morning when I got off the boat and he shook my hand and said to me 'HELLO SATCHMO'. I had never heard the name before. Satchelmouth, yes.

So consistent is this 'Satchmo' explanation that it seems wise to accept it, although research brings up little in its support. Percy Mathison Brooks was editor of the *Melody Maker* in July 1932 when Armstrong arrived. Had he invented a nickname, even unwittingly, he or the paper would have mentioned the fact when they found out. But they did not, and it appears from a scrutiny of *MM* files that the first the paper heard of its re-christening of Louis was when he publicized the story. Issues of the *MM* prior to Armstrong's visit make no reference to the nickname, though, and we can find none in print at all before 1932. Then, in the August number announcing his presence in England, come several mentions of his trumpet, 'Satch'-Mo'. It was evident from two or three recordings on which he spoke that Louis addressed the instrument by name ('Watch it, Satchel-mouth', for instance, on the 1930 record of *You're Driving Me Crazy*). In preparing advertising or editorial copy, some-body probably had the idea of abbreviating it to Satch'-Mo' to impart a tang of black dialect. Certainly Henri Selmer's ad for August told us: 'Satch'-Mo' is a Selmer "Challen-ger" Trumpet.' A main feature was illustrated with strange drawings, one of which had Louis saying to his horn, 'Speak to 'em, Satch'-Mo'.' And in his report Dan Ingman wrote of the instrument 'which he calls "Satchmo", a con-traction I am told of "Satchel Mouth" '. Ingman was the paper's Technical Editor, but he knew and still knows noth-ing of his colleague's part in the contraction. The following month's *Melody Maker* carried several reports without a Satchmo among them. Selmer had by then switched the name from instrument to man ('Louis "Satchel-mouth" Armstrong is going strong with his new Selmer...'). Percy Brooks helped Selmer with their advertising copy for the *Melody Maker*, which seems to strengthen the chance ab-breviation theory. 'It sounds the sort of thing Brooks would have done,' said Ingman. 'He certainly did not meet Louis at Plymouth and say "Hello Satchmo".'

A curious story, because Armstrong himself possibly didn't start using the form 'Satchmo' until some time later. On the other hand, perhaps he or his trumpet had the name already. Edgar Jackson, who was also with the *MM*, wrote:

It seems that Louis' memory let him down. Brooks and your

annotator ... had for some time known Louis as Satchmo
from having heard him called that in 1928 by the American
musicians in Fred Elizalde's dance orchestra at the Savoy
... it will probably never be known who thought it up.

When I put the puzzle to Louis, he was unrepentant.

Maybe Percy Brooks mis-spelled it or he himself abbreviated
the name to Satchmo. Anyway to me, Percy Brooks deserves
all the credit for my new name. We all had a laugh when I
asked a musician why he called me Satchmo when my name
was Satchelmouth. 'It's because you got more mouth,' he
told me. We had lots of nicknames when I was a kid in New
Orleans, and they called me that because they thought my
jaws was like a satchel, you know, a doctor's valise. But I
had a million names. But to me it was Percy first called me
Satchmo, and I love it.

A great many boys who ran loose and battled in the
streets attracted the attention of the New Orleans police or
juvenile courts, and Louis was no exception. He has spoken
of his quartet posting lookouts to warn of approaching
cops, especially if the boys were venturing into Storyville.
After selling coal and singing for hours he still had steam to
let off. Then, on the last night of 1912, he was arrested for
disturbing the peace. One New Orleans player suggested
that the authorities had been after him for some time,
probably because of 'unsatisfactory home influences'. Louis
admitted that rough stuff had a place in his life, though he
always preferred music.

I remember running around with a lot of bad boys which did
a lot of crazy things. As the saying goes, your environment
makes you. My life has always been an open book. There's
nothing for me to hide. I have respected everybody as best I
could ever since I was a little shaver. Many a time I would
be with kids in my neighbourhood and they would play
Follow the Leader. So if they would get into any kind of
trouble, I would be in trouble also. If they would steal something and get caught, I was in trouble the same as they.

Savvy? You must realize it was very shaky all the time during my days coming up in New Orleans. Especially those early ones. They were rough. You had to fight and do a lot of ungodly things to keep from being trampled on. Sure I had fights and did a number of rough things, just so I could have a little peace or elbow room as we used to express it.

All boys were bad in those days – you'd better believe it. The kids from the Third Ward were so bad until they carried their pistols on them in holsters just like those real cowboys. And you think they won't shoot to kill? Huh! Mayann used to tell me, 'Son, don't fight, don't fight.' So I was arguing with a boy one day in school and, thinking of what my mother told me concerning not fighting unless you had an excuse, I told this kid, 'OK, since you want to start a fight, hit me.' And he did – right in the eye. Damn near blinded me. But where he made his mistake, he kept standing there to see what I was going to do, while I was feeling for him because I could not see at all. Finally my hand touched him. Yes, you're right. I hung him. I swung on that so-'n'-so's jaw and head and etc. From that time on I got the name of being a bad boy.

On the New Year's Eve of his downfall the quartet was singing strenuously, in the hope of parting revellers from their nickels, when from across the street near Rampart and Perdido came a young boy firing a cap pistol practically in Louis' face. Louis was carrying a real gun on his hip. Encouraged by shouts of 'Go get him Dipper', he produced it and replied with a few cannon-like shots. They clinched the contest but, the next he knew, the arm of the law was around him and he was taken away. Published accounts of this event have been surprisingly contradictory, considering that he wound up in court. He was sentenced to serve an indefinite term at the Colored Waifs' Home, for discharging firearms within the city limits. The dates most commonly given are 31 December 1912, or 31 December 1913, but Sam Charters suggests 4 July 1915.

Armstrong's references to 'that New Year's Eve of 1913' led to mistakes. Other factors make it hard to be positive about when he entered or was released from the Home. The head of the New Orleans Jazz Museum told one of us that Satch was in the Home on two separate occasions. 'He was,' said Clay Watson. 'He came out and went back again.' The truth may be that Louis was released in the care of his father, then taken back until he could stay with his mother. A sidelight is thrown on the matter by his description, in the second autobiography, of the 'honeysuckles all in bloom' when he arrived at the Home. This would seem to be premature, even in a mild climate, if Louis was admitted in early January. In a taped interview, in which I [M.J.] tried to clear things up, he answered '1912, the first time' to a question about the arrest date. Then, 'Well, I went in January and I stayed all 1912, no, I stayed all of 1913, and I got out in June of 1914. So I stayed out there a year and a half.' In a follow-up answer, relating the incident in full, he wrote:

New Year's Eve, 1912 – I was arrested for celebrating with my stepfather's big old rusty .38. Shooting up into the air, blanks, cartridges, which everyone has fun on New Year's Eve. No crime. Of course Hell will break loose if you should get caught with a gun, let alone shooting one. Anyway it was New Year's Day when they took me from the Juvenile Court to the Waifs' Home. I don't remember being taken to the Waifs' Home twice. Maybe my memory's bad. It has been so long.

When the detective came up behind Louis and took the pistol out of his hand he felt that his world had ended. 'I was just a kid, twelve years old. Oh but I cried.' Later he saw it as a significant turning point which led to music lessons and, as a result, 'a beautiful life'. In the reformatory he was taught by two amateur musicians, 'Captain' Joseph Jones, director of the Home, and warden Professor Peter Davis. These lessons did not start immediately, however, for it was as a reward for good behaviour that he was permitted to play, in turn, the tambourine, snare drum, alto horn and bugle before graduating to the much-wanted cornet. Peter Davis, who taught the fundamentals of music, deserves the larger share of credit for setting Louis on the road, although 'Cap' Jones claims to have given him his initial trumpet lesson. When the Captain, who was 'Pops' to the inmates (is that where Louis got his 'Pops' habit from?), died in 1957, there was a headline to proclaim 'Satchmo's Discoverer Dies at 76'. Engagements prevented Satch from going to the funeral. But he sent a contribution to the family and said 'Joe was a fine man'. He had been back to the Home on several occasions as an honoured guest. Jones's widow later presented to the Jazz Museum the cornet Louis learned on. Peter Davis died 30 April 1971, aged 91.

Few historians have unreservedly accepted Louis' statements about learning to blow in the reform school. He seems too good to have started with bugle calls. Bunk Johnson supplied the heaviest ammunition by saying that he showed the youngster how to play 'until he begin understanding me real good'. Bunk described in detail how Louis, aged about eleven and in short pants, would steal into a honky tonk named Dago Tony's and sleep behind the piano until Bunk came on to play. It sounds the kind of thing Louis might have done, and Albert Nicholas says he first heard him playing on Bunk's 'expensively engraved trumpet'. Samuel Charters writes that Louis was playing a little before the school, where 'he got his first formal training'. Bechet, too, recalled that Satch was playing 'a bit before he went into that Jones school', and there has been more, similar, circumstantial evidence. We do not have much faith in it. The recollections of Jones, Davis and Armstrong himself dovetail convincingly. And why should Louis have lied about it? His story first appeared in *Swing That Music*, where it is the same in almost every particular as his later versions. Although a number of Crescent City pioneers are named in that book, Bunk is not among them. Johnson spent only a few years in New Orleans during Louis' time, and was rarely seen there after 1913; Louis must have been very young if he did follow him.

All the same, as far back as 1938 Louis said 'Bunk is the

53

man they ought to talk about. Man, just to hear him talk sends me.' Admiration is not in doubt. But some of Bunk's utterances must have made him blink when that leathery old trumpet king made his remarkable late comeback. 'A short while after that, well, Louis would get arrested for goin' in the Basin swimmin'. So when he went to Jones' Home, Louis could play,' said the veteran in 1942. 'He didn't learn at Jones' Home. He learned with Bunk. And he'll tell you.' The sentences have a poetic sort of balance but Louis did not corroborate them. Later he denied them comprehensively.

– As for Bunk Johnson, he didn't even know me when I was a kid. In fact he didn't have time to bother with us kids. Joe Oliver did, and I love him. Bunk told it all wrong. I never went into anywhere by the name of Dago Tony that I know of, so forget about me in short pants hiding behind a piano in a Honky Tonk. The 'Peelers' (Police) would beat your legs off with their sticks for doing something like that, though a kid might get by with long pants if he looks old enough. And I never was arrested for going in swimming as Bunk said. He made all that up. Now don't get me wrong. Bunk was a beautiful man on his cornet, but I could never get close to him like I could with 'Papa' Joe. I never had a lesson from him in life. He was too busy drinking that port wine.

No, my teaching was in the Home by Mr Peter Davis, and that was the start of my career. The first horn I blew was in Jones's home. It was a bugle. They made me the bugler of the institution. I learned all the calls including Reveille, Taps and the Mess Calls. Then they gave me my first cornet in the Waifs. I learned so rapidly until they made me leader of the little old brass band. And I could read all the music. Sometimes we used to go out into the town on a parade, and one day we went up in my old district. When the parade passed my corner – Liberty and Perdido – there was Black Benny, a bass drum player who used to carry a pistol and look after us kids, and all those tough characters that practically raised me. They passed the hat around and picked up a lot of money and dumped it into my band cap. I gave it to Mr Davis, who led that band, and when we returned back to the Home and counted all that money we had enough to buy brand new instruments for every member of the band. And that's quite a big-size band. Nice wasn't it?

So forget Bunk's statement. I did learn to play the cornet in the Colored Waifs' Home for Boys. And after I got out Papa Joe Oliver took over, quite naturally. He was always my idol. I liked the way he did things (musically anyway). My man Joe – God bless him.

At the end of his stay in the Home, Louis knew how to play – marches, tunes like *Home Sweet Home*, the brass band repertoire played with a ragtime flavour – and he already had the broad taste which helped him through the years to cope with different bands, shows, symphonic situations, anything that was hurled at him. The details of his release are obscure. In one account his mother had him released through the intervention of a 'boss man'; according to another, he was discharged into the custody of his father and stepmother who lived at Miro and Poydras streets. In either event, he was moved around (he frequently spent periods with his grandmother Josephine throughout his childhood) and was soon back in the one-roomed house with Mayann and Beatrice. It is likely that these sporadic disappearances gave rise to the confusion about when he started playing in relation to his sojourn in reform school. He was still fourteen and had finished his education. He owned no instrument but borrowed or hired a cornet if he needed one for a 'play'. For the next few years he worked at various day jobs: delivering milk for the Cloverdale Dairy, selling papers once more, collecting for a scrap merchant, unloading banana boats and his old job of selling coal – often to the inhabitants of the Storyville cribs. He enjoyed his coalman's work because it enabled him to hear his favourite music at places like Pete Lala's in the District, and often to educate himself in other aspects of local low-life. While taking in his buckets of coal, Louis would also take his 'little peek'.

He was rarely performing musically at this time – he hardly touched a trumpet for eighteen months or two years – but kept his mind busy listening to bands at Economy or

Funky Butt Hall, at Lincoln Park or anywhere music could be heard cheaply. Oliver, as we have been told, taught him more than anybody else did about jazz. Louis said the older man looked out for him and acted like a father ('I sure was like a son to him. That's why I called him Papa Joe'). In 1917, Louis played in an Oliver-type group which he led with drummer Joe Lindsey. It used to do gigs that the King passed on, and before that Louis was taking engagements himself when they were offered. 'Any time a cat would lay off,' he remembered, 'they'd say, "Run get Little Louie." I went up real quick then because I was crazy about the music and pretty fast on that horn.' So fast, it seems, that there were times when Papa Joe – who gave the boy his first cornet, an old York he had no further use for – had to counsel his pupil to cut out the fast fingering and 'play more lead'. Oliver showed him musical exercises, too, and practised duets with him; but this tuition, though it must have been vitally important to his development, hardly explains his prodigious ability. Louis learned at an astonishing speed; he could play anything he could whistle, and he impressed people from the very beginning. Trombonist Preston Jackson said he heard the young Armstrong, and trumpeter Kid Rena, in the Waifs' band playing for the opening of a school playground.

Now my public school was Thumy Lafon. Now I'm coming to Louis. I saw him though I didn't know who he was during this time. There was a large lot there, square and full of debris and stuff, so they decided to fill it up and make a playground – which they did. Now here comes Louis: he was in this little band from Jones', you might have saw the pictures of it, the Waifs' Home band? I didn't know his name but he was outstanding then. If anyone had told me that this particular boy standing up there, two or three years older than me, that some day I'd be playing trombone in his band, I'd have said they were crazy, because I wasn't even interested in music.

Of course Louis worked with other fine players, and he

listened attentively enough to Jimmy Noone, Zue Robertson, Buddy Christian and the rest of King Oliver's men to be able to pronounce them years afterwards 'the hottest jazz band ever heard in New Orleans between the years 1910 and 1917'. Influences and tutorship notwithstanding, Armstrong advanced rapidly to a stage at which we can be forgiven for thinking that there never was anyone who could have taught him.

His first steady professional engagements were at Henry Ponce's and at Matranga's. The latter, a tavern with music on Perdido Street, was managed by an Italian named Henry Matranga. Louis reckoned he was seventeen when he played there. He termed it a real honky-tonk, whose customers were well used to trouble. Ponce's was no Sunday school either, and Louis related in the *Satchmo* autobiography how its boss, who was afraid of nobody and liked listening to blues, shot up three or four toughs one Sunday morning and put them all in hospital. As for Matranga's, it filled up with local hustlers and out-of-town workers in the early hours. Characters like the chicks with 'big stockings full of dollars' were partial to Louis' music; 'they always dug the way I blew them blues'. Shootings and police raids were not unusual.

> When they raided the honky tonk [Louis wrote], they put everybody in the Black Maria and they would take us down to the Parish Prison. Sometimes we'd be in a few days, sometimes more, until the owner (Henry Matranga) came down to pay the fine or get us all out on bail.

But Louis was always protected, or told to duck when the bullets started flying.

The years of 1917 and 1918 were eventful for Armstrong and for all the sporting people of New Orleans. Storyville was closed down by the US Navy on 14 November 1917 and, though musicians continued to find work, the employment situation was seriously affected.

Well, the story is that some sailors from the naval yard in

Algiers got foolin' around in them cribs in the District [Louis remembered]. One or two of them got themselves killed, so the navy clamped down. They made all them whores and pimps and madams leave their homes there. Some of the prostitutes looked like children. You know, they spent the best of their days down there. That's right.

The closure was one reason for the migration of jazzmen north during the war years and after. King Oliver had joined trombonist Kid Ory in a band which became the most famous of its day. This was the band that carved the Lindsey–Armstrong sextet in a bandwagon battle. Joe Oliver had warned Little Louie to stand up if the bands ever met, but one day Louis forgot and his band took a 'terrible beating'. And this was the band he joined when Oliver left, early in 1919, to go to Chicago.

Having studied Papa Joe for so long, and knowing all the band's pieces well, Louis was equipped to take over. Now he was able to put into practice everything he had heard his tutor do. The band worked at Pete Lala's on Sundays, at the Co-operative Hall on Mondays, and at various private dates in between. When he wasn't playing with Ory, Louis accepted funerals, parades and any gigs that came his way. He 'commenced to get known' at Matranga's but became 'real popular' during the three months or so he spent with Ory. For most of 1918 he had kept the coal job going. It appears that his motives were only partly financial; the war was still on and the orders, he says, were 'Work or Fight'. Louis, only eighteen, went on selling coal. Besides, there were pretty girls to be seen, though the official District had been shut down, and Louis declared he was full of fire 'even with the shovel'. At any rate, he quit the coal trade on Armistice Day, 1918. Before the year was up he had married Daisy Parker. She frequented a particularly vicious dance joint across the river in Gretna called the Brick House, where Armstrong sometimes played on Saturday nights. The gig paid well, with tips from the drunken patrons thrown in, but the bad side was that 'you could get your head cut off, or blown off, if you weren't careful'. As

58

always, Louis was careful. But he noticed a pretty little brown-skinned Creole girl who had 'the stuff in her eyes' when she watched him playing. He got to know her easily. 'She was doing the best she could for herself in this tonk; it was business with her. And for me another mash.'

The marriage just held together, with the help of a few separations, until Louis left the home city in 1922; but his devotion to music made him a poor candidate, and he realized it. 'My early chicks (sweethearts) were all local gals,' he wrote. 'I did not have too many, though. I loved my horn too much.' What Daisy, who could neither read nor write, knew best was how to 'fuss and fight'. To increase their initial difficulties, the neighbours annoyed Mayann by asking if she would allow her son to marry a whore. She, to her credit, told them Louis had to live his own life; let him get on with it. Fifty years later he re-created the scene for us.

When I married Daisy (my first wife) she was a prostitute from across the river from New Orleans (Gretna, La.). She was twenty-one years old and I was eighteen at the time. And the way those tough men such as gamblers, pimps, etc., got along with their wives and whores, that was the same way that I had to get along with Daisy. That was to beat the hell out of her every night and make love in order to get some sleep. That was supposed to be love. And the Lord was with me. She was so mean and jealous. And to my surprise I awakened one morning and Daisy had a big bread knife laying on my throat, with tears dropping from her eyes, saying, 'You black son-of-a-bitch, I ought to cut your Goddamn throat.' Hmm. That's why I always said the Lord was with me. Many times she and I went to jail from fighting in the streets, and my boss would have to come get me out. Now you can see why I don't remember just how many times that I went to jail. It was a common thing in those days. I can proudly say though that I didn't steal – much. I didn't have to, and I was so busy trying to keep from getting hurt and blow my horn – those blues they liked then – until stealing never crossed my mind.

The mentions of blues-playing scattered through Louis'

letters are enlightening. Like Oliver, Johnny Dodds, Mutt Carey and many another New Orleans musician, he was an expressive blues handler. This seems to have been obligatory in a man expecting regular employment in the lower-class tonks. The Oliver band, when Armstrong joined it and it recorded, was very much a blues band. Though he took infrequent solos on Oliver's records, what we do hear of his playing is firmly grounded in the blues tradition. So too, naturally, are his accompaniments and solo interludes on recordings with Bessie Smith, Alberta Hunter, Clara Smith, Ma Rainey, Trixie Smith, Ida Cox, Sippie Wallace, Maggie Jones, Chippie Hill, Nolan Welsh, Hociel Thomas and other exponents of blues song.

While still in the Kid Ory band, Louis was employed on excursions out of New Orleans on the Mississippi riverboats. Each trip lasted from about eight in the evening until midnight. The pattern of his career is not quite clear, but he was doubling the boats and other musical jobs around town until he took the train (his first time right away from home) towards St Louis in May 1919.

Piano-playing Marge Creath, who became Mrs Zutty Singleton, met Armstrong in St Louis at this time, and she recalls a very diffident young man.

He was on the boats before Zutty, and on Monday nights Zutty and I used to go on the steamer to hear Marable's band. And Louis was so shy, as soon as he got off the stand he'd run down to the first deck – the band played on the second deck – and wouldn't talk to anyone. So one night a bunch of us said we was going to get him. He was down to the waterfront, and just kept his head down and didn't have anything to say. That was really the first time I met him.

He didn't hang around in St Louis; did know my brother, but he was quite shy and never seemed to associate with anybody but musicians, and we never got to know him real good. He wouldn't talk to the girls and I don't think he even went with any of the girls in St Louis. I can see him right now; we were telling him how we loved his playing and he kept his head down, didn't want to talk. When I got to know him, when Zutty went to Chicago, he was altogether different.

These paddle-steamer journeys proved valuable experience for Armstrong, and he increased his music-reading facility as he played long hours with 'a bunch of the finest musicians'. They included David Jones (mellophone), Baby Dodds (drums) and Johnny St Cyr (banjo and guitar). He remained with the Streckfus Line boats until September 1921, when he and Baby Dodds were dismissed. Louis worked diligently with this larger, nine-piece, orchestra, and relished the change of scene as the steamers brought him to the different places up river. He later gave Marable credit for breaching a few of the hard and fast colour barriers existing in all those southern regions, saying that this was the first black band to play many of the smaller towns. 'The ofays were not used to seeing coloured boys making fine music for them to dance by.' Evidently black jazz had not penetrated far outside the major cities by 1920. In conversation not long before his death, Louis repeated that 'somewhere up around that time' he had met 'the great Bix Beiderbecke' at Davenport, Iowa. 'That's where the Streckfus boys used to keep all their boats, and I'll never forget meeting Bix, a nice kid then.' He also spoke nostalgically of Jack Teagarden, whom he ran into on the docks in New Orleans. He had never heard of him then, but liked him. Although there was some mixing in the old days in New Orleans, meetings between white and black musicians were not commonplace. Louis could not be sure if he ever met Wingy Manone – the white New Orleans trumpet player who was born in 1904 and sometimes played in Storyville as a youth – before they got up north. He knew they had not blown on the same stand. 'I imagine white and coloured jammed together in the early days in New Orleans,' he wrote, 'but I don't remember it. What I do remember is the time Henry Zeno, a coloured drummer, died. He was so famous in the Red Light District cabarets that there were lots of white as well as coloured musicians at his funeral.'

61

Through the decades since then, it seems that Teagarden remained a special favourite of Armstrong's. Louis loved his singing, playing and his personality. He told *Life*'s Richard Meryman in 1966, 'He was from Texas, but it was always: "You a spade, and I'm an ofay. We got the same soul. Let's blow" – and that's the way it was.'

Talking to the BBC's Geoffrey Haydon, Armstrong offered this opinion and story: 'Look at Jack Teagarden now. Who played no more blues than Jack? He was somethin' wasn't he? I know one story where a friend of his made him a nice bridge, but every time he went to work he'd put them teeth in his pocket. Say: "Boy, you goin' to sit down one day and bite yourself to death." That's what he did. He wouldn't play with 'em; he blew better, you know.'

When Louis received a telegram from his idol, Joe Oliver, asking him to join his band in Chicago, it set the seal on all his hopes and ambitions. He had been offered jobs away from home before – by Ory and Henderson – but was either unable to accept or doubtful of his readiness. 'I'd never leave New Orleans except for Papa Joe. When he asked me to join him at the Lincoln Gardens – it was about August 8 in 1922 – there was nothing or nobody could hold me. I was with the Tuxedo Band then, playing parades and funerals, and had just done my last funeral over in Algiers, Louisiana, that day.' The summons was not a surprise because letters had been exchanged between Oliver and his 'stepson', and, sending for Louis one day was a recurring theme of Oliver's correspondence. Zutty Singleton, already a close friend of Armstrong's, explained: 'Louis first got a telegram from Fletcher, and he answered Fletcher and said he wanted to bring me with him to New York. Fletcher told Louis that he'd had a drummer for so long and everything, and when Louis told me, I said: "I can't play with all those kind of guys." He said: "Man, you got rhythm." Finally Oliver sent for him, and he told me, said: "Zutty, I got to go. Man, Baby Dodds is drumming with King Oliver." He said: "So I got to go up there, got to leave you." Boy, it was wonderful. But I sure hated for him to leave.'

In Chicago Louis at first felt lost and homesick. The Creole Jazz Band sounded even better than he had expected. He wondered if he would ever measure up to such formidable talent as that possessed by Johnny and Warren (Baby) Dodds, Honore Dutrey, and Joe himself. The records show that he did. Though he played the role assigned to him by Oliver, his individual 'voice' kept breaking through the highly disciplined music. 'This newcomer', wrote the Chicago *Defender* of Armstrong's debut, 'brought us an entirely different style of playing than King Oliver had given us. He was younger, had more power of delivery, and could send out his stuff with a knack.' The knack opened a new chapter for the newcomer and for the music he graced. New Orleans saw him again in 1931, after that not for a further long period. As Bunk Johnson succinctly put it, 'Louis went north, and made good.'

Everybody from New Orleans Can Do That Thing

If Louis felt pangs of loneliness and uneasiness mixed with his elation at joining the most wailing band in Chicago, they were not long-lasting. Thousands of black Louisianians had migrated from the south during and after World War I, and many had settled in the Windy City. Among them were acquaintances, mostly musicians, from New Orleans who had found a better standard of living up north. All but one of the Oliver band members were from down home. Honore Dutrey, the Dodds brothers, Bill Johnson and Oliver himself – all were New Orleans men. These out-of-towners from Dixieland were not popular with Chicago musicians or their local union branch, but this didn't stop them being in demand. Louisiana was where the finest jazz players were bred. As the old Hot Five disc, *Gut Bucket Blues*, proclaims : 'Everybody from New Orleans can really do that thing'. The down-homers – or at least some of them – made Armstrong welcome, and the King looked out for him and insisted on him eating meals at the Oliver home.

Musically, the situation was only briefly daunting. Louis listened on his first night in town, and rehearsed next afternoon before taking his place on the bandstand for the first time. He quickly proved his worth. The rapport achieved by Joe and Louis, the two-cornet breaks and leads and occasional solos, soon became talking-points among lovers of the new music. Any young jazzman would have felt proud of a place in such a band. It was a commercially successful unit which had a strong following of dancers and other nightlifers at the Lincoln Gardens, one of the largest and most popular dance and cabaret spots. Picturing the place in Oliver–Armstrong days, Robert Goffin wrote:

> Only early comers could be sure of getting seats. The tables near the band were usually reserved for regular customers, who demonstrated their admiration ... by making themselves familiar with all the numbers, following the orchestra's rhythm, and generally going wild with enthusiasm.

And Preston Jackson again:

> Now when Louis joined Joe Oliver, the first ten rows at the Gardens was nothing but musicians. You could see such people as Paul Mares and the New Orleans Rhythm Kings, Muggsy Spanier, the Dorsey Brothers and musicians from a couple of other white bands that arrived. Also the fellows from that particular school in Chicago – George Wettling, Frank Teschmaker and that bunch. Well, all those were young, and they used to come over and listen.

For Louis the experience was 'a dream come true', and it must have been a pleasurable one for Oliver, who had so consistently befriended the gifted young player.

As Oliver had hoped, his Little Dipper proved an immediate asset to what was already the best hot band in town. The story of Armstrong joining the Creole Jazz Band has been told many times, not least by Louis. That first night, he was 'all ears, sitting up there listenin' and figurin' to myself, and almost before I could turn round Joe Oliver and me was playing duets and crackin' out trumpet breaks together'. These short licks and codas can be heard on a number of the band's recordings: *Snake Rag* (both versions), *Weather Bird Rag, Sweet Lovin' Man, Sobbin' Blues, Alligator Hop, Working Man Blues* (both versions), *Southern Stomps* and *I Ain't Gonna Tell Nobody*, and they were a source of mystified delight to the more musically inclined patrons of the Lincoln Gardens in 1922 and '23.

Louis remembered:

> All the white cats from downtown Chicago, Bix and all of
> them boys, would come by after their work and sit up by the
> band and listen until the place shut. They didn't understand
> how we did it, without music or anything. I had second
> trumpet notes for all them riffs and breaks we made. So
> many you hear today were originated by Joe Oliver, and I
> had notes for every one of them. Couldn't nobody trick us;
> the musicians thought we were marvellous.

There is ample evidence that this was so. Drummer
George Wettling, for example, has said: 'He [Oliver] and
Louis Armstrong had some breaks they played together
that I've never heard played since. I don't know how they
knew what was coming up next, but they would play those
breaks and never miss.'

Or trombonist Preston Jackson: 'Did those two team
together? When you saw Joe lean over towards Louis at
the first ending you would know they were going to make a
break in the middle of the next chorus. And what breaks
they made.'

Or clarinettist Buster Bailey: 'Louis upset Chicago. All
the musicians from Isham Jones's big band, for example,
came to Lincoln Gardens to hear the band Joe had, and
especially to hear Louis . . . King Oliver and Louis were the
greatest two trumpeters I ever heard together.'

Bailey went on to explain the secret of this novel duet
technique: 'What Joe was going to make in the middle
break, he'd make in the first ending. Louis would listen and
remember; then when the middle came, Oliver and Louis
would both take that same break together.' Early in 1924,
when Bailey toured with Armstrong in the Oliver band,
there were two clarinettists in the line-up. Buster and Rudy
Jackson, the other reedman, tried out the Oliver–Armstrong system on clarinets. King Joe didn't care for this,
according to Jackson's recollection, and forbade them to
repeat the attempt. The implication is that the leader was
jealous, but Louis painted a different picture.

They said: 'Aw, we can do that.' So the band's playing, and Buster says, 'now let's get it,' and they're concentrating and arguing about 'it's a wrong note, man.' Well, by the time the break comes, they're right in the middle of an argument. They never did get together!

From many contemporary accounts we know that Oliver was fond of putting on a show, and well aware of the commercial value of imitating, on cornet, with the aid of various mutes, cups, buckets, glasses or bottles, the sounds of a baby crying, a child talking, a rooster crowing and other farmyard noises, even a preacher and congregation. He was known as a 'freak' player and great gut-bucket man, full of jokes and riotous ideas.

A two-trumpet team was nothing new in jazz history, but we can be sure Oliver came up with something fresh in the way he used his. Any competent pair of musicians could have knocked out a series of breaks without missing, and hardly raised an eyebrow among the Chicago cognoscenti. What marked this duet-work as superior or, as was often said, sensational? To begin with, it went far beyond breaks. The voicing of the cornet parts, in relation to themselves and the whole flowing ensemble pattern, was clear and 'correct' yet subtly inventive. As dominant lead voices, the two cornets sang out the melody with superb lift and attack, urgent expressiveness tempered by restraint, and a proper regard for the continuity, balance and unity of the band's collective improvisation. As a matter of demonstrable musical fact, the Creole Band's performances on records were not improvised in the real sense of the word; but the effect of spontaneity was given – by various little deviations from the arranged parts, for example, or by highlighting Dodd's clarinet embroidery – and it seems reasonable to write of these ensemble variations as group improvisations in a New Orleans style.

Then, too, there was the personalized manner of the delivery. Every performance of classic New Orleans jazz depends on the personality of each player as well as on his willingness to submerge some of his individuality for the good of the ensemble. Thus no two classic or traditional bands, made up of different personnel, can sound alike, even if they play the same material. For sure, the execution of the Armstrong–Oliver duos was unlike anything the Chicagoans had seen or heard before. Both men were jazz giants, musicians with ears, memories, abilities out of the ordinary, and it can be assumed that their sheer presence was commanding.

So visually as well as aurally these cornet interpolations caught the imagination of Lincoln Garden patrons. The Creole Jazz Band was a cohesive unit playing closely organized and semi-arranged music. Solos were few, and the seven members would be rocking along in buoyant ensemble, tied together by a common spirit and the need to listen, paying little attention to the music sheets (if there were any) since they knew these compositions intimately. Then the instrumental interplay would give way to a two-bar break – taken by clarinet, trombone, cornet or whatever was favoured – which provided a release from the tension created by the collective effort. Sometimes the arrangement called for the two cornets. 'Then Joe and Louis stepped out,' wrote Frederic Ramsey in *Jazzmen*, 'and one of their breaks came rolling out of the two short horns, fiercely and flawlessly.' To the onlookers it was a bit of a puzzle, one which provided a moment of contrast and surprise, of liberation from the polyphonic statement of the theme, almost of light relief. Small wonder they waited for, and applauded, these crafty little duets which must have come as novel dramatic effects in those far-off early '20s.

The Lincoln Gardens were invariably crowded from dance floor to balcony. 'People belonging to all classes of society attended,' was how one musician put it. 'Doctors, lawyers, students, entertainment people, musicians, people of all colours were found there. When packed, the Gardens could hold a thousand customers. This loyal audience meant that the Lincoln Gardens were able to sustain, besides a group as fine as Oliver's, a cabaret said to run to half-a-dozen acts, including well-known singers like Ethel

Waters. The whole review might feature, according to entertainer Tommy Brookins, 'at least 60 people: chorus girls, Creole dancers, et cetera'.

It was before an appreciative 'sporting' crowd, well seasoned with musicians as we have heard, that King Oliver was able to present his protégé and his unbeatable three-man brass team.

I don't know of another band [Louis said] that had two trumpets at that time, but I guess Joe decided to have two because he figured I could blend with him, because he liked me and wanted me to be with him. He probably wouldn't have sent for anybody else. There wouldn't have been another trumpet player in New Orleans he'd think about, but he sent for me because he knew I could blend with him.

Oliver's confidence in his former pupil was justified; when they got together on the bandstand they 'really made something of it'. The musicians in front of the band might not have been able to tell which break the cornettists were going to play next, or when the choice was made, but for Joe and 'his boy' the matter was simple. Armstrong explained:

We weren't reading any music. Joe had a way of making up the break he was going to take while he was playing the lead, and I was on to his playing so well that I just figured my second to it and I'd just go about my business ... and when the break came it just was there, and the musicians ate it up.

He amplified this description of the method they 'stumbled upon'. The King would lean towards him, 'moving his valves on his trumpet, make notes, the notes that he was going to make when the break in the tune came. I'd listen . . . and when the break would come, I'd have my part to blend right along with him.' Another explanation is that during the chorus before the two-horn break, Oliver sang or softly hummed the phrases he would be playing in Louis' receptive ear.

69

For Armstrong, the years with Papa Joe were educative and inspiring – some of his most thrilling days, as he confessed more than once. Joe's was a real New Orleans band, dedicated to the creation of well-balanced, unexhibitionistic music, for Oliver was a firm believer in ensemble jazz. In that sense he was a disciplinarian, who once told an incoming player: 'I wants you to be a band man, and a band man only, and do àll you can for the welfare of the band.' Louis would have needed no such direction. His musical and social background resembled Papa Joe's and his outlook on jazz must have been very similar. When he joined Oliver in the summer of 1922 – usually held to be July, although Louis has repeatedly referred to 8 August as the date on which he received Joe's wire – he joined as a bandsman, not as a soloist. Expecting nothing else, he could scarcely have been disappointed.

The suggestion is often made that Oliver recruited his former pupil in order to protect his own reputation. By keeping this doughty contender as an auxiliary in his own outfit, Oliver felt safe from serious competition. That theory is based on fragile circumstantial evidence. Oliver had been away from his home town some four years, and could hardly have guessed how far the pupil had advanced. Why should he fear a distant, upcoming competitor? Was he not the talk of the Chicago jazz brethren, a great musician, a true cornet king?

If Oliver thought his supremacy was threatened, why did he invite the potential rival into his territory? Of course, Armstrong might have been tempted out by another bandleader; that possibility is supposed to have prompted Oliver to act. Against it is Louis' assurance that he had turned down offers before and would leave town for no one but Joe. Against it also is the weight of almost everything we can learn about the characters of the two men and their regard for each other. Armstrong never doubted that Mister Joe wanted him because of the relationship formed back home before 1919. 'After all,' he argued on Oliver's behalf, 'look at the progress he'd made in Chicago. He didn't *need* to send for me; he was top man.' And another time: 'Oliver was *the* man in Chicago; he had the town sewed up.'

Maintaining the band's superiority required sending down south for fresh talent from time to time, and so Armstrong was brought up to the South Side to maintain the Creole Jazz Band's lead over its competitors. 'During those times New Orleans was like a reservoir,' Preston Jackson has told us. 'You see there was Chris Kelly, Punch Miller returned from the army. Papa Celestin was still around – never did come north at that time – and there was Sam Morgan, Buddy Petit and Kid Rena. Joe Oliver could reach down when he needed trumpet players and come up with one just as good as the one he'd lost.'

What does not appear likely is that Oliver was moved by timidity, fear or jealousy. Louis and most of his contemporaries have described him as mild, helpful, considerate, if somewhat vain, and happy-go-lucky at that period in his life. If his motive in importing Louis into his band was selfish, it is far from obvious why he insisted on encouraging the youngster's musical curiosity and desire to learn. Soon – perhaps as soon as he heard Louis' virile cornet turned loose – Oliver may have experienced some of the discomfort of a man sitting on a hot stove. The attractions of having this extraordinary musician in the second trumpet chair would have been brought home each night with searing clarity. In time Joe came to feel safer with his protégé in the same band. Louis never denied this, nor that he began to find Oliver's musical restrictions irksome. By the end of his stay a number of things had happened to the band and to Louis. He had made his first recordings, played his first solos on record, begun to reach a wider audience. He had even married again. To Oliver goes the credit for helping him in all these achievements, as well as for summoning him up north in the first place.

The prince of New Orleans trumpeters had left his home and everything he knew and moved north to join the King. When he went to the station to catch the train to Chicago, friends and well-wishers came along to see his departure. Though happy for the local boy, some were disappointed because he was not to star in his own right. Others had warnings for him. Joe Oliver was in trouble with the musicians' union, they cautioned. (This was probable as he had already been fined on the West Coast for employing players who had not been cleared by the union.) To Louis, totally inexperienced in union matters, all this meant nothing.

The boys from the Tuxedo kept telling me I shouldn't go, because Oliver's band was out of the union and was scabbing ... that old phrase. I said it didn't bother me none, that whatever Papa Joe was doing, why, I wanted to do that same thing. I lived for him. So I took the train, with my valise and my cornet case, and when I got out at Illinois Central Station I couldn't see Joe or anyone I knew to meet me ... damn nearly went right back on the next train. You know, first time in a strange city, and all them tall buildings. It was a bad moment for me, I'd have gone back home, but he left word with a porter to guide me to the place. All I knew was Lincoln Gardens, Chicago. I went there, and when I dug this band, swingin', I nearly didn't go in.

Tommy Brookins remembers the welcome Louis received on the South Side.

The news spread like wildfire among the musicians who hurried that same evening to Lincoln Gardens. It wasn't that Louis' name was then known, but the musicians were aware of the fact that a young trumpet player had just arrived from New Orleans and was playing with Oliver.

Preston Jackson remembers the day of Louis' arrival for a different reason.

At night I was usually sitting behind Dutrey. Now he was afflicted; he was in the navy during World War One and was locked up in that powder magazine, and it affected his lungs. So whenever he begin to have trouble breathing he'd look back and say: 'Pardner, you want to play a little for

72

me?' I'd have paid him for the pleasure. So I happened to be sitting on the stand one night in 1922 and heard Joe say: 'Well, Dipper's coming with me tomorrow.' And, as true as his word, Louis walked in. He had on a brown suit with box-back coat, and a sailor straw hat, and carrying tan shoes. It seemed like he weighed 200 pounds or a little better. I had the honour to be introduced to him. Yes, there was bad blood between the Chicago men and the New Orleans musicians due to the fact that we had most of the work, except the theatres, locked up.

In a 1950 interview in *Record Changer*, Louis was shouting the praises of his idol as loudly as ever.

No trumpet player ever had the fire that Oliver had ... He was most serious about that horn. A lot of the boys in those days played a little rough, and they kept that bottle on the stand. The more they nipped the rougher they got. But Joe Oliver didn't drink, he could blow all day long.

Without doubt Louis found satisfaction and inspiration in the tightly co-ordinated approach of the Oliver band. Typically, he set out to improve his technique and enlarge his theoretical knowledge. In this, as in his domestic affairs, he was assisted by Oliver. Louis, for his part, was grateful, and not just for the advice. 'I thought so much of him, and what he did for me. I used to have all my meals at his house, eat just like they did – big pot of red beans and rice, half-loafs of bread, and a ham-hock. Drink sugar-water or lemonade. That's what we'd all have.' Both these giants of jazz were also champions at the table, and Mama Joe – Mrs Stella Oliver – knew how to provide the food they liked best.

It was Oliver who introduced Louis to his second wife and drew her attention to his musicianship, an action which had far-reaching consequences. Lillian Hardin was a trained pianist and an ambitious young lady, and before very long she was to replace Mister Joe as Armstrong's minder and guru. Often, in interviews, Louis would imply that Miss Lil was in the Lincoln Gardens band when he joined it, but he was telescoping occurrences from his past. She had already worked with Oliver at the Dreamland and Pekin Cafés – the latter a tough place favoured by mobsters and their bodyguards – and travelled with the band in 1921 to play in a West Coast 'jitney' dance hall. But she left at the end of that run, not in the best of health it was said, and the piano spot was filled by another girl player, Bertha Gonsoulin. Explaining the situation, Lil (Hardin) Armstrong wrote:

> Late in May, 1921, King Oliver's band went to San Francisco, Cal., to play a six-months engagement at the Pergola Ballroom (949 Market Street). When the job closed I returned to Chicago, but the rest of the band stayed out there an additional six months. Oliver brought Bertha Gonzales back to Chicago in 1922 and it was then that Louis joined him at the Royal Gardens. Some months later Bertha left and I went back with the band.

By the time the Creole Band came back to the Gardens, however, the old hangout on 31st Street and Cottage Grove Avenue had been redecorated and rechristened the Lincoln Gardens Café; and the piano replacement is usually, and we believe correctly, referred to as Gonsoulin. She is supposed to have evolved her keyboard style from the example of Jelly Roll Morton, then out in California, and with his help. If so, it should have fitted in felicitously with Oliver's conception of jazz.

Bertha must have joined the band at the end of '21 and stayed eight or nine months. She made a reappearance, as Bertha Gonzolon, with the rediscovered Bunk Johnson, in 1943, but remained an obscure figure, dismissed by Ross Russell as 'a weak substitute for the proper accompaniment'. I [M.J.] don't think I ever heard Armstrong speak of her. Rudi Blesh has even reported that Oliver asked her to meet Armstrong's train in Chicago – 'because', Blesh says, 'in a real New Orleans band the pianist could have dropped dead with the mishap unnoticed'. (The Creole Jazz

Band was on duty at the hour Louis was expected to arrive.) 'Minnie Mouse' – as this young lady was called by the bandsmen – is said to have actually met Armstrong and escorted him to the hall; but it seems more likely that the only person Louis found waiting for him was the redcap.

What happened to Bertha? Lil said, 'I don't know her. She didn't like Chicago – something happened – and she went back to San Francisco. I never heard her play. We were always working the same hours.'

Miss Lil

Anybody endowed with Armstrong's musical abilities and trusting disposition, and unversed in the politics and chicanery of the entertainment business, was bound to attract numbers of counsellors who would seek to direct him professionally. Up to this time Oliver – 'always to me a fantastic fellow', said Louis once – had given him the guidance, reassurance and concrete assistance he needed. Armstrong always wanted to look up to someone – a sort of father-substitute – and Papa Joe filled the bill during his teenage years and early twenties. It was somebody else's turn now that Louis was approaching the brink of self-realization. That somebody, as it turned out, was no father-figure but a girl of around Armstrong's age, Lillian Hardin, who had studied music at Fisk University where she was class valedictorian. Lil, from Memphis, Tennessee, picked up on jazz after she moved with her family to Chicago in 1917 and began working with Delta jazzmen at the Dreamland on 35th and State.

Before falling under her gentle influence Louis toiled happily and rewardingly for many weeks at the Gardens. The 'green-looking country boy' was getting his boots laced, not only learning from playing with his idol but accustoming himself to the ways of the big city. During this settling-in period he received an unexpected visit. His mother, advised that her son was ill and even feeling suicidal up north, had packed necessary belongings in two bundles and entrained for Chicago. Upon making a few urgent enquiries she wasted no time in seeing for herself what shape he was in.

We were sitting on the stand getting ready for the show one night [Louis recalled with some relish]. Lights up, you know, and everybody waiting when what should we see cutting across that floor but a familiar figure. My God, it was Mayann, walking past the tables, the waiters, coming straight towards me. Just walked across that dance floor looking at me, watching nobody else. Joe said, 'Ah, here comes the hen.' I couldn't hardly believe my eyes. She came right up to me, pointing, and said she'd heard I was doin' bad.

Like I told you, somebody who'd been to Chicago let her know I was in a poor job, hanging my head and cryin', which was all lies, so mama had rushed up there looking for me. She said, 'Son, they told me you was fairing out so bad I had to come up to see about you.' Naturally I told her I was all right, very happy with the band, and Papa Joe dedicated a number to her and we went on back to playing.

Referring to his mother's sudden appearance in the Lincoln Gardens, Armstrong once told Barry Ulanov: 'When she saw what a fine job I had and how big and fat and happy and healthy I was, she cried. She spent the rest of the night right on the stand with us and we all missed cues and muffed stuff, we were so happy.'

When she caught the train for Chicago, Mary Ann Armstrong intended to be back home within a few days, but Louis was so pleased to see her he made her stay on.

I got her an apartment at St Lawrence and 45th and bought her a lot of nice clothes and everything. And I enjoyed that just as well. She liked Chicago but I guess she got homesick. One day she decided to go back to New Orleans, saying, 'My church is waiting for me.' I couldn't hold her. And she went back to her home and a little later on took very sick, and I lost her. We did what we could, and I sure am glad I had the chance to do something for her before she passed.

The exact dates of these events are unknown. Goffin has written of Lil being in the band when Mama Armstrong visited town, which would make it the autumn of 1922 or later. But Lil denies this with finality. 'Louis and I were not married when his mother came to visit him; in fact Bertha Gonzales was still playing piano with Oliver at that time.' It is not on record just when Lil returned to the band. 'Late in the summer' is the guess of Walter Allen and Brian Rust.

Mayann's death occurred some time afterwards, as is shown by Lil's remark 'it was later that Louis' mother became ill. I went to New Orleans and brought her to Chicago to join us. She died in this house on East 44 Street I'm still living in – the same house that Louis and I purchased in 1925.' In his book *Swing That Music* Louis noted that his mother 'died very young – in her early forties'. By that time, of course, he had a new wife to think about.

Miss Hardin was not unknown to Louis, nor he to her, before she took over the piano stool from Bertha Gonsoulin. Papa Joe had seen to that. He had sent photographs to Louis in New Orleans; Louis had replied that he liked Miss Lil and to tell her so, which provoked that lady's curiosity.

Finally, while I was working at the Dreamland, Joe brought Louis over to meet me. I'd been hearing from all the musicians about him – Little Louis, they'd called him – and what a good player he was. So they brought him in and 'Li'l Louis' was all of 226 pounds.

Naturally the pianist was surprised. In a reminiscent note to *Down Beat*'s '50 Years With Armstrong' issue, she said that Louis didn't stay long in the cabaret that night, and didn't play. If he had it would have fastened her attention, no doubt. As it was, she didn't entertain 'any romantic ideas at all at that time'. Louis, on his part, remembered the smart-looking brown-skin and was wary of meeting her after his 'tell Miss Lil I like her' message; nevertheless he went with Oliver and approved of what he heard at the piano – and saw, if Lil is to be relied on.

In a TV interview Lil spoke humorously about Armstrong's size and style. 'How come you call him "Li'l Louis", big as he is?' she had asked the other musicians. 'Well, he's been following us around since he was a little boy,' they replied.

I wasn't impressed at all [she said], I was very disappointed. 226 pounds. I didn't like anything about him. I didn't like the way he dressed; I didn't like the way he talked; and I just didn't like him. I was very disgusted. So he came on the bandstand – I don't know if I should tell this or not – and I used to, you know ... girls wore garters on their stockings, so when I'd sit down to play I would roll my stocking down so the garter was below my knee, for circulation. And the first thing Louis spied was my knee. And he was looking, and I said: 'This guy's got ideas he'd better not put into words.'

They didn't meet again for a month or two, and not regularly until she moved across to Oliver's band at the Lincoln Gardens. Then her interest in the newcomer was aroused by a remark of Oliver's.

One night he told me: 'You know this Louis, he's a better trumpet player than I'll ever be ... As long as I keep him playing second to me he won't get ahead of me. I'll still be the king.' I said, 'Oh, yeah?' It didn't mean anything to me because Louis didn't mean anything to me either. But I started to listening, to try to see if there was any difference, but I couldn't tell any difference because they played their solos together – Louis would play a second to everything he played ... I really couldn't tell.

The band stayed at the Gardens until late February, and then began a tour of the Middle West. In the Starr Piano Company's studios in Richmond, Indiana, they made their first recordings, for the Company's Gennett label. Nine historic tracks were cut on 6 April 1923: *Just Gone, Canal Street Blues, Mandy Lee Blues, I'm Going Away To Wear You Off My Mind, Chimes Blues, Weather Bird Rag, Dippermouth Blues, Froggie Moore* and *Snake Rag*.

All were interesting compositions, and three were band originals by Oliver. They were numbers the musicians knew well and 'had down', but drummer Baby Dodds said that the boys were nervous in the unfamiliar surroundings of the Gennett studio. That included the leader – 'Joe was no different from any of the rest' – but not the lady, for 'the only really smooth-working person there was Lil Armstrong. She was very unconcerned and much at ease.' Maybe this self-confidence stemmed from the years of study Lil had put in before meeting Louis. Certainly she was a remarkable person, able to read music fluently and write it down, and help with the arrangements and compose good tunes, in addition playing adequate jazz piano with the four-in-a-bar beat which was not all that common in those times.

Lillian was not yet Mrs Armstrong, of course, but if she had thoughts in that direction they were probably spurred on by what she noted at that first recording session.

We all had to blow in this great big horn, the old style. And in trying to get the balance, Joe and Louis stood right next to each other as they always had, and you couldn't hear a note that Joe was playing, only could hear Louis. So they said, 'Well, gotta do something,' and they put Louis about fifteen feet over in the corner, looking all sad ... he thought it was bad for him to have to be separated from the band. I looked at him and smiled to reassure him that he was all right. And then I said to myself, 'Now if they have to put him that far away in order to hear Joe, he's got to be better.' Then I was convinced.

Louis' instinct was right, since a New Orleans band should be grouped together for the necessary unity in performance. He confirmed Lil's account: 'to show how much stronger I was than Joe, he would be right in that horn, blowing, and I would be standing back in the door'; but he added that Oliver was no longer in his prime (he was not quite 38 years old) when those records were made.

Hearing those first Gennetts today we realize that Armstrong's part could have been a fraction more prominent. On the later sides, his share of the ensemble pattern is more clearly heard. He may have moved in a little or increased his volume, or – as Lil suggested at one time – simply projected his sound as an actor would do until his voice was audible in all parts of the room.

I [M.J.] shall not attempt to examine the records individually; they are described elsewhere in the book, and Gunther Schuller's *Early Jazz*, Martin Williams' *Jazz Masters Of New Orleans*, Rudi Blesh's *Shining Trumpets*, Wilfrid Meller's *Music In A New Found Land* and Leroy Ostransky's *The Anatomy Of Jazz* contain good critical studies. As early as 1942, Hugues Panassié, in his book *The Real Jazz*, wrote shrewdly about Oliver's records:

> The extraordinary thing about these interpretations is the perfect equilibrium which the musicians achieve in improvisation, and the grace and melodic clarity which reigns from the beginning to the end. Listen, for example, to the sublime *Canal Street Blues* ... Is there anything more moving than the singing of the two trumpets, enriched by the singing counterpoint of Dodds' clarinet?

Not everyone agreed. A 1943 critique in *Jazz Music* complained:

> Although Oliver's was not the first New Orleans group to use two cornets, the practice, we feel, destroyed the perfect balance of the 'classic' instrumentation. By doubling the power of the tenor voice a responsibility was thrust upon the clarinet it could not, tonally, fulfil ... As we may only judge the band by its recorded performance, it would appear that the addition of a second cornet was a liability rather than an asset. With two cornets of different power, the question was further complicated.

This is to some extent true. The controlled cut and thrust of three-part interplay in the New Orleans ensemble is liable to be impaired by doubling up the melodic lead. In

81

practice, much would depend on the degree of variation indulged in by the lead players and their qualifications for this task, demanding as it did a sensitive ear for harmony and the many rhythmic and melodic nuances of New Orleans style. Armstrong and Oliver were outstandingly qualified, and the critique above allows room for several complimentary references to the imaginative integration of the cornet lines.

It is indeed surprising to discover an artist of Armstrong's phenomenal virtuosity playing a secondary role with such conspicuous success. The ability to sublimate his individual ardour to the dictates of scrupulous performance – a remarkable gift in one possessed of so strong an artistic personality ... At first hearing the listener is apt to overlook the younger cornetist's contribution. Thoughtful listening, however, brings to light a score of moments which owe their brilliance, in no small measure, to Armstrong's cornet.

Again, of *Mandy Lee Blues* (a blues in name only), after mention of the melodic nature of this music:

In conventional manner the cornets state the theme during the first chorus ... Without preamble the second chorus is introduced, and here the two cornets commence to enrich the melodic line. With the improvisatory spirit abroad the rhythmic section adds stress to the basic pulse. In this sequence, too, we glimpse Armstrong, *second* cornet. With rare fidelity he matches his tone, his vibrato, to Oliver's, weighs his accents with selfsame precision. On hearing this performance we begin to appreciate the astonishment these improvised cornet duets aroused in audiences of the time.

This critic of nearly thirty years ago had perforce to base his judgements on recordings, mostly dubbings, of questionable fidelity. This led to some under-valuing of Oliver's personal contribution, as player and bandmaster. It was he who imposed his taste and sense of order on the Creole Band's music. Today we are better served by reissues, but as we never heard the band in person we cannot achieve more than a partial knowledge of how it sounded in real performance. The sessions were nerve-wracking, the balance was imperfect, recording techniques were somewhat rudimentary and, whenever a train was due on the tracks which lay outside the studio, recording had to stop. Further, the choice of programme and duration of each number were to some extent determined by the requirements of the Gennett people. It is surprising how much lastingly fine music found its way into the grooves of those archaic shellac discs.

The band went on to record further titles for Gennett, OKeh, Columbia and Paramount, all during 1923. As well as their indication of the singular flow and coherence of the ensemble, these records give us most of our knowledge of Armstrong the 22- and 23-year-old trumpet player. He arrived in the studios already a fully-fledged musician – how good we cannot say for sure, since his artistry may have been held in check and his sound was, in any case, inadequately captured by acoustic recording. There is, however, no hesitancy about his well-made second cornet parts, when they can be followed closely, and nothing diffident about his various solos. In spite of accusations that Oliver refused to feature Louis, we hear his first recorded solo, the fourth strain of *Chimes Blues*. It is not an inspired example of extempore playing, for Louis sounds as if he is following a written variation. Oliver rehearsed his music fairly thoroughly, so almost all the solo passages would be prepared variations performed from memory. Even so, Louis' personal debut on disc shows a poised rhythmic character and a tonal urgency which proclaim unmistakably that it is Louis Armstrong at the business end of the cornet.

On 5 February 1924 Louis Armstrong and Lil Hardin were married. Louis had divorced his Daisy and had been 'walking out' with Lil for some months. 'And the musicians, as soon as they found out we were dating, they all quit speaking to us almost,' Lil recalls. 'They didn't like it because they knew I was going to start something.' Lil worked hard on Louis' sight-reading. 'I thought the best thing to do was to get him away from Joe,' she revealed in *Down Beat*. 'I encouraged him to develop himself, which was all he needed. He's a fellow who didn't have much confidence in himself to begin with.' Lil was not in a minority in her belief that Louis surpassed Oliver in tone, ideas and technique. Musicians' memoirs, when they touch on the Creole Jazz Band, are loaded with similar opinions. Tommy Brookins said:

It was necessary to wait till Joe Oliver was sick to have a real idea of the talent of Louis ... believe me, Louis really played, showing everyone present all he knew, all his tricks, and he received after each song trémendous acclamations ... Hearing Louis after Oliver it seemed that Louis was more powerful. Opposite the young Louis, who was already prodigious, Oliver's style rapidly appeared to us to date a little.

Preston Jackson did not feel that Armstrong got enough chances. 'Joe seldom featured Louis, knowing that Louis could show him up. Therefore Louis would never have been as famous as he is, had he continued to play second trumpet to Joe Oliver.' Buster Bailey made it plain that, showcased or not, Satch soon became something of a sensation. 'What made Louis upset Chicago so? His execution, for one thing, and his ideas, his drive.' Armstrong, at that period, was at least the equal of Oliver and probably his superior as a player; but King Joe had done much of it first. He was Louis' principal model. Moreover he was, in the words of Burnett James, 'in a number of significant respects the father of jazz trumpet playing'.

The shortcomings of the early recording situation, which militate against a true assessment of Armstrong's capabilities at that date, also preclude a full, fair judgement of Oliver's worth. We can hear what he thought fit to play and direct on those recordings. We know that his choice of material, and the tempos at which it was to be performed, was exceptional, and also that his phrases swung well, but we would be hard put to it to express a firm opinion on the

84

power or beauty of his tone or the extent of his prowess as a soloist. Outside the studios Oliver took solos of a type not heard on any of the almost forty sides he cut with the Creole Jazz Band. He was celebrated for those on which, in Mutt Carey's phrase, he made his horn sound like a holy roller meeting. Mutt's use of cups and buckets to mute his trumpet was inspired by Joe Oliver – 'the greatest freak trumpet player I ever knew'. He admired both Oliver and Armstrong enormously, and could compare them knowledgeably with each other and with the rest of the Crescent City pioneers. Asked, in an interview, to nominate the greatest trumpet player in jazz, he said there was no question ... Louis.

You see, he tried to make a picture out of every number he was playing, to show just what it meant ... I remember once when Louis came out to Lincoln Park in New Orleans to listen to the Kid Ory Band. I was playing trumpet with the Kid then and I let Louis sit on my chair. Now at that time I was the 'Blues King' of New Orleans, and when Louis played that day he played more blues than I ever heard in my life ... I always admired him from the start. I give Freddie Keppard and Joe Oliver credit too; they were great boys, but there's no one who ever came close to Louis. No, Louis was ahead by a mile.

After enumerating some of Armstrong's virtues – playing from the heart as he felt a number at the time, playing it as he would sing it, and vice versa, filling all his notes and hitting them correctly – Carey went on:

There's nothing freakish about Louis' horn. He fingers what he wants to play and there are no accidents in the notes he brings out ... Louis set the pace for the whole world for trumpet players. Joe and Freddie did their bits but they never could touch Louis. God knows, both of them were good but what the heck, man, they never could touch Louis ... Now at one time Freddie Keppard had New Orleans all sewed up. He was the king, yes, he wore the crown. Then Louis got in and killed the whole bunch of them ... Now

LOUIS ARMSTRONG'S
125 Jazz Breaks
for
Hot Trumpet

Throughout the world the name of Louis Armstrong is known to thousands of musicians. It is accepted by interpreters of jazz and commands at all times a place of honor. During the past few years jazz music has come into international vogue. Armstrong was among the pioneers who brought it into popularity and has been a big factor in keeping it to the front. His influence is felt everywhere. Hundreds of jazz cornetists, who by the way, are an important feature in all dance orchestras, have adopted the Armstrong style of playing. Many of the greatest hot men we have today, men who have made enviable reputations as recording artists, will tell you they conceived many of their tricks and ideas from the Armstrong style of playing. His ability is enthusiastically endorsed by all the great and near great.

The breaks in this book depart in principle of production from any breaks on the market. They are genuine inspirations obtained, not by the old method of the artist writing down his breaks one note at a time, but from actual recordings. Special phonograph recording apparatus was employed to make them. They are red hot inspirations extracted from red hot jazz recordings.

If you want to get hot and stay hot, memorize these breaks. They will prove invaluable to all jazz cornetists as they can be used in playing any and all dance melodies.

Publisher's Note.

Buddy Petit was a boy who had the ideas like Louis but he let the liquor get the best of him. He never was as powerful as Louis but he sure had ideas and feeling. He was no high note man either.

Commenting on Oliver's records, Carey embraced them all in this statement:

86

I haven't heard a single one that comes close to sounding like Joe's playing in person. I don't know what it was but I'll tell you the truth, I don't believe that it is Joe playing on the records sometimes. It never has sounded to me much like Joe.

One person never went on record as saying Armstrong could outplay King Oliver. That was Little Louis, constant in his admiration and respect for the man he classed as a creator, a player with unlimited ideas who influenced scores of musicians and failed to win the recognition he deserved 'in the mentionings in Jazz History'. Armstrong was advised from several directions, even before his marriage to Lil (but more forcefully afterwards), to strike out for himself. He found the advice painful, and his unwavering loyalty left him learning the tactics of the game from the King, never out-blowing him or dominating the music unless he had been assigned to that role, deepening his understanding of the essential disciplined freedom of the New Orleans idiom.

Although Louis was profoundly influenced by Lil he still resisted the pressure she put on him to leave Oliver. Lil said she thought Oliver sent for him partly for selfish reasons. ('He was going downhill – otherwise why would he have done it?'). Louis countered by saying he didn't look at it that way. 'He still played whatever part he had played, and I always played "pretty" under him.' Another time he wrote that she and Oliver were both working on him. Joe, he said, held him back for a while 'and the boys didn't understand it at first, but I guess the King knew what he was doing'. He argued, pertinently, that Oliver 'always insisted I had something special, and that's how Lil Hardin became interested in me'. Lil had Satch rehearsing with her, practising classical pieces, playing church recitals, and thinking about going his own way stylistically and professionally. 'She didn't want me to copy Joe, liked me to play the way I felt it,' said Louis. 'He tried to play some of Joe's solos, but they sounded different,' said Lil. 'Joe always played with a mute, and Louis played clear and straight.'

'She told me I could play better than Joe and should have a chance to play the first chair,' said Louis.

Shortly after the wedding, at Chicago's City Hall, the Oliver band went on a tour of Pennsylvania, Ohio, Wisconsin and Michigan. By now the personnel had changed. Bill Johnson had gone some while before, and Dutrey and the Dodds brothers had left late in 1923, after, it is rumoured, rows with Oliver about money and his use of 'outside' men on record dates. Armstrong once said that Oliver's men were always talking about striking for something or other. It has been suggested that the Dodds brothers and Dutrey were dissatisfied because he didn't give Louis enough chance to shine. Louis' explanation was simply that the King wished to take the band on the road 'at real good money' and half the band declined, preferring to stay in town.

Lil had something else to say about the money. She alleged that Joe Oliver was receiving $95 apiece for his players and handing them $75. 'So Johnny and Baby threatened to beat him up.' Through the years stories have circulated of King Oliver coming to rehearsals with a big gun in his pocket. As guns were then a common coin of existence, in a hustling community where, in Al Capone's words, 'nobody's on the legit', this is not unlikely. If Lil's version of the circumstances is correct, he can be forgiven for arming himself against threats. One of the Dodds brothers might have been 'dressed'. She remembered that Oliver brought his pistol to work in his cornet case every night. Not surprisingly, perhaps, the aggrieved members gave their notice – but not Armstrong, 'always so crazy about Joe' as Lil granted. He agreed to stay, so Lil stayed too. Those who left were easily replaced, for at that date the King could still get top men.

Other factors entered into these band changes. The manageress at the Gardens had apparently asked Oliver to use saxophones 'like the band across the road'. The reedmen he brought in towards the close of '23 were Rudy Jackson and Buster Bailey, both saxophonists from the rival Sunset

Café. Jackson claimed, however, that during his spell at the Lincoln Gardens he seldom played his saxophone. Like a good New Orleanian, Oliver preferred the clarinet; but if the lady wanted saxophones, saxophones she should have.

Thus Jackson and Bailey took part in the north-eastern tour, and it was then they tried to outdo Joe and Louis with the duet licks. In Jackson's memory this shook the King considerably and he ordered them to cut it out. 'He was the leader,' said the clarinettist in a 1947 interview, 'and if he wanted the clarinets to play breaks together he'd tell them when to do it.' Lil and the two saxophone players felt Louis was wasting his time with Joe, and dropped hints to this effect 'at every possible opportunity', but Louis would not budge. Interestingly enough, Jackson gave no support to the view that Oliver kept Louis out of the limelight. On the contrary, he declared that on one-night bookings the King left Louis with a good share of the lead playing, and often wandered off the bandstand, leaving his second cornetist in charge.

Armstrong was probably doing a few vocals, too, and evidently some dancing. 'I used to do a little comedy dance then; I'd slide and fall, like I was going to hurt myself.' As Rudy Jackson told it, the singing and humour, as well as the playing, were popular with the crowds. Before long it was being suggested that Louis should lead the band, which, not unnaturally, upset Oliver. Though very fond of Louis, Joe did not like the idea of his attracting so much attention; but, beyond his peak as a player, he could do little about it. Sometimes he found, Jackson stated, that his band was not wanted for an engagement unless Armstrong was in it. Sensitive to these currents and anxious to please Joe, the younger man deliberately toned down his playing and took a back seat.

On that tour nothing was settled about his departure, but when they got back from the honeymoon-cum-working trip Lil told Armstrong firmly that she had no desire for a husband who was a second trumpet. 'What are you talking about?' he asked. 'Well, I don't want to be married to a second trumpet player. I want you to play first,' she replied. Armstrong, a patient man at most times, tried again. 'I can't play first, Joe's playing first.' Lil brought the argument to an end with grim efficiency, according to her own account. 'I said "That's why you've got to quit." He said "I can't quit Mr Joe; Mr Joe sent for me and I can't quit him." I said "Well, it's Mr Joe or me".'

The end of Armstrong's first job in Chicago was in sight. The band played more out-of-town dates in May and June, six weeks of them, and during this tour Louis' mind was made up for him. Returning to Chicago by train from a gig outside the city, Lil, Bailey and Jackson – apparently the chief conspirators – prised Louis away from Oliver for a talk. At last they persuaded him that it was to his advantage to make a move. After a long argument he agreed to try his luck away from the King, but was 'greatly perturbed' at the thought. He wouldn't tell Oliver himself, understandably, so Jackson went to where Joe was sleeping and woke him up with the tidings. Rudy and the others expected the bandleader to 'go raving mad', but he took the news quietly. Oliver was no stranger to bad luck, and from that year on he was to suffer misfortune on an increasing scale. The thought of losing Little Louis must have been a dismaying one, but we have Jackson's word for it that the King merely said he knew Louis was a better player than himself, also that he was lucky Louis liked him enough to have stayed so long.

It was the end of June 1924 when Armstrong handed in his notice. The impression often given in jazz writings is that he left Oliver and at once joined Fletcher Henderson's orchestra in New York. Lil told it differently, in an interview with Geoffrey Haydon.

Louis asked 'You made me quit – now what you want me to do?' I said 'Just go on out, round the musicians, find out who needs a first trumpet-player.' So the first place he went to was the Sunset. They had a band – quite a society band – called Sammy Stewart. So he went and asked him and said that Sam barely turned his head, told him, 'No, I don't need

90

anybody,' and Louis came back home.

I said to go out again tomorrow, somewhere else. 'Don't worry, they'll soon be eating at your feet.' I heard that Ollie Powers was putting a band in Dreamland, and Louis went there and Ollie said, 'Yes, come on, sit there and play with us.' So Louis played and Ollie liked him and he hired him. When he came back and told me I said, 'That's good. How many trumpet-players in?' 'Just one.' I said, 'Oh, then you'll be first.' And Louis said, 'Girl, you're sure crazy.' But he rehearsed and opened up with the band and they did very well. Because when Louis was the only trumpet-player he played what he had in himself.

Miss Lilly had won.*

Lil Hardin Armstrong

---

* Lil Hardin Armstrong died on 27 August 1971, while taking part in a Louis Armstrong Memorial Concert held in Chicago.

91

Big Apple and Back

At this stage of his life, still only 24 years old but now married, Satchmo found his career taking off rapidly. He was moving steadily up a ladder whose base was held by Lil Armstrong, watching him climb. Viewed in the short term, however, his progress was not consistently upwards. The branches of entertainment which gave employment to jazz musicians could not be expected to bear fruit indefinitely. The Chicago *Defender* printed its first notice of a Vitaphone talking picture in November 1926, and early the following year it warned musicians that theatre business was declining all over the country. Times were to get rougher for other businesses, too, before the decade came to an end.

For one reason and another, but mainly because musical tastes tend to change with each generation, the public for small-band hot jazz – never large – decreased rapidly during the later '20s. The demand was for larger bands and sweeter, less challenging, music. So Chicago became a scuffling city for the jazz fraternity, and many who had trekked from the Mississippi valley up to the middle west to follow the work now migrated towards the big cities in the north. Even Armstrong, who recorded and worked regularly, knew days when he had nothing.

Playing jazz was still a gigantic kick for him. He enjoyed nearly all his jobs, particularly the Dreamland one with Ollie Powers. Powers (real name Powell) was a singing drummer, who died in 1928; Louis played trumpet at his funeral service. He might well have stayed with Powers, but in September 1924 he received a telegram from 'Smack' Henderson in New York, and agreed to go there to join him. Henderson's was almost certainly the highest-ranking black band in the land – for all that its jazz-playing ability was slight; but to work in it meant status hitherto unattainable for a relatively unschooled musician like Louis. The money, said to be $55 a week, was less than he had been getting with Oliver. Going into the big-time would compensate for that, though, and his working wife must have been a help to the family finances.

It is a little surprising that after she had master-minded Armstrong's exit from the band, Lil wished to remain with Oliver or was permitted to do so. In every respect the King appears to have been an unflappable and dignified sort of figure. The night Louis gave notice, Oliver told Lil, adding, 'I didn't get yours.' She replied that she wasn't quitting. Joe shook his head and said he didn't understand why Louis was leaving. Lil thought, 'I wonder if he figures that I made Louis do that.' But what she said was: 'Don't worry, he'll be back with us soon.' To herself she added, 'Over my dead body he will!'

Preston Jackson gave Lil credit because Louis was known only in Chicago and the south, not nationally, before he went out for himself. 'I felt if it wasn't for Lil, Louis would not be where he is today.'

Perhaps Oliver believed that she was right and that what happened was inevitable. Armstrong could look back, a quarter of a century later, and decide that he had reached a position from which he felt it was time to move on, and Oliver thought so too. 'He couldn't hold me, I couldn't stay where I was.' His career was being handicapped, and his creative energies were being confined, although it took somebody else to make him realize it. Thinking back after 46 years he stressed Lil's part in his progress:

If she did engineer my life, she had a perfect right to. We married and heard the preacher when he said to love, honour and obey. And to me that's what was happening ...

93

I listened very careful when Lil told me I should play first cornet. Play second to no one, she told me. They don't get great enough. She proved she was right, didn't she?

Having achieved Louis' independence from Oliver, Lil Armstrong worked with the band for a month or two, then quit in order to join her husband. 'I was nosing around, listening and looking, and noticed all the signs for Fletcher Henderson. I didn't see Louis' name anywhere,' Lil told Geoffrey Haydon. 'So I said to Louis, "Well, you situated all right? I'm going back to Chicago."'

Louis travelled to New York on 29 September 1924. When he accepted the invitation he had no idea what to expect; but Henderson had asked for him the second time and he decided he'd better go – three years late, as he put it. Lil had improved his music-reading, building on the foundation he gained from David Jones on the Mississippi showboats, but he still found some difficulty initially in the special arrangements in Fletcher's book. He rejoiced in the atmosphere of Harlem, however, and was stimulated by the prospect of fitting in with a four-man brass section in his first big dance band.

The size of this band, like much else in Louis' story, is open to question. It was a fine twelve-piece band at the Roseland Ballroom according to *Swing That Music*. Richard Hadlock writes that 'in Henderson's eleven-man organization he found high ensemble discipline and contact with a wide variety of musical materials that extended well beyond even the ambitious arrangements Louis had played in riverboat orchestras.' Well, it numbered eleven very shortly after Armstrong came in, but it seems likely that there were nine men at the time he joined. 'We had a nine-piece band, which was the standard thing in those days,' wrote Kaiser Marshall, the drummer with Henderson. And he was more specific: 'the regular set-up was two saxes, two trumpets, one trombone, banjo, piano, drums and tuba. Fletcher wanted to try using three trumpets, and that was why he sent for Louis.' Henderson had, in fact, been using three

94

trumpets on records for some months before Louis' arrival, Joe Smith filling the third chair. Buster Bailey, one of Joe Oliver's reedmen, joined Henderson at the same time, having been recommended by Louis.

As befitted a band of its reputation and popularity – it was described by the black press of the day as the 'greatest, not at all like the average Negro orchestra, but in a class with the good white orchestras' – Henderson's group recorded frequently. It visited the studios when Satch had been installed for just one week; on that occasion the ensemble numbered eleven, including Louis and Buster Bailey. Two titles were made that day, and before the month was out six more had been cut, at two more sessions.

A fund of information survives on the subject of Louis' thirteen months with Smack. He shook the New York jazz world as he had Chicago's a year or two earlier; other 'name' bands, such as Sam Lanin's, played opposite Henderson at the Roseland, and their musicians spread the word about the fabulous new trumpet player. So did Smack's men, no doubt, and people like Rex Stewart, the cornetist, came in again and again to look, listen and wonder. 'Then Louis hit town. I went mad with the rest of the town. I tried to walk like him, talk like him, eat like him, sleep like him,' Rex enthused. 'Finally I got to shake hands and talk with him.'

Duke Ellington said that when Henderson came in with Louis 'the guys had never heard anything just like it'. Don Redman swore that Armstrong's style and feeling changed the band's conception of music. This can be detected in their records, if they are listened to in sequence, from Before Louis to After. The earlier records are almost without exception undistinguished, but their mediocrity is shattered from time to time by the emergence of Armstrong, quickly coming to terms with the unfamiliar surroundings, soloing fiercely in a setting very different from Oliver's lusty ensemble. These solos impressed and inspired musicians who had not heard him in Chicago or caught him with the Henderson band. Bill Coleman said:

95

When I was nineteen I first heard Louis on a record with Fletcher Henderson. One of the most disappointing nights of my life was when Henderson was making a tour and came to Cincinatti, and Louis was not with the orchestra ... But Louis made up for it when I first heard him in person at the Savoy Ballroom in New York a few years later. I was hypnotized, paralysed and knocked out when I heard him. I could not believe that one man could get so much out of a trumpet, yet I was seeing and hearing it done.

That, roughly speaking, is the impact that Armstrong's cornet made on any musician when first confronted by it head-on. His 'hot' ideas and tone, and especially the bold yet relaxed manner in which he attacked his phrases, had their effect on Henderson, his arrangers, such as Redman, and his bandsmen. After exposure to Louis' New Orleans style of improvisation and 'attack' – the swinging element of jazz or 'hokum' music was then sometimes defined as 'attack' – Fletcher's star soloists had a few altered notions to digest on the art of 'jazzing it up'.

Kaiser Marshall threw interesting light on the first meeting of Satch and Smack's men.

I remember the day that Louis showed up for rehearsal. We were up at the Happy Rhone Club, a night club at 143rd Street and Lennox Avenue that we used for rehearsals. The band was up on the stand waiting when he got there, and Louis walked across the floor. He had on big thick-soled shoes, the kind policemen wear, and he came walking across the floor, clump-clump, and grinned and said hello to all the boys.

He got his seat and opened the book for the third trumpet. Now Fletcher Henderson's book wasn't one that just anybody could open up and read at sight. He had a lot of difficult arrangements there ... They were pretty fancy arrangements, and although Louis was a good reader at that time, he had a little trouble at first. He would make a mistake and jump up and say: 'Man, what is that thing?' Then everybody laughed and Louis would sit down and play it right the next time. After he made one mistake he didn't make it

Above The street, Jane Alley, in which Louis was born on or around the year 1900. This shot is taken from the Alley looking towards Gravier Street with Perdido Street behind.

Right Lulu White's Mahogany Hall—a famous 'sex emporium' at 235 Basin Street, once known as the Hall of Mirrors—as it looked shortly before being pulled down in 1949. It was the last Basin Street brothel to be demolished.

Above Family group in New Orleans, 1919 or 1920. Louis, his mother, Mayann, and sister Beatrice—often called Mama Lucy.

Opposite Satchmo, as he looked on his 1932 visit to Britain. He was renowned for his large 'Windsor' tie knot, also for his gold wrist chain.

Fate Marable and his Riverboat Orchestra—Marable (piano), Johnny St Cyr (banjo), Louis (cornet) and Baby Dodds (drums).

'Creators of Jazz', self-styled. The Original Dixieland Jazz Band in London, possibly at the Hammersmith Palais de Danse, 1919. (L. to r.) Russell Robinson, Larry Shields, Nick La Rocca, Emile Christian, Tony Sbarbaro.

Above Louis with Jack Hylton (on his left) and orchestra.

Opposite Creole Jazz Band, probably early 1923, with (l. to r.)
Baby Dodds, Honore Dutrey, (rear) King Oliver, Louis
Armstrong, (rear) Bill Johnson, Johnny Dodds and Lil Hardin.

Ory's Original Creole Jazz Band in California, *c.* 1922. Probably Ben Borders (drums), Kid Ory (trombone), Mutt Carey (cornet), Wade Whaley (clarinet).

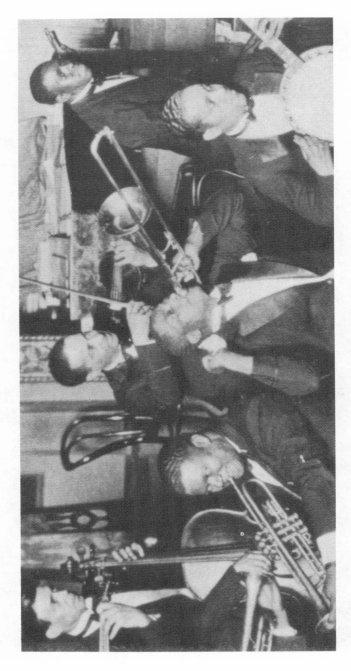

Erskine Tate's Vendome Orchestra, Chicago, 1926/7, with Louis on trumpet, Tate (violin) and probably Frank Ethridge (banjo).

Armstrong's Hot Five in 1926: Louis, Johnny St Cyr, Johnny Dodds, Kid Ory and Lil Hardin Armstrong.

Above Louis with (centre)
Johnny Collins and (l.)
bandleader Henry Hall.

Right Freddie Keppard, an
early photograph.

Above   On Parade: Kid Shots Madison (l.), who was raised in the same district as Louis, and Bunk Johnson ready for brass band duty.

Opposite above   Pianist–arranger–bandleader Fletcher Henderson, nicknamed 'Smack'. He is seen here on stage at the Apollo Theatre, New York, early in 1937.

Opposite below   Les Hite's band, Hollywood 1930. Lawrence Brown (trombone), Louis, Hite, Lionel Hampton (drums) and probably Henry Prince (piano).

Above Preston Jackson; picture taken in Chicago, 1943.

Left Henry Red Allen, photographed in New York, 1960.

Opposite Louis Armstrong and his orchestra, 1936/7, with Louis flanked by vocalists Bobby Caston (l.) and Sonny Woods. Luis Russell, who led the band, is sixth from the left.

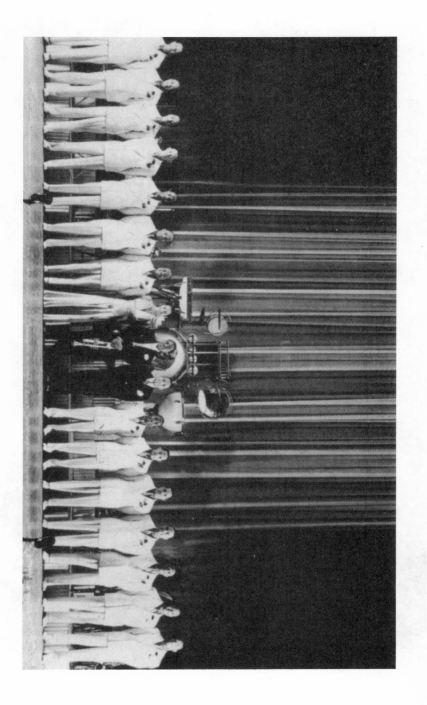

Above The Armstrong–Russell band's rhythm team in posed action: Russell (piano), Paul Barbarin (drums), George 'Pops' Foster (string bass) and Lee Blair (guitar, played left-handed).

Below Melody Maker get-together with American bandleader–arranger Benny Carter in London, 1936. Behind Carter is Leonard Feather with (l.) MM Editor Percy Mathison Brooks and Technical Editor Dan Ingman.

again. We got along fine ... Everything went fine on the job. Louis played mighty well, and the more he got a chance to read that music the better he was. He was always a good showman.

Henderson's interpretation of the welcome Louis received differed in emphasis. 'The band at first was inclined to be a bit reserved towards the new arrival,' he said, 'and there seemed to be a little tension in the air. At rehearsal he was perplexed by the trumpet part I gave him to a new arrangement of a medley of beautiful Irish waltzes.' Louis' 'studying out of books' with his wife had increased his repertoire, but medleys of Irish waltzes were not quite what he had been used to – the reason, perhaps, why he was tried on them so soon. His tactics, faced with the strangeness of the material and the company in which he found himself, give off a familiar echo. He did his best to make everybody laugh.

Henderson went on to recount how the band parts were well supplied with expression marks, and how in one place the music was marked *fff* with a diminuendo down to *pp*. Louis blasted through the orchestration without heeding the dynamics, and Smack stopped the band and asked his new recruit if he had noticed the letters *pp*. Armstrong retorted, 'Oh, I thought that meant "pound plenty".' It dissolved the tension, and shows that even way back Satchmo used to give his fellow men a few belly-laughs at sticky moments. Henderson admitted that some of his players were a little too stiff for Armstrong, who only relaxed properly when a band scrap developed, and trombonist Charlie Green and tuba-player Ralph Escudero had their coats off for the fray. Then Louis began to feel at home.

Louis' own references to the band have differed in tone, as memories will according to mood. In conversation he more than once intimated that his stay with Smack was agreeable despite the fancy arrangements and big-headed attitude of some of the band's personalities.

The first thing they gave me to play was *Waters Of Min-*

97

netonka, I'll never forget that, written out by hand. Made me nervous at first, all of them masters like Kaiser Marshall, Big Green, Don Redman and Coleman Hawkins, famous musicians in that big town. Later I thought I was in heaven for a while. 'Course I felt a little homesick.

Buster Bailey confirmed the homesickness, saying that Louis had been scared to move to New York. 'He liked Chicago. It was the same with me. The first week ... we both said, let's go back to Chicago.'

The Henderson musicians possibly found Armstrong rather gauche and unsociable in his ways. Marshall said they kidded him about his long underpants and thick-soled shoes. 'He had to take so much about those drawers that he finally said to me, "All right, I'll take them off, but if I catch cold in the winter time I'll blame it on you." '

Louis didn't drink or smoke much, if at all. He wasn't one for carousing or big spending, whereas Smack's musicians were swells and probably earning more than he was. Kaiser Marshall spoke of them being in the money, with bonuses for record dates and extra dance or party bookings.

Sometimes, after we finished at the Roseland, we'd go up to Harlem and play from 2 to 3 in the morning; it meant $25 a man just for that hour of playing ... We all lived high; we were a top band and we had top wardrobes. The boys used to wear English walking suits that cost $110, $7 spats and $18 shoes. Things were good in those days.

Louis never went around much then. He was working hard and saving his money. At first he liked New York, but later he wanted to go back to Chicago to be near his wife, settle down and organize his own band. He used to write to his wife every day.

Lil had returned home after a few weeks, but still made occasional working visits to New York.

With Henderson, Louis appeared at the Apollo, the Roxy and other theatres. In June 1925 they left New York on a tour of New England, and by September were back in the Apple at the Renaissance Casino, then home to the Roseland. This was to be Louis' final week with Smack. He 'cut out' during the first week of November and rejoined his wife in Chicago.

The reasons stated for this drastic decision have been many and varied. Henderson's version was that Louis said he wished to return to Chicago to form his own band and that they parted on the best of terms. Armstrong professed that he felt unhappy on Broadway but, on the other hand, got a terrific thrill from being invited to play one night at the Savoy Ballroom in Harlem. Sometimes he enjoyed life in New York, sometimes he wanted to be reunited with his wife in Chicago; she eventually pressed him to return and play first trumpet in her band.

Another reason advanced – though this only began to be heard about twenty years after Louis and Smack parted company – was Armstrong's growing dissatisfaction with his colleagues. It may be that he felt an outsider. Henderson found Louis 'pretty much a down-home boy in the big city' who took a ribbing from the band and endured it good-naturedly. The down-homer said the men regarded him out of the corners of their eyes at their first encounter. 'They simply ignored me to an extent, and so I don't say nothing to them. But I'm saying to myself, "This bunch of old stuck-up . . ." ' Their initial coolness, however, disappeared after he was able to prove what he could do. Later on, Henderson and Louis made conventionally polite noises about each other when asked for an opinion, and there is some evidence that the bandleader had treated him with consideration. Louis, too, praised the jazz musicianship of Coleman Hawkins and Charlie Green to third parties, though it was noted in one account that at the first rehearsal Hawkins didn't have much to say. These two pace-setters never became 'tight' associates; they met in London nearly ten years later in unusual circumstances, and didn't have much to say to each other on that occasion, as we shall see.

99

Smack's band became notorious in later years for its lack of discipline – men dodging rehearsals, turning up late on jobs, drinking to excess. Such conduct may well have alienated Armstrong, a supremely conscientious musician if not a stiff one. In a discussion with Barry Ulanov he remarked, out of the blue, when talking about Henderson's band, 'When them cats commenced getting careless with their music, fooling around all night, I was dragged, man.' To prove this was no momentary slip of the memory, he repeated the charge to Richard Meryman twenty-one years later. 'After a year the cats ... started goofing – drinking, didn't care. I was always very serious about my music, so I went back to Chicago.'

In a way it turns a minute piece of jazz history over on its head, and we should consider the possibility that distance was lending disenchantment to Louis' view. The self-portrait in this book reveals an even harsher view of the whole episode, Satch talking of having to endure cutting-up on the stand, and lamenting the fact that his singing was 'out' so far as Smack was concerned. This accusation is surprising because Henderson took credit for encouraging the budding vocalist. 'He asked me if he could sing a number. I know I wondered what he could possibly do with that big fish horn voice of his, but finally I told him to try it.' Fletcher wrote. 'He was great ... I believe that was the first time he ever sang anywhere. He didn't sing with Oliver, I'm sure.' He didn't sing on the Oliver records, certainly, and Lil Armstrong said 'I don't remember Louis doing any singing in the Oliver band. Surely one would have been used in the Gennett sessions?' Louis, however, used the phrase 'all the singing that I did before I joined Fletcher', and emphasized that it 'went down the drain the whole time I was with him'.

As it happens, the breaks he sang on the first take of Henderson's *Everybody Loves My Baby* represent his first recorded vocal efforts. Louis sang and played this song in a featured spot at the Roseland on vaudeville nights; in fact, he won first prize with it in the Thursday evening talent competition, and Marshall asserts that from then on the crowd used to shout for Armstrong every Thursday night, and he would play his horn and sing his songs. Maybe Louis wondered why he was never allowed to record his show version of *Everybody Loves My Baby*.

Rex Stewart talks of the night Henderson and Louis came into the place where he was working and sat together and listened to him play. There is no doubt that to Rex, Louis was already the Great Man. When Satch was quitting the band, he rang up Stewart, telling him to be ready to join it in a fortnight's time. So in awe of Armstrong's ability was Rex that he refused, and his bandleader, Elmer Snowden, had to sack him in order to get him to accept the job, months afterwards, although Stewart still insisted that he couldn't stand the pressure. If Louis had that effect on a tough cornet-man like Rex, it is hard to conceive what he did to lesser exponents; yet at this particular time he obviously felt under-appreciated. 'You know, being an underdog in a band is a bad thing,' he told us. 'Of course in every band there's always pets. They're the ones that can't even blow their noses let alone their horns. Tch, tch. Life's a bitch, ain't it?'

The letters from Lillian Armstrong – growing more urgent in tone as the months passed and Henderson's orchestra failed to get to Chicago – were probably the primary cause of Louis' retreat from New York. She had fixed up a job for him at Bill Bottoms' Dreamland (there was also a Dreamland Ballroom in Chicago) at $75 a week. 'My wife had the band there and she said I'd gotta come home and join it,' Satch once disclosed. 'I said I was doing all right where I was but she insisted, saying, "Come now or don't come at all." So I gave in my notice.'

Lil corroborated this. She told Louis she was putting in the band and featuring him on trumpet. It was a good job, playing lead and at a high salary, but Lil realized he wasn't rushing to take it. She indicated that he must choose between New York and her, and Louis said okay. He didn't want to come, confessed Lil, adding that he was 'having a ball with that Fletcher Henderson band and chorus girls'. Goffin's biography says that Louis was becoming infatuated with a dancer named Fanny in New York. Lil's ultimatum succeeded, even though the bond between her and Louis had loosened. 'I was yellow and didn't know about them threats,' he explained from a position of superior wisdom 45 years later. 'So I quit and went on back to Chicago.'

In this first New York stay Armstrong scored a success only with musicians and those dancers and music fans who bothered to note who was playing what. He commented once that five years after his visit Broadway finally accepted him. The experience, however, had been vastly worthwhile for him professionally. In the year with Henderson he gained confidence, improved his knowledge of reading and interpreting a score, learned many new tricks of showmanship, and picked up ideas from dozens of musicians he heard and, in some cases, recorded with.

New York was the last of Louis' universities. There were still finer points of the music game to be mastered, and he was as eager as ever to learn them, but he returned to Chicago a marvellous and mature all-round musician. Once back he launched himself on a variety of enterprises which established him as the jazz sensation of the city. A long series of recordings by his Hot Five and Hot Seven, the first made under his own name, carried his reputation beyond the United States to wherever jazz records were sold. They were soon to be rated by connoisseurs in many parts of the world as the most advanced of all performances in the rough-and-ready or gutbucket style. To this day they are recognized as absolute classics in their field. In the opinion of thousands of collectors they have never been bettered.

They were not the first outstanding discs to feature Armstrong, though it could be maintained that they were the first to show inescapably that his conception of music was all his own. In New York he recorded abundantly, and of none of the records could it be said that his performance, where he was featured, fell flat. More than forty sides were made with Henderson. Most were tedious, and many lumbered along until the clear-cut tone and shape of a vibrant, vital cornet solo brought life to the waste land. From these, interesting on account of the glow Louis imparted, it can be seen that he was already emancipating himself from Oliver's example without essaying an abrupt change of manner. *Money Blues, Mandy, Carolina Stomp, T.N.T.* and *Sugarfoot Stomp* are merely a handful of those on which his cornet punches free of the rhythmic confines of Henderson's band.

Of more consequence to students of music – and probably to Armstrong, since they reverted to the spontaneous type of jazz-making he loved and excelled at – were the quintet sides cut with Clarence Williams' Blue Five and a similarly constituted group, with Lil on piano, known as the Red Onion Jazz Babies, after a New Orleans dive named the Red Onion. In spite of the acoustic recording, which muffled the tone of Armstrong's cornet, these tracks give a clear enough representation of his authority and expressiveness as both solo and lead player. We may guess his relief at being temporarily released from Henderson's stuffy arrangements and the orchestra's rather choppy approach to swing. He was back in the informal setting, driving out a New Orleans lead. His improvisations point ahead, hinting at audacious ideas to come very soon; yet at the same time his lead, breaks and solo work on *Terrible Blues*, for instance, remind us that he had forgotten none of Papa Joe's training. *Cake Walking Babies* is another matter. No one before had ever swung a lead as violently as Louis did on the remake of this tune. This was for Armstrong a time of stylistic dichotomy; he was beginning to break old ties but was still firmly in the tradition (note the solidity of his lead on the Jazz Babies' *All The Wrongs*). The virtuoso was on his way, but these were intermediate steps in his path. Oliver still swayed him powerfully.

In much the same way as the Blue Five and Red Onion performances, Armstrong's work on a number of records by blues singers illustrates the movement he was making during '24 and '25 towards greater timing subtlety and freedom of expression, while still employing the fundamentally sober 'singing' approach of Oliver and other New Orleans trumpeters. Louis' gripping background cornet (although background is not really the word for some of these displays of incipient virtuosity) can be savoured on the rightly-extolled records with Bessie Smith, although his playing with Ma Rainey, Maggie Jones, Chippie Hill, Clara Smith and Trixie Smith is also noteworthy. Bessie Smith was the outstanding singer of the era, and the meeting of these two exceptional personalities produced music which, at its peak, reaches the highest musical and emotional level. Panassié observed, as many have done, that the cornet provides more than accompaniment, its part being 'every bit as important as Bessie's part'.

Recently some critics have put down these recordings because, it is argued, the sheer compelling power of Armstrong's responses imposes a mood, a pattern or a certain logic of his own on what should be solely the singer's interpretation. While I respect the argument and see the objection, I cannot be converted by it, because the music is so good. What are we to look for? A copybook interpretation of the ideal balance to be struck between vocal call and instrumental response? Or music which projects and communicates, leaving us with a heightened appreciation of the possibilities of the blues form? From Bessie's touching opening stanza of *St Louis Blues*, where her majestic voice is answered by melancholy chords from Fred Longshaw's harmonium, and poignant cornet statements whose economically chosen notes seem to imply all that has been left out, the music sweeps slowly along its course with perfect continuity.

We are told that Bessie Smith was less than ecstatic about Armstrong's contribution, preferring the more discreet lyricism of Joe Smith. This preference may not have much significance, however. Most great artists are egotistical, even arrogant, about their art, and she would be likely to feel happiest with musicians who did not, or could not, steal more than a fraction of the limelight.

Louis may well have learned a few swift lessons from the Empress of the Blues. There were pointers, too, to be picked up from Sidney Bechet, perhaps the only jazzman in the mid-'20s who could live with Louis in a no-holds-barred ensemble improvisation. These two strong men knew each other from pre-war New Orleans and to a large degree shared a common musical background. They met again in New York on several Blue Five and Red Onion record sessions, where their impassioned playing, separately and together, provided all the most scorching moments.

Jazz-making, even when disciplined by tradition, is a competitive undertaking which has as much to do with personality as with technical facility. The twice-recorded *Cake Walking Babies From Home* tells its own tale and demonstrates how quickly Armstrong learned from experience. On the earlier, Gennett, version with Lil on piano, made in December 1924, he leads admirably but sounds hard pressed to hold his own against the sheer force and abandon of Bechet's soprano saxophone; but on the Blue Five's *Cake Walking*, recorded some two weeks later for OKeh with virtually the same routine and personnel, he has manifestly discovered how to make the running. Young Louis plays like a demon, with every nerve and ounce of energy concentrated on the job in hand, and the legacies from Joe Oliver are well to the fore. The soprano leaps and roars as exuberantly as before, but at the close Louis must have put down his horn with the satisfied feeling of a gladiator who has just taken care of the strongest lion in the country.

Just Glad to Play

The Chicago *Defender* announced, in an advertisement on 14 November 1925, that Lil Armstrong's band was featuring 'The World's Greatest Jazz Cornetist, Louis Armstrong'. Musicians in Chicago had been admiring him since his Oliver days, but now even larger numbers were attracted to see him 'blast out those weird jazz figures'. To all intents and purposes, he was playing lead for the first time – with an eight-piece group led by Lil from the piano. Soon he was doubling from the Dreamland to the Vendome Theater, where Erskine Tate led the Little Symphony Orchestra, a 15-piece ensemble with strings. At the Vendome, a movie house, Armstrong played for silent pictures, did the show and still further improved his reading of music. It was here, also, that he started to play trumpet regularly. He had previously tried it in the New Orleans days, but in 1922–5 used trumpet-cornet – a Harry B. Jay model, as used by Muggsy Spanier and George Mitchell.

It was December when Armstrong started at the Vendome. He said he used to switch chairs with Tate's brother, Jimmy, who played first trumpet, and while he was playing lead 'got pretty good on all my classics'. Each Sunday one member of the band would have a feature spot. When it came to Louis' turn he liked to solo on *Cavalleria Rusticana*, then jump into a jazz tune.

I was at home then, 'cos that's what they hired me for, anyway, them hot numbers. That's when I could hit 50 high C's and more, maybe pick up a megaphone and sing a few

106

choruses on *Heebie Jeebies* or sump'n. There weren't no talkies, and we used to cue them silent movies; had music in front for everything that happened. It was beautiful. Helped me a lot and got my stage career under way.

During this second period in Chicago, Lil and Louis were together and, in spite of the normal disputes of married life, Armstrong remained very much under his wife's influence. Lil was a working wife and her earnings were useful; Louis said they made good money between them in the years of '26, '27 and '28. It was soon after his return from New York that they bought the house on 44th Street, as well as an automobile and 'some lots on Lake Idlewild'. He was starting to get wilder in those days, as he moved a little higher up the ladder with each new professional offer, but he was still taking Lil's advice. He had doubts about his competence to read the overtures played by Erskine Tate's orchestra; Lil assured him he could do it. When business slackened off, and he entertained the idea of working with King Oliver at the Plantation Café, she vetoed the plan. Sometimes it seems as though Lil had an ambivalent outlook on the King. She admired him at first and was proud to be invited to join his band. She did much work for the band – composing, writing down arranged passages and helping out in other ways. Oliver appeared to be fond of her, but Lil could not have thought much of his playing, and her knowledge of the New Orleans idiom was scarcely sufficient to enable her then to grasp his importance as a leader and organizer. When the young white musicians used to pack the bandstand area to listen to the Creole Band, and sometimes sit in, she would wonder what they admired so much. 'It was really funny to me because I didn't know what they were trying to get – what it was that they were trying to listen to,' she said in 1956. 'Now I know.'

Her puzzlement didn't prevent her from forming the opinion that Freddie Keppard was superior to Oliver as a player. 'I think he had a better tone; in fact, I know he did. I liked him better.' She remembered the time Keppard took

Louis' trumpet and tried to blow him down. Then it was Armstrong's turn. His wife urged 'Now get him,' and she vowed that never in her life had she heard such trumpet. 'Just hear him play when he's angry,' she said, adding that nobody else ever asked Satch for his trumpet.

Then there was Jabbo Smith, who, according to Kid Ory, came looking for Louis 'with blood in his eyes'. Not surprising, this, since Jabbo was an extremely fast and heated trumpeter – the 'Dizzy Gillespie of that era', in Milt Hinton's words. When both had had their blow, Jabbo is alleged to have said, 'I'm gonna get a trombone'. Preston Jackson confirmed the Jabbo Smith incident for us, and recalled another contender, Memphis trumpeter Johnny Dunn.

You see, Johnny Dunn was pretty high at that time, and Louis, he'd played with Fletcher in New York and had then left Fletcher 'cos Lil had the job at the Dreamland. So everybody in Chicago said, well, Louis' back. And so Johnny Dunn strolled in there one night and asked for Louis' horn. Louis gave it to him, and when he got it back just blew him out of the place. Yes, he did the same thing with Jabbo Smith but of course it was a little closer than with Johnny Dunn.

Trumpet-player Hot Lips Page described one of the many subsequent trials of strength:

I remember I was eating with Pops in a restaurant when I overheard four young cats arranging to cut Pops that evening. Man, it was to be murder; when one guy's lips gave out, the other would take over. Pops never looks up from his fried chicken, but that night he let those cats start and as they played he pulled up a little café table and set a chair on it and climbs up and let go. Those four cool guys faded out one after the other, put their horns away and just slunk out.

Armstrong seemed to have within him both a broad streak of artistic pride and determination and an opposing lack of resolution and confidence in his personal life, which could hardly fail to lead to occasional inner clashes. There is something not quite in order about the behaviour of a man who overcomes every obstacle in his profession, and vanquishes all competitors, then goes home to be ruled by his wife. Armstrong, in the middle '20s, deferred to Lil in most matters. Since he worked with her, and then for her, the position did not go unnoticed.

It was bad, Lil confessed later, because the other musicians kidded him about his wife being the leader. 'Look out, your wife'll fire you,' they used to joke. Sometimes they called him 'Hennie' – short for 'hen-pecked'.

> The band men called Louis 'hen-pecked' [said Lil] because I had too much to say and do about his actions, dress and just about everything ... And it embarrassed him and he became so hard to get along with at home and on the bandstand. I would get ready to start the band off and he'd have all the musicians on one side, telling them a damn joke. And I got after him about it, and he said, 'Well, if you don't like it, fire me.'

As for Louis, he looked back on it this way:

> The guys who called me Henpeck all the time were broke all the time. And I always had a pocket full of money. Lots of outside people tried to interfere with Lil and my marriage which I personally thought was unfair. After all, the woman was my wife. All of those kuniving, inquisitive, two-faceted people started interfering in our personal love and business, etc. We were both young and Lil with the better education and experience only did what any wife would do. Everything she bought for me were the best, clothes the very best and her suggestions were all perfect. I appreciate them all.

Armstrong's stint with Lil at the Dreamland came to an end and he joined Carroll Dickerson early in '26. This was the moment he thought of going back to Oliver on second trumpet, an action he regarded almost as going home, but Lil once more put her foot down. He went on doubling with

Tate at the Vendome, and it has been suggested that he started dabbling with Alpha Smith, a young maid who worked for a white family, at the theatre and elsewhere. Alpha took over a major role some years later. For the time being, Armstrong's second marriage remained on and off. 'Whenever we'd break up, we'd draw all of our money out of the bank and split it up,' he wrote. The break-ups were further complicated by Clarence Armstrong, son of Louis' cousin, Flora Miles. Louis had helped bring up Clarence ever since Flora died, and he installed the boy in his Chicago flat in '25 and subsequently in the new house with Lil. Throughout the marital disruptions Louis continued to care for Clarence, whom he adopted, although Lil tells us she doubts whether the adoption was ever made legal. Later he set up the younger Armstrong family in a flat in Chicago.

Apart from domestic upheavals these were happy, jumping years, with Louis so busy, most of the time, that he could choose his engagements. The Lincoln Gardens, he said, Dreamland and Sunset, 'were the cabarets I played through the years, and I stayed so long they brought up the years'. He may have worked again for Ollie Powers – 'a great friend to me and fine entertainer' – around this period; he certainly went into the Sunset Café with Dickerson's big band on 10 April 1926 and saw the year out playing the two jobs, Sunset and Vendome – which was nothing out of the way for a New Orleans player.

At the Sunset, on 35th and Calumet, Louis played alongside the pianist Earl Hines – with whom he was to strike up one of jazz music's most memorable partnerships – and with such musicians as Shirley Clay (trumpet), Pete Briggs (bass), Tubby Hall (drums) and an old sidekick, trombonist Honore Dutrey. He went to work at the Café after the theatre show, which began at 7 pm, and played until three or four in the morning. It was at the Sunset that Louis met Joe Glaser, later to become his manager, and saw his name go up in lights outside the place. He was appointed leader by Glaser, already a budding talent-spotter, early in 1927.

110

The band, billed as Louis Armstrong and his Stompers, soon made its name with the clubgoers. Louis left Hines the job of musical director and, given half a chance, the effervescent Earl used to refer to the outfit as *his* band. He spent plenty of time directing because the Sunset ran a large floor show with star singers, dancers and the obligatory show girls, as well as a Charleston competition on Friday nights. Louis and Earl remained there until the latter part of the year, when they quit abruptly, after, it was rumoured, Hines fell out with Glaser. Meanwhile, in April, Louis had left 'Professor Tate' and, after a short rest from doubling, began a four-month engagement with Clarence Jones's Orchestra. He recalled that the last cabaret he worked at was the Sunset.

I went out to the Vendome and then to the Metropolitan Theater. After Clarence Jones I went out to the Savoy Ballroom with Carroll Dickerson. Played a few more places for a while, and all that took a few years. I moved to Chicago in 1922 – was with Henderson in 1924, and when I had to go home from New York, that was my home in Chicago – and didn't leave again until 1929. That's how fast it was in those years, and how much work there was around Chicago. We saw some hard times, too, but I always had a job.

In addition to all his regular work, Louis was playing sporadic solo dates and making rafts of records. Between 12 November 1925 and 12 December 1928 he cut more than 60 titles with his own small groups, as well as many more with Johnny Dodds, Lil's Hot Shots, Erskine Tate, Carroll Dickerson and divers blues artists.

He was tremendously prolific at this stage of his life, turning out brilliant recordings at remarkable speed and then, very often, pouring out music for eight hours each night; music which, as almost everyone who has heard it will agree, established a new high-water-mark for jazz creativity and excitement. The records – the Hot Fives and Sevens and the blues accompaniments – helped to extend Louis' fame throughout the country and far abroad. The

111

Hot Five series stands as one of the great achievements of jazz. Readers are directed to André Hodeir's *Jazz: Its Evolution And Essence*, in addition to the books already recommended, for a detailed analysis of selected Armstrong small-band records of this time. Among these records are a few inferior or badly flawed products, but also such masterworks as *West End Blues* and *Potato Head*. The sides were made quickly and informally, with none of the gravity of musicians laying down works of art. Jokes and studio chat were left on, mistakes too, and various novelty effects were sometimes tried, with calamitous results. Armstrong's story about Johnny Dodds being too nervous to utter a word (see 'Satchmo Says') conjures up the atmosphere of high-spirited abandon which prevailed on these truly amazing sessions. The trumpet is on no performance less than distinguished, and on many superb.

Asked if he realized that the Hot Five dates might go down in jazz history, Louis would say no, they weren't trying to prove anything, they were just glad to play. He had a story about the day the trombone player got so carried away that

> he ran off from that big horn – we were supposed to play everything into that horn you know – and he went 'way back in the corner and started blowing. We had to pull him back, he thought he was on the stage. Man we laughed ... spoiled that take. No, we wasn't serious at all as far as money and things like that.

This sums up Armstrong's approach as well as anything: always serious about his music but seldom about the circumstances in which it had to be made.

One quality of these records is indicated by the remark 'just glad to play'. The joy of playing, not affected by the melancholy content of some of the compositions used, seeped into almost everything the group recorded. Armstrong was happy to be home among musicians he knew and understood, playing a type of music which evolved directly from the collective improvisation of Oliver's band

112

and the New Orleans-style groups he had recorded with in New York. Significantly, the instrumentation of the Hot Five was that of the Blue Five and Red Onion Jazz Babies, though without a soprano saxophone, and the personnel consisted of musicians who had worked with Oliver and, with the exception of Lil Armstrong, came from New Orleans or nearby.

While Armstrong expressed pleasure in working with men who could read music [Wilfrid Mellers has written], it is clear from the recording of *Heebie Jeebies* that familiarity with notation is subservient to the heat of the moment. Human contact is the music's inspiration ...

Armstrong was at last free to do what his heart and head told him was possible within the old New Orleans framework. The singing, which he complained was overlooked by Henderson, was tried out almost at once (the Hot Five's *Georgia Grind*) and was extended as Louis got used to his independence. Although the early vocals have a harsh tonal quality and noticeable inflexibility, compared with his singing two or three years later, they are a vital part of his jazz-craft and go back to the fountainhead of his musical talent – his ability, as a boy, to sing or whistle anything that was played to him.

Armstrong's approach on the Hot Fives was not his approach outside the studios at that period, so far as we are able to tell. This suggests strongly that the more frenzied trumpet heard on Erskine Tate's recordings of *Static Strut* and *Stomp Off, Let's Go* is an approximation to what Louis was serving up during 1926 and 1927. The part he played in expanding the boundaries of traditional jazz technique, and finally, in a sense, destroying the conventions on which the style depended for its strength, has already been acknowledged. It is worth remembering, then, that on his records he observed for a while these very conventions (or most of them) just as they were being eroded all around him. Oliver himself was using a trio of saxophones and

Armstrong was building up big-band experience. Nevertheless, Louis surrounded himself with home-town musicians and sent to the West Coast for Kid Ory in order to ensure that the 'cellar' department was in capable hands. He even continued to record on cornet after changing to trumpet with Tate. It may be that he was not just asked but firmly instructed to make records of that kind. No full and unvarnished account of how these compelling sessions came into being has been handed down. Richard M. Jones, an A & R man for OKeh, set up the dates, but he would hardly have been the prime mover in this deal. (Bud Jacobson, then a 19-year-old clarinettist and alto saxophonist around Chicago, claims to have persuaded E. A. Fern, OKeh's chief executive in Chicago, to record an 'all-star' quintet led by Armstrong.)

The Hot Fives – and their immediate successors – were good sellers, hot properties for the General Phonograph Corporation, which owned OKeh. *Heebie Jeebies*, the first hit, is said to have shifted 40,000 copies within a few weeks of its release. Other titles notched up very handsome aggregate sales. They were eventually marketed in Britain and elsewhere in the world; most of the later issues came out in Britain on Parlophone between 1929 and 1932 and remained in the catalogue for nearly thirty years.

OKeh publicized their successful artists by different and enterprising means. For 12 June 1926 they announced an OKeh Race Record Artists' Ball with Richard M. Jones in charge. Butterbeans and Susie, Chippie Hill, Sara Martin, Sippie Wallace, and Lillie Delk Christian were among the singers booked. The bands of King Oliver, Erskine Tate (both, in fact, recording for Vocalion at the time), Doc Cooke and others were to be present, as was, of course, the Hot Five. There was a rumour that twenty-one bands would join forces for a finale on *Cornet Chop Suey* and *Come Back Sweet Papa*, but this proved unfounded. It does, however, show the popularity that these two early Hot Five items had already achieved. This would have been the Hot Five's only public appearance, but there is no evidence that the Ball ever happened.

These records of Armstrong's were enormously influential, not because they still adhered to some of the New Orleans conventions but precisely because they broke away from others to reveal fresh jazz possibilities. In a perceptive review of Louis' entire 1925–30 output as bandleader, Victor Schonfield calls this music the most avant-garde jazz of all time. 'Avant-garde does mean revolutionary, and in these records he created not just masterpieces of black music but also the basic conception of improvisation which has governed it ever since.' Writing of *Cornet Chop Suey*, he continued, 'Armstrong discovered a style which reduced everyone else's to the level of accompaniment, and which riveted all the attention on his trumpet.' This is why *Cornet Chop Suey*, like a dozen or two more recordings, became a model for thousands of jazz trumpet players.

Many trumpeters who were 'coming up' at that period have admitted their indebtedness to Louis, live, on record, or both. Bill Coleman, Roy Eldridge, Rex Stewart, Muggsy Spanier, Lips Page, Max Kaminsky, Kid Howard, Wild Bill Davison, Red Allen – the list could be trebled. Bill Coleman's reaction, when asked to select a favourite disc, shows an attitude towards Louis which is typical of these men:

Armstrong was my first inspiration, and I listened to all of his records I could get hold of. The Hot Fives and Sevens ... they're all so great, you know, *Cornet Chop Suey, Potato Head, Keyhole Blues, West End, Basin Street*, that I could have chosen any of dozens. *Knee Drops* is one of many I like that Louis did in the '20s ... I think that's my real favourite. It has special memories for me. I had started then, been playing for a few years, but I used to copy Louis' records. Oh yes, in fact if he played a bad note, I'd put that in as well ... In the beginning I modelled myself on him. I couldn't get away from those ideas he had when I was trying to find my way of playing.

There have been plenty of trumpet players since then that I admire but I still say Louis is my favourite because of all the things I learned from him ... Now this particular number, *Knee Drops* ... It's in B flat. I used to play it on my horn along with the record, and eventually got to the place where I could play it along with Louis note for note. My tone may have been different but the improvisation, I had that. And, of course, it was something to play. Oh, Louis had some technique, and harmonically he was years ahead of his time. Take this record: when he plays the introduction he makes a phrase any trumpet player of today would consider modern, and when he comes in on his solo he plays some very unexpected things. Then there are the wonderful breaks in the last chorus ... All these old records with Pops, I knew them. *Money Blues* with Fletcher Henderson, that was my first impression of Louis.

The mention of *Money Blues* serves as a reminder that Pops was influencing droves of musicians before he started recording under his own name. Pianist Sammy Price said that in his youth many jazzmen took inspiration from the instrumental portions of vocal blues records. 'It was Louis who liberated the music. You must remember that in the early days of Ma Rainey and Bessie Smith, instrumental solos were just beginning – he emancipated the jazz musician.' Confirmation came from Jack Teagarden. 'I remember the first Louis record I ever heard, *Cold In Hand Blues*. I was down in Texas and all the musicians stood and listened to it over and over again. I guess that just about everywhere else, too, musicians were listening to Louis' records.'

One who was, trumpet player Max Kaminsky, tells this story (in a BBC interview):

In the middle '20s my sister bought a phonograph, and in those days when you bought one they gave you free records – that was the come-on. The records would be 'race records', meaning they were made for the black people. So my sister used to play these records, and the first time I ever heard Louis he was playing behind Maggie Jones on *Good Time Flat Blues*. My sister used to go round the house singing, 'Miss Lizzie Green from New Orleans runs a good time flat' – and that's how I first heard Louis Armstrong. Never forgot that song.

116

Of course record-making was just part of the day's work for Louis. The day was often so long that he spent only a few hours at home. This widened the rift with Lil, but they continued to record together until the close of 1927. That December saw some of the hard times Louis spoke about, but they did not last long. After leaving the Sunset, for reasons unstated, he and Hines and drummer Zutty Singleton decided to go into the club business on their own. They took a year's lease on the Warwick Hall, on 47th Street, and opened their club, paying a monthly rent of (it was said) $375. The Savoy Ballroom, some two blocks away, had its grander opening on the same night as the Warwick and killed it before it could get off the ground. The trio tried another place, this time on the West Side in the toughest part of Chicago, and put on a dance. This was also a failure, apparently owing to some rough-housing that took place on the premises, and they all went back to working for other bandleaders. Hines later remembered:

Louis was wild and I was wild, and we were inseparable. He was the most happy-go-lucky guy I ever met. Then Louis and I and Zutty ... formed our own group, and I don't know what happened but we like to starve to death, making a dollar or a dollar and a half apiece a night. So we drifted apart ...

This interlude cured Armstrong of bandleading – except in the record studios and on odd gigs outside – for about a year and a half. He was never one of nature's organizers, and his first band (apart from the one he co-led with Joe Lindsey back in New Orleans) came to him by chance. This is the way Louis described the acquisition.

The leader at the Sunset, then one of the most popular night spots on the South Side, was Carroll Dickerson. The boss of the place, Joe Glaser, one day gave the band to me. Overnight I became a leader. Never tried to. That's how you get carried away.

The well-informed Preston Jackson supplied some background information.

Glaser was manager of the place, in fact his mother owned the building, and at this time Joe and Carroll Dickerson had agreed to disagree. It seems like a certain film actress went into the Sunset's ladies' room, and naturally the men's room and the women's room was adjacent to one another, and the wall between, it didn't quite reach to the ceiling. So Carroll was in there, and he threw what we call a grenade in this profession – that's a note – over the wall and the wrong person got hold to it. See, this was a movie star; she told her husband about it and he told Joe, and it ended up in a fight. So Joe fired Carroll and gave the band to Louis. And that's the first beginning of Louis Armstrong being a bandleader.

By this time he was beginning to make some real money. During the year with Dickerson at the Savoy his reputation grew, and the management had to raise his salary in order to hold off a rival offer from Henderson. In the autumn of 1928 he worked out of the Savoy Ballroom, going to St Louis for what must have been one of his earliest engagements as a solo guest star (he had already done a solo spot at the Savoy in Harlem during the Henderson days). He went to play on the *St Paul*, fronting Floyd Campbell's band for a two-day riverboat excursion, for a reported fee of $100 a day and expenses. Campbell's band, reinforced by its formidable trumpet soloist, engaged in a battle with the Alphonso Trent Band. The steamer became so overloaded – five thousand people were on board, it was said – that it was forced to return prematurely and perilously to St Louis. This traumatic experience may have provided some of the material for the paddle-steamer panic stories Louis told, with varying detail, in both his autobiographical books.

The Dickerson band had broadcast regularly from the Savoy, and these airings, together with Armstrong's sensational recordings, built up Louis' name in many parts of the country. Some idea of his personal popularity is conveyed by an anecdote of Art Hodes about a basketball game between the Dickerson band and a team representing the Clarence Black orchestra, which played opposite them at the ballroom. Louis, who weighed 210 pounds, couldn't buy a basketball suit to fit him. Finally, he and another member of the team turned out in their bathing trunks.

When we went out there we upset the joint [Louis declared]. But that game tore me up. I didn't know it took that much wind to play the game. I was so tired when that ball did get in my hands, and Zutty yelled out 'Dribble it,' well, I put it against my chest and ran to the basket. Then I missed. They told me all of the rules I broke. You shoulda heard them fans howl.

That night, feeling tired and ill 'with the grip', Armstrong made his way slowly to the Savoy to work. He was met by a swarm of admirers who pushed and pummelled him in their enthusiasm, then carried him shoulder-high through the crowd to the bandstand. According to Hodes, it was the most ecstatic display of fan feeling he had ever witnessed. Though exhausted and in pain, Louis held nothing back when the band started. He was the people's choice, and he would 'blow his brains out' to thrill them. But he stayed in bed for a week or more after that night.

Though Louis was now a star, he found work becoming scarcer during the months that followed. The ballroom's management had got into trouble, and couldn't or wouldn't pay the Dickerson band properly. There was talk of OKeh's Tommy Rockwell picking up the reins of Louis' career. The order of events in early 1929 is unclear, but Rockwell certainly sent for Louis to come to New York.

He recorded with Luis Russell's band in March and also with a mixed group which cut *Knockin' A Jug*. Kaiser Marshall, Jack Teagarden, Eddie Lang, tenor saxophonist Happy Cauldwell and pianist Joe Sullivan had been alerted for the date. Eddie Condon, who had something to do with assembling this unusual gathering, was in the studio too. Kaiser Marshall later wrote:

We had been working the night before and the record date was for eight in the morning, so we didn't bother about

119

going to bed. I rode the boys around in my car ... and we had breakfast about six so we could get to the studio at eight. We took a gallon jug of whisky with us.

When the blues number was done, the recording man asked for the title. Louis didn't know, since it had been created on the studio floor, but seeing the empty whisky container he said, 'We sure knocked that jug – you can call it *Knockin' A Jug*.'

By April, Armstrong was back in Chicago working as a single at the Regal Theater. Within the next month or so he was asked by Rockwell to travel to New York again for a job in a Vincent Youmans show then tentatively called 'Horseshoes'. When he broke the news to Dickerson and the other musicians, they made it plain they wanted to stay together and all take a chance on the Apple. They elected to put his name up front, since he was the principal drawing card, and move the band – lock, stock and library – by road in Louis' old Hupmobile roadster and three more 'shorts' owned by bandsmen. On the appointed day this curious cavalcade set out by sometimes circuitous routes for the east. The scene must have been like something from a hip musical version of *The Grapes Of Wrath*. After saying goodbyes to friends, the entire band, with most of their possessions and petty cash, piled into the four cars and drove away from a Chicago which was becoming associated in their minds with tiring conditions of work and poor pay.

What ailed the Savoy Ballroom cannot be diagnosed from this distance, but it was facing some fresh competition by this time – including that of the large, luxurious Grand Terrace, which had opened in December 1928 with Earl Hines leading his own band. Talking pictures had arrived, and the public's taste in music was on the swing – away from 'swing', as it happened, and towards the sweet sounds which were almost to drown hot jazz in the long Depression years.

The crime syndicate played a powerful part, since they

120

had hands in the tills of most, if not all, of these 'entertainment' venues and directly controlled many of them. What connection Al Capone may have had with the Grand Terrace was not specified by Hines, but he spoke of the big man as a frequent visitor. 'He liked to come into a club with his henchmen, order all the doors closed, and have the band play his requests. He was free with $100 tips.' Other jazzmen agree that Big Al and most of the gun toters preferred sentimental numbers, so it may be that as the mobs moved in the righteous music was squeezed out.

Zutty's wife Marge, the sister of trumpet player Charlie Creath, vouched for the fact that her husband was employed by gangsters in Chicago during the later '20s.

They were in control. I remember Zutty playing at a big sort of political affair which was run by the gangs. The bands had to play, and they didn't get paid anything. Zutty took me to this big affair, and that's the first time I saw Al Capone. Zutty showed him to me, and said: 'There's Capone's gang, and the other bunch, Bugs Moran's.' When the Moran gang came in, Capone's gang, they all got up from the table, like I guess they had their hands on their pistols. And the other gang, they all sat down. But it was a nice affair, but the musicians didn't get a nickel.

And this place where Zutty worked on the West Side was run by gangsters. They were nice to him, though. One of the guys had heard him drum and they asked him to put a little band together and come in there. It was a joint, but the football players hung out there. Yeah, they were nice to the boys in the band and everything but they ruled with an iron hand, you know. And they didn't bother him when he got a better job, because they liked him.

If Armstrong noticed what went on upstairs (or in the back rooms) in the places where he worked, he kept it to himself; but, like the rest of the jazz and dance musicians playing in Prohibition clubs, he had experience of the shooter brigade and brushed with them now and then. Relations between Louis and his managements seemed to be the only thing that brought him face to face with gunmen. Hines said that Armstrong 'once changed managers and was threatened with gangster violence. After that he hired two bodyguards who protected him on and off the job for many months.' Earl did not state when or where this happened. Once I [M.J.] asked Louis. He wouldn't elaborate, but told me 'all that stuff came later, before New Orleans'.

Gangsters notwithstanding, Chicago's jazz age was in decline by 1929. Armstrong, sooner or later, would have opted for New York. In fact, his rather dilapidated car led the procession out of Chicago during the May of that year. As Zutty Singleton recalled:

> We loaded all the stuff in the car. Finally Lil made a loan on something and got $20 for each of us. That was some trip. We had a couple of vibraphones – tied them on the car and they got all rusty. We didn't know enough to make stops, to play. Louis was really coming then, but we didn't stop. When we got to New York, we didn't have nothing. Next morning [Wellman] Braud helped us out...

Lil Armstrong was still the family treasurer, and Louis said that he raised the $20 a head on something or other, took $20 for himself, and left his savings at home with Lil and his Clarence.

> We went up to New York in those raggedy automobiles. Supposed to go alone but we didn't want to leave one another so I took the whole band up. The money ran out and everything, but we took our time, saw the country, and just made it to New York. We didn't know nothin' about business, but we kept our heads up.

The bandsmen – pianist Gene Anderson, saxophonists Crawford Wethington, Bert Curry and Jimmy Strong, trumpeter Homer Hobson, trombonist Fred Robinson, Mancy Carr the banjo-player, bassist Pete Briggs and of course violinist Dickerson and drummer Zutty Singleton – 'lazed their way' east, stopping at Detroit, Toledo, Cleveland and Buffalo. They spent time seeing Niagara Falls. There was no urgency, because no one except Armstrong had any work to go to. When Dickerson's car was involved in a collision, it was abandoned and he and his passengers had to be accommodated in the remaining three vehicles. At every place they called they were given a 'wonderful welcome' by musicians made aware of Louis' talent by the Savoy broadcasts. He hadn't reckoned on the power of the airwaves, otherwise a few gigs might have been fixed up to tide the travellers over financially. 'We didn't know nothing about radio then, or how far it reached. So it was all fun. The cats were so glad to meet us that we didn't need spending money.'

In New York he informed Tommy Rockwell that he had a band with him. Rockwell was displeased but promised to see what he could do. In late May Louis was in Philadelphia, briefly reunited with his former bandleader, Smack Henderson. As for the show which Louis had gone east to join, the New York *Age* reported that:

Louis Armstrong was supposed to be the first cornetist in the orchestra, and Russell Smith, second cornetist. [We have the word of Ben Webster and many another Henderson bandsman that 'Pop' Smith ranked with the finest and most experienced lead trumpet men of his day.] In fact it is alleged they were so seated at a rehearsal, and after a number had been played, either Dr Felix, who is said to have arranged or composed the music, or the conductor, is alleged to have told Armstrong to change chairs with Smith. This placed Russell as first trumpet, Armstrong second. The number was replayed and the decision was made that Armstrong was not adapted to the show business and his seat was declared vacant...

For a while, Louis and the band were under-employed, but they played a few dates at the Audubon Theater, deputizing for Duke Ellington's orchestra, and at the Savoy Ballroom in New York. By June, Louis was leading at the Savoy, with Dickerson still MD. Then came an engagement at Connie's Inn with the same band, and soon he began doubling at the Hudson Theater in 'Hot Chocolates', a revue staged by Connie Immerman of the Inn. Louis joined Leroy Smith's orchestra for this production, and a musician who saw the show says you could detect a new lift in the music when Louis came in. His feature number was a newly-written song by Fats Waller and Andy Razaf, *Ain't Misbehavin'*, and this quickly became a success for Armstrong and the composers.

When the Connie's Inn job folded the Armstrong–Dickerson band broke up, Louis and some of the men staying in New York and others returning to Chicago. By the end of 1929 or the beginning of 1930 Louis was fronting the Luis Russell band. Early in 1930 he worked with a new band, made up of musicians from Mills' Blue Rhythm Band, and during this year in New York he continued to record quite frequently – with Russell's orchestra, the Dickerson orchestra and then what is sometimes known as the Coconut Grove Band. He also toured briefly with Luis Russell's men, for by this time Rockwell was booking him, when the chances came along, as a solo attraction in front of other people's bands.

It was in this way that Armstrong visited the west coast for the first time. An offer was received in July 1930 for him to play as 'cabaret soloist' at Frank Sebastian's Cotton Club in Culver City, California. The offer appealed to Louis. Once again he started travelling, but now he was on his own and heading towards Hollywood's rosy horizon.

Days of the Vipers

During this period, from 1929 to 1931, Armstrong emerged clearly as an interpreter of popular songs, and as an individual 'name' attraction. Early jazz players never remained aloof from the popular repertoire, but the entire scope and influence of popular music altered with its nation-wide (sometimes world-wide) dissemination by radio, the cinema and the juke-box. As jazz became more and more involved with popular music, commercial interests moved in at every level. The peaks of New Orleans jazz and folk blues on record were reached at a time when the styles had very little attraction for any but black Americans. Subsequent expansions of these idioms led to the expected change and decline. Not everything was lost; artists of originality and real talent moved with the shifts of social habits and public taste and continued to express themselves honestly and uninhibitedly in an idiom familiar to, or designed to appeal to the new, bigger audiences. Armstrong was one who met the challenge posed during the great depression years, and survived professionally and artistically.

He started recording popular songs and ballads early in 1929. *I Can't Give You Anything But Love* (March), was followed by *Ain't Misbehavin'* and *Black and Blue* (July), and later by *Some Of These Days* and *When You're Smiling*. The beginnings of a more sympathetic vocal style can be detected in the *St James' Infirmary* he recorded in December 1928. Louis was not alone among jazzmen in performing hit songs of the day. He made a few boring records, but they represented a very small proportion of his

125

output. In general he played as well on these new band tunes as he had on the old.

These 'commercified' songs helped to spread Louis' reputation. Though a big name among musicians even as far back as Henderson days, he was still not known to more than a fraction of the public until 1929 or 1930. The situation was summarized by Paul Eduard Miller: 'These waxings [the Hot Fives and Sevens] became immensely popular in the Negro sections of urban areas. But only the habitués of Chicago's night life heard the great trumpeter in person during the next three years – probably his peak period.'

Mezz Mezzrow tells numerous stories in *Really The Blues* of Armstrong's growing fame in Harlem during the winter of 1929 and 1930. Mezz, who was constantly in Louis' company then, talked-up Pops' records in order to get them played on some of the first juke-boxes in Harlem. Soon the record man was back asking for more titles. Mezz recommended *Ain't Misbehavin'*, *Black And Blue*, *Some Of These Days*, *After You've Gone*, *St Louis Blues*, *Rockin' Chair* and *Song Of The Islands*. 'They all hit the juke-boxes fast, and they rocked all Harlem,' he relates.

'Everywhere we went we got the proprietor to instal more boxes, and they all blared out Louis ... The Armstrong craze spilled over from Harlem right after that, and before long there wasn't a juke-box in the country that Louis wasn't scatting on.' These titles were some of his earliest successes in Britain, too, and they helped to take him over the ocean.

The late Marshall Stearns wrote in *The Story of Jazz*: 'The story goes that as late as 1928, a survey of collectors at Princeton indicated that only one possessed any recordings by Louis Armstrong, and this collector was considered a specialist in pretty rough stuff.' The early jazz-collectors – almost exclusively young, white, middle-class and conventionally educated – tended to go first for white jazz, typified by the groups led by or featuring Red Nichols, Miff Mole, Bix Beiderbecke, Joe Venuti, Eddie Lang, Jack Teagarden

126

and the Dorsey Brothers; but by 1930 the 'coloured style' exemplified by Ellington, Russell, Henderson, the Chocolate Dandies and a few more bands began to exercise a considerable influence on the various jazz sects springing up in both the United States and Britain.

Armstrong was one of the prime contributors to this black take-over, and there is no disputing that the records featuring him as virtuoso soloist with supporting big band brought him this breakthrough to a larger, not predominantly black public. As the popularity of hot jazz passed its zenith, Louis and hundreds more jazzmen instinctively shifted ground slightly to accommodate public demands.

Louis made his trans-continental train journey to California in the early summer of 1930. He had several reasons for going west. The break-up of Dickerson's band and a quarrel with his old drumming friend Zutty Singleton are said to have disillusioned him. The idea of working in front of a strange band, with no hang-ups on account of the other musicians' behaviour, may have seemed particularly enticing. Perhaps management and marriage problems were looming too. Relations with Lil were very strained. 'That's when things started going oozy-woozy,' she said. 'We weren't agreeing on anything, see?' Louis, when faced with extra-musical troubles, often leaned towards travel. Anyway, what he remembered afterwards was wishing to see Hollywood and find out the kind of welcome he would get from musicians on the coast, and from the actors and celebrities in the film city.

At Frank Sebastian's New Cotton Club, which had opened in 1927 in Culver City, a suburb of Los Angeles, Armstrong appeared with a house orchestra contracted by Sebastian and led, for a few weeks after his arrival, by trumpet-player Vernon Elkins. Les Hite finally took over the leadership. In the band were at least two exceptional young jazz players: Lawrence Brown, a 22-year-old trombonist with an exquisite tone, and a 21-year-old drummer named Lionel Hampton. Armstrong often laughed about the 'little young fellow who played around with the bells when we went into the recording studio'. He already rated Hampton a first-class drummer, and Lionel idolized Louis.

I worked and recorded with Louis [Hampton said later] when we were at the Cotton Club, and I've never heard anyone play the stuff that he played on trumpet there. No other musician has contributed as much as Louis, the greatest living force we have in jazz ... who has influenced the whole music business. Satch has put down the key for everyone.

Like many percussionists, Hampton had learned to play xylophone and marimba. He was induced to try the vibraphone by Armstrong, ever on the lookout for unusual effects. He spoke of the Cotton Club episode thus:

We used to hear all the other bands on records; then we'd taken down all their parts and play 'em. All the big movie stars and everything came out there; so they brought Louis Armstrong in to be the star of the show. Louis just came by himself, brought his music and had us play with him. As the drummer in the band, this really was a great experience for me, playing behind Louis. This started me playing the vibes, because I made a recording session with him, and when I went in the studio there were some vibes in the corner. At that time, drummers were just striking one note occasionally on the vibes, as it was fairly new. And Louis said, 'Play something on that.' By me knowing the percussion, I thought of playing jazz, right there on the keyboard ... That was how I came to be the first to play jazz on vibes. Then I made an introduction with Louis on the vibraharp, and that was the first time that four hammers were ever played.

The first recordings Armstrong made with the Elkins band, *Ding Dong Daddy* and *I'm In The Market For You*, featured no vibes; nor did *Confessin'* and *If I Could Be With You*. The band was not a stunner, but its beat was keen enough on such swingers as *Ding Dong* – a remarkable example of an extended trumpet outing – and its overall strength sufficient to coax from Satch some of the most endearing performances of his recorded career. We include in this category such 'commercified' numbers as *Confessin'*, *If I Could Be With You* and the wondrously gentle but hot *Just A Gigolo*. Incidentally, Hampton's multi-mallet work can be heard on *Memories Of You, Shine* and *Gigolo*.

By the time these later tracks were cut, Les Hite was in charge of a new band. Only Hampton remained from the Elkins personnel, but the changes made little difference. Magical trumpet constructions were built one after another, with a noticeably blander tone, using less vibrato, than Louis had employed in his small-band days. *You're Lucky To Me, Sweethearts On Parade, You're Driving Me Crazy, Shine* ... these are a few of the good old good ones Armstrong enjoyed making with Les Hite's band. The 'chop suey' conversation with Hampton on *Crazy* always amused him. 'That was some funny stuff. A nice little record. That Chinese talk really gasses me.'

These, like *Ain't Misbehavin'* and *I Can't Give You Anything But Love,* became big sellers for him. Their influence was widespread. 'We played all Louis Armstrong's things note for note,' the trumpeter Cat Anderson told Stanley Dance. 'In school, all the trumpet players played *Shine* and made a hundred C's with the F on top.' There was no room for the hundred C's on the recording, of course, but Louis used to blow them out at his stage and ballroom appearances.

These were the records which abruptly turned Buck Clayton on to Louis' talent. Previously, in Kansas, Buck had heard of him but was not really familiar with his work.

Then, in Los Angeles about 1931, I was walking down the street when I heard a record being played that Louis had just made. The record was *I'm Confessin'* and I just stopped right there and listened. I wouldn't walk any further, because it was such a beautiful interpretation. And that's what struck me first, how pretty it was. I admired that record so much – not so much for the execution and all that, which he was known to have, but just for the beauty of it.

Some of the saxophone passages are cloying to jazz

129

tastes, and this excess of sweetness stems from Armstrong's almost notorious admiration for the Guy Lombardo orchestra. 'Now you dig that *Sweethearts*,' he pointed out. 'It reminds you of Lombardo ... When we were at the Savoy in Chicago in 1928, every Saturday night we'd catch the Owl Club, with Guy Lombardo, and as long as he played we'd sit right there ... We didn't go nowhere until after Lombardo signed off. That went on for months.'

Lombardo advertised 'the sweetest music this side of heaven' and Louis said that was what he played. He added that he often sat in with the Lombardo band in Chicago during the '20s. 'And that was before the first mixed session was ever put on record, so what does that make me?' he asked.

The inherent sweetness of a melody, or its treatment by band or arranger, has never stood in Louis' way. He was unavoidably confronted with a greater number of vocal chores as the popular song assumed more importance in the jazzman's repertoire. His method of dealing with them was unique, or nearly so. 'In the singing of Louis Armstrong and Fats Waller,' wrote Sidney Finkelstein, 'a frequent deliberate harshness serves as a sardonic commentary on the idiocy of the words and the sugariness of the tune. Louis' "scat" singing, of nonsense syllables, makes this point clear, for since the words are really meaningless, why use them?'

Victor Schonfield raised the subject of Louis' alleged commercialization – when he deserted the New Orleans formula in order to 'sell himself' as 'World's Greatest Trumpeter with supporting band' – and thoroughly demolished it. Of Louis' early big band recordings he writes:

But far from having gone commercial, he shows he was not only the trumpeter with the most fire and soul, the most inspiration and technique, and the richest and most personal tone – from now on every soloist tried to find his own unique sound – but had raised jazz singing to the same expressive level. Both aspects are at their peak on *I Can't Give You Anything But Love*, which spells out just how little patience he had with 'ballads' in those days. Tin Pan Alley slop is torn apart into an other-worldly fantasy of moans, mumbles and scat, with only traces of the original words or melody.

Louis was looking for other means of expressing himself, even if the basic vocabulary was the same as he'd used before the big band period, and he was interesting himself in obtaining fresh material and working out new ways of tinkering with it so that it fitted him comfortably. This joy in playing is particularly marked in the recordings made in Los Angeles, and it is easy to believe that Louis was delighted by his first stay on the West Coast. He remained there until spring 1931, and said afterwards that he felt happily at home in Los Angeles. The band broadcast nightly from the spacious Cotton Club, which was often filled. Among the patrons was a generous sprinkling of movie actors and show people, including of course musicians from all over California and sometimes from further afield.

We had little arrangements [Lawrence Brown said], and we'd take different choruses. If he [Louis] got tired he'd just say 'take one' or 'take another' or 'take two'. He was the kind of musician you could sit there all night and listen to and be amazed at the technique, the poise, and just everything. People used to come from 'way up around Seattle to hear him. Every trumpet player at that time tried to play *one* of his choruses.

Trumpet players used to try to sing some of his choruses, too. Buck Clayton was one who learned a few of the vocals because, as he put it, 'Louis was famous for them. I've seen women faint when he was singing.' The slightly sardonic streak in Armstrong's humorous make-up is exemplified by his insertion of a racial joke in the lyrics of Irving Caesar's and Leonello Casucci's *Just A Gigolo*, though his modest piece of word-play passed almost unnoticed outside the black community.

131

As Clayton explained:

> One of the songs I learned note for note and word for word was *Just A Gigolo*. Louis changed the words a little bit at the end and instead of singing 'another gigolo' he said: 'When the end comes I know, they'll say just another jig I know.' It kind of stirred up some people, especially the NAACP back home. Well, you know the word 'jig' often means a coloured person, which isn't too bad a word really; we use 'em, words like 'spook' and 'jig', or at least we used them in those days, not so much now. But that's just the way Louis was; he put his own little version in there.

One way and another, these nine months were prosperous, halcyon months for Satchmo; but at the end of March 1931, a cloud was cast over the days of sunny success. He had an unexpected encounter with the law, and spent nine or ten days in the Los Angeles county jail.

Tea, muggles, reefers, and a dozen more names for marijuana, were common parlance among jazz musicians and friends who were 'vipers'. This word has a period ring today, but was much used (as was the tea) in some jazz circles during the '30s. It found its way into quite a few tune titles, among them Mezzrow's *Sendin' The Vipers*, Stuff Smith's *If You're A Viper* and Fats Waller's *Viper's Drag*. The rest of the marijuana-smokers' jargon infiltrated respectable society by way of record labels and catalogues and music publishers' lists. *Golden Leaf Strut, Muggles, Texas Tea Party, Chant Of The Weed, Song Of The Vipers* and *Smoking Reefers* are random examples of 'celebratory' recordings made in the '20s and '30s.

Louis was caught with some stuff and sentenced in March 1931. He never recounted the story of this affair until shortly before his death, when he agreed to 'tell it like it wuz'. Here, for the first time, is that story:

> Speaking of 1931 – we did call ourselves Vipers, which could have been anybody from all walks of life that smoked and respected gage. That was our cute little name for marijuana,

132

and it was a misdomeanor in those days. Much different from the pressure and charges the law lays on a guy who spokes pot – a later name for the same thing which is cute to hear nowadays. We always looked at pot as a sort of medicine, a cheap drunk and with much better thoughts than one that's full of liquor. But with the penalties that came, I for one had to put it down though the respect for it (gage) will stay with me for ever. I have every reason to say these words and am proud to say them. From experience.

Now I'll relate a few incidents from the West Coast in California when Vic Berton (the top drummer then in all Hollywood) and I got busted together. It was during our intermission at this big night club which were packed and jammed every night with all sorts of my fans, including movie stars. Anyway, while Vic and I were blasting this joint – having lots of laughs and feeling good enjoying each other's company. We were standing in this great big lot in front of some cars. Just then two big healthy Dicks (detectives) came from behind a car – nonchalantly – and said to us, we'll take the roach boys. (Hmm.)

Vic and I said nothing. So one Dick stayed with me until I went into the Club and did my last show, he enjoyed it too. Because when he and I were on our way down to the police station we had a heart to heart talk. First words that he said to me were, Armstrong I am a big fan of yours and so is my family. We catch your program every night over the radio. In fact, nobody goes to bed in our family until your program's over. And they're all great – which I was glad to hear, especially coming from him. Ha Ha. Then I confidentially told him – Since you and your family are my fans they'd be awfully sad if anything drastic would happen to me, the same as the other thousands of my fans. So please don't hit me in my 'chops', when he said to me, why, I wouldn't think of anything like that. That's all I wanted to hear. Immediately I said, OK let's ride. I also told him – after all I'm no criminal. I respect everybody and they respect me. And I never let 'em down musically. Hell, he said, you ain't doing any more 'n' anybody's doing. It's when they get caught is when they're found out.

Then this Dick confidentially told me, he said, Armstrong, this wouldn't have happened if that band leader – he probably smoked marijuana himself – who's playing just up the road from you, and the big name that he's supposed to have, didn't get jealous because you are doing bigger business than him. So he dropped a nickel on you (meaning) he dropped a nickel into the telephone and called us and stoolpigeon on you. They sent me and my partner to come up for the assignment, and when we found out that you was the one we must nab (arrest) it broke our hearts. They told me, you must understand we can get you six months for a roach (meaning) the stub of a joint of gage. That's why they laughed when I pulled my whiskers and said to them, Ooh no, don't do me no favor such as that. I was so relaxed on the way down to the station until I forgot I was being busted.

When we reached the police headquarters there were several officers, including the man at the desk, sitting around. And the minute we came through the door they all recognized me right away. They too had been diggin' my music nightly over the radio. Oh boy, were those guys glad to see me. They gave me one look (with glee) and said, What'ta' hell are you doing here this time of night away from the club? So we yakity yakity while I was being booked. That's one reason why we appreciated pot, as y'all calls it now. The warmth it always brought forth from the other person – especially the ones that lit up a good stick of that 'shuzzit' or gage, nice names. Now, when it came to summing it up, the difference between the vipers and those using dope and all other kinds of drastic stuff, one could easily see who were actually dope addicts. First place – they were never clean, and they stays dirty-grimey all the time. Show most addicts a bucket of water and they'll run like hell to keep it from touching them. But a viper would gladly welcome a good bath, clean underwear and top clothes – stay fresh and on the ball.

We didn't do much drinking lush. When we did we always figured that pot would cut liquor any time. And being physic minded like we were we would take a good laxative (of some kind) and keep our stomachs cleaned out, because that good stuff we were smoking gave you an appetite. And drinking makes you eat like a dog. A good cleaned out stomach makes one feel like any human deserves to feel, and I've always been physic minded. Mayann (Mother) used to tell me and Mama Lucy (my sister) always stay physic minded. You may not get rich but you won't ever have those terrible *ailments* such as cancer etc. And she would go out by the railroad tracks and pick a lot of peppers – grasses – dandelions, etc. and she'd bring it home and boil that stuff and give us kids a big dose of it. And my gawd – we'd make sprints to the toilet and afterwards feel 'oh so good', all cleaned out 'n' stuff.

Every time I'd 'light up' with a cat (viper) I'd mention laxatives and was happy to know that everybody got the message. Because for a while we were drinking Abalena Water. It came from a well in Abilene, Texas. We drank that well dry, so had to get another kind of physic. So we started taking Pluto Water, which was great. Then here come this book – a health book written by Gaylord Hauser. When I read down to the part where he recommended some 'herbs' – herbal laxatives – I said to myself, 'erbs, – Hmmm, these herbs reminds me of the same as what my mother picked down by the tracks in New Orleans. Right away I went to the Health Store and bought myself a box of Swiss Kriss and took a big tablespoonful – make sure and see if it worked me the same as the other laxatives. Yes it did. Wow! I said to myself, yessindeed, this is what I need from now on – and forsake all others.

But back to the time I was busted on the coast. I spent nine days in the Downtown Los Angeles City Jail, in a cell with two guys who were already sentenced to 40 or 45 years for something else. Robbery, pickpocket, or whatever they were in for, didn't make any difference to me, and they cared less as to what I was in for. The most important thing was we were so very glad to see each other. Because it was a week ago I was blowing some good shuzzit with both of those characters. We reminisced about the good ol' beautiful moments we used to have during those miniature golf days. We'd go walking around, hit the ball, take a drag, have lots of laughs, and cut out.

Anyway, one night real late – those two cats started fighting amongst themselves over something, and the first words they said to me was, move out of the way 'Pops', we don't want to hurt them chops. And they fought their asses off until the jail keeper came and stopped them. One of them bit the other's finger off. They were intelligent, highly educated guys too. And they loved Pops' horn. It was actually a drag to me when I had to leave them in their cell and go to trial.

135

They also expressed sadness. So we finally said goodbye.

As we walked through the cellblocks, where prisoners of many many nationalities were locked up, they looked up and saw me walking with this great big deputy sheriff and (en mass) they hollered Louie Armstrong over 'n' over. They also hollered sing *Old Rockin' Chair*, etc. etc., and I smiled and said, Fellers I don't have time right now, nothing but to concentrate on what I am gonna tell this judge. They all laughed and cheered, saying Good luck Louie. On the way to court we stopped at the clothes room to pick up the suit I went in there with. The man handed me my suit, which was torned all through the lining, looking for some stuff I guess, stronger than pot. Referring to me, he said, Why this man is no 'Heeb' (their word when talking about dope fiends).

So I got to trial. Everybody were there – which takes in my boss, manager and a whole gang of lawyers – and I said to myself that I was straight. Meantime the Chicago papers were all on the stands, with big headlines saying Louis Armstrong will have to serve six months for marijuana, and things like that. The judge gave me a suspended sentence and I went to work that night – wailed just like nothing happened. What strucked me funny though – I laughed real loud when several movie stars came up to the bandstand while we played a dance set and told me, when they heard about me getting caught with marijuana they thought marijuana was a chick. Woo boy – that really fractured me! Every night I would run across those same detectives who arrested me, glad as ever to see me, and me back on the mound blowing again.

Now I'm back in the club, and everything's running along very smoothly when one night the washroom boy comes up to the bandstand and says there is a white boy in the washroom who wants to see me in there. I asked who it was, and he said, I don't know but he just came up from the south and he had a large croaker sack (meaning Burlap bag) full of something that he said is especially for you. (Hmm.) I went into the men's room and there was this fine ofay musician (a good one) who's father was a big judge down south, so you can easily see he was well off. He led me to the corner and showed me this sack. It was full of gage in the rough – dirty looking and had to be cleaned.

He said, Louis this muta (one of the names lots of the

Fays used) came from out of the back yard where the chickens trampled all over it, so it should be well seasoned. He and I went to the hotel over on Central Avenue, rolled up our sleeves, cleaned it real beautifully and rolled up one a piece. We dragged on down halfway to a 'roach' and he was right. When we got on down there we could taste the cackling, the crowing and the other things those chickens did. Beautiful.

We finished at the club with a big closing night, and a big farewell celebration from everybody. With a promise to return, which I did a year later, I left the coast – arriving home in Chicago on a Sunday morning. Had a sleep up into the afternoon, then had my supper while listening to some of my records. Lil was out visiting some place. The door bell rang. I went to the door and found one guy standing there, pointing towards four other youngsters getting out of the car. I said Boys, I'm very glad to see you. It's been a long time. The minute they came in they told me, Pops, we came to serenade you. The boys pulled out their guitars, ukes etc. and wailed awhile with a perfect beat which lifted me up just beautifully. Then they put up their instruments, one cat pulled out a big 'bomber' – lit it – took two drags and looked straight into my eyes as he passed it to me, saying, Pops, we all feel you could use this stick after all you've been through. I said, Aw boys, Y'all didn't have to do this, reaching for that joint at the same time. Each of them pulled out a stick a piece and started blowing and talking about a lot of interesting things.

That moment helped me to forget a heap of ungodly things. Made me have the right frame of mind for my opening day at the theatre on the South Side, which was really something else. After all, the vipers and fans in Chicago thought I was actually serving time from the incident on the coast with my boy, Vic Berton, whom I still think is the greatest drummer of all times. So the theatre was packed to the rafters. They came to hear what their boy Louis had to say, and when I was introduced you can imagine the house coming down with thunderous applause which lasted for a whole gang of minutes. Made my heart flutter with happiness.

Soooo, when they quieted down I said Yea, you thought I was. But I wasn't. And that did it. Such yells ... Dipper,

Satchelmouth, etc, we're glad to see you back. We went into our show and every tune was a gasser. We did three shows a day, each one packed 'n' jammed. After two weeks in Chicago I formed a band and went on the road, playing theatres in different cities and towns.

One stop was the Royal Theater in Baltimore, Maryland, located in a poor Negro neighbourhood. The people were so poor until they couldn't afford to buy hard coal. When we arrived in the town it was as cold as a well-digger's you-know-what. Freezing. Well, I heard about these people who were too poor to get coal to keep themselves and their kids warm, so I bought some for them. Yass I did. Went to the coal yard, ordered a ton of coal and had the company to deliver it to the Lobby of the Royal Theater. Then I had all of the folks who needed coal, to help themselves, it made them very happy. And they made it their business to come backstage and thank me personally – of course it all caused me to stick out my chest with pride. I came up through life the hard way just like those folks.

As we always used to say, gage is more of a medicine than a dope. But with all the riggermaroo going on, no one can do anything about it. After all, the vipers during my haydays are way up there in age – too old to suffer those drastic penalties. So we had to put it down. But if we all get as old as Methusela our memories will always be of lots of beauty and warmth from gage. Well, that was my life and I don't feel ashamed at all. Mary Warner, honey, you sure was good and I enjoyed you 'heep much'. But the price got a little too high to pay (law wise). At first you was a 'misdomeanor'. But as the years rolled on you lost your misdo and got meanor and meanor. (Jailhousely speaking.) Sooo 'Bye Bye,' I'll have to put you down, Dearest.

[signed] 'Soul Foodly, Satchmo'.

138

Sweet Sunny South

Early in his career Armstrong realized that bands are worrisome things, whose organization and day-to-day running should not concern him. He therefore worked to a rough rule-of-thumb, preferring to lead a band which was directed by another musician, who would take care of musical arrangements, rehearsals, hiring and firing and complaints in general. Especially the complaints, because Armstrong could never be bothered with all the extra-musical headaches of keeping a band together. Besides, as he often observed, it makes a man too many enemies. Sometimes he had a hand in picking musicians for his bands, but the actual hirings were done by the office or, as in past times, the band's director.

When Louis returned to Chicago in April 1931 he did take a hand in the selection of musicians for a ten-piece band which worked with him in Chicago and then in New Orleans and on tour until March 1932. It was really the first big band that he had made up 'on purpose', which had not been turned over to him ready-made by someone else.

It was constructed and run with the help of the trumpet player, Zilner Randolph, who was MD and orchestrator-in-chief, and guitarist Mike McKendrick, who kept the men on time and in order. Both were dependable musicians who were to be associated with Armstrong again. The band stayed together, with possibly one personnel change, for a year and played together pretty closely, displaying on occasion an incisive beat and stolid sense of discipline within its capabilities. This was no star line-up, and sometimes its performances sounded dull and routine, but what mattered to Louis was its reliability and all-round competence, also its temperament on tour, and he was to call this band the happiest he ever led. With it he recorded about two dozen titles between April 1931 and March 1932. Different takes of several tunes were made and released, and these show the amount of variation admitted to his 'set' method of executing a solo in the recording studios. Original interpretations of many songs that are now standards were cut at that time. Louis' first recorded onslaught on the somewhat vapid lyrics of *Sleepy Time Down South*, which became his signature tune, was made then. *I Surrender, Dear, Them There Eyes, When Your Lover Has Gone, Between The Devil And The Deep Blue Sea, Georgia, All Of Me, Love, You Funny Thing* and *Blue Again* are among the innocuous Tin Pan Alley concoctions he took over and introduced to the record-buying public as jazz vehicles.

A few of the tunes Louis overhauled were from films, or songs well known for other reasons, and a few had already achieved hit status. Others again, newly written, he helped to steer into prominence. Today we forget, if we ever knew, which were which. What we remember are his emancipated treatments. Melody and meaning, though perhaps unprepossessing in the first place, are transmuted by the Armstrong alchemy into precious material.

When Louis left Los Angeles, after the marijuana contretemps, he went to work straight away at the Regal Theater in Chicago. The job had been booked by Johnny Collins, described by Louis simply as 'my latest manager'. Where Collins came from, who he was connected with, where indeed he went after he left Armstrong's affairs finally in 1935, these are riddles on which we can shed no light. It might be illuminating to hear his version of those few years with the trumpet king, but, in trying to find out about him, we ran into absolute blankness. He was last heard of more than a decade ago, probably in Florida. Louis told us he never heard directly from Collins and seldom if ever thought about him. From accounts and photographs, it seems he was several years Louis' senior, and he may now be dead.

The period during which Collins and Armstrong were in cahoots was eventful to the point of danger. Armstrong had already done some travelling, but was usually resident at one place or another for months on end, sometimes for a year or so. There had been tours, with Oliver and Henderson and Russell, but never of long duration. Even the journey to California was followed by a protracted residency. But after Collins' appointment, Satch was kept mostly on the move, and the scope of his travels widened significantly. We shall see why.

In recalling the viper days Armstrong referred to going on the road with a band after a fortnight in Chicago. This is not quite accurate. His new band, which for a year had the appearance of permanency, was assembled in mid-April for an engagement at the Showboat Café, a new cabaret on the Loop once known as the Cellar. There Louis played for a time and enjoyed the kind of exhilarating success to which he was beginning to become accustomed. *Sleepy Time, Little Joe, Walkin' My Baby Back Home, Them There Eyes* were some of the songs he fractured nightly at the Showboat and over coast-to-coast radio. Another was *You Rascal, You*, a vaudeville-type ditty well suited to Louis' eccentric vocalizing, which on records surprised audiences in Britain as well as all over the United States. The band went into the OKeh studios on 20 April and again soon afterwards. These were deadly quiet days in the record business – the recording activities of such a great Negro star as Bessie Smith, for example, had slowed almost to nothing – and Louis was one of the few lucky jazz artists who continued to visit the studios regularly in the years following the Wall Street collapse. As we have suggested earlier, slump conditions were not the only cause of this decline in jazz music's fortunes; the trend in the public's musical tastes was towards the new popular songs of the dance bands and crooners. Had Louis not changed his

141

repertoire he would have sunk into obscurity like so many jazzmen. Had he changed his way of singing and playing, the records he made might well have sunk without trace. But he did the first and not the second.

On one of these recordings, *When It's Sleepy Time Down South*, he committed the solecism of uttering the word 'darkies' which he found in the lyrics. Nobody said much at the time, for every popular singer was likely to do the same if he came within tonsil distance of *Sleepy Time, Mississippi Mud* or any of a score of plantation-style titles. But, Louis being Louis, his recording remained in currency and he went on singing the song, to the increasing distress of white liberals and 'brothers' who were then careful to speak of 'coloured' or 'Negro' people or, perhaps, of 'ebony' races and other such euphemisms. For a period, 'spade' was permissible, but this was soon jumped on when it appeared in print. As you might expect, Louis continued to employ it in conversation and was in trouble on that score, too. Later, when the error of his ways was driven home to him, he altered the offending 'darkies' to 'folks'. But he grumbled that he had only been singing the lyrics: 'I didn't write the song.' How odd that it should be his theme tune and that the original 1931 recording was to be considered, on grounds of taste, virtually unreissuable for many years.

But in the Chicago of 1931, Armstrong had more pressing business on his mind. His unexplained departure from New York and Chicago the previous summer could have been caused by the application of heat from some quarters – matrimonial, union or management – and, if so, history was about to give him an encore. Things were looking bright for Louis at the Showboat, and jealous eyes peered in his direction from New York.

In his thirty-odd years Louis must have seen plenty of action from knives, revolvers, blackjacks and brass knuckles. He realized it was tough to argue persuasively with somebody who is holding a gun, and had long ago learned that when gang disputes broke out, intelligent men took to their heels. He never said any more about these adventures than he had to, but what he used to say, when reminded of this chapter in his affairs, was that it happened back in the Showboat or, more often, 'All that was before I went back to New Orleans.' His persistent association of New Orleans with this episode makes an interesting subject for speculation. But, before speculation, some facts. First the date: this cannot be established precisely, but the night of the 'pressuring' must have been before 25 April. On that day two stories on Armstrong appeared in the black press. The New York *Age* reported 'Louis Armstrong and his band broadcast over station WIBC in Chicago last Sunday morning. The King of the Trumpet is now appearing nightly at the Showboat, Park and Lake, in Chicago.' According to the Chicago *Defender*, Messrs Weil, Fiore and Ryan were arrested on a charge of trying to extort six thousand to ten thousand dollars from Louis. Weil denied the charge, saying he was 'only trying to get him to change managers'.

Robert Goffin wrote up the gun scene fairly vividly in his *Horn Of Plenty* biography. He claimed Louis was summoned to the dressing-room, where he found a stranger with a beard and a pistol. The mobster, named by Goffin as Frank Foster, is said to have prodded Louis with the weapon and told him he was 'leaving right quick for New York' to play a date at Connie's Inn. Louis objected that Mr Collins had not mentioned this engagement. He was advised to forget Collins and to confirm the New York date on the telephone there and then; or else! Louis agreed, said Goffin, made the call, and was 'thanked cordially for his acquieseence'. After the false-bearded visitor had gone, Collins turned up with the police. He admitted he was having trouble with New York, forbade Armstrong to go there, and told him he'd been offered a theatre date in Chicago for two months.

'I ain't goin' to New York,' was Louis' reply (in the book). 'But get this straight – I ain't staying in Chicago neither ... I'd rather take a walk through the cemetery at midnight.' So Collins signed Armstrong up for the Suburban Gardens in New Orleans. The trombonist in this band was Preston Jackson, who gave us this account:

I'm playing at the Savoy, one night only, and at intermission I stand up against the wall and suddenly there's Louis Armstrong. He say, 'Hya Nosey.' He called me Nosey always and I called him Nosey. We talk and he says he's going out to Sebastian's in Hollywood. 'And when I get back and form a band, you're my man.' I was happy to hear him say that but didn't think any more about it. Within a few months he was back and looking for me.

So we rehearsed about two weeks and opened up at the Showboat, where we stayed about a month, broadcasting every night. And that was a terrible place; that's where Louis had some trouble. You see, that man had a whole lot of trouble of different natures. Now we're there – he's with John Collins now, had some kind of dispute with the Connie's Inn – and one night he gets a phone call from New York. As he enters the booth a gangster puts a gun in his stomach and tells him he's going back to New York. Louis told him he wasn't. Well, he didn't shoot Louis. But thereafter, a squad brought Louis to work each night and brought him home.

As a result, Louis quit Chicago for the best part of a year. Otherwise he would surely have stayed on to enjoy the advantages of a residency and the adulation of the Windy City jazzmen, who came to the cabaret in impressive numbers to pay respects to the greatest of the jazz trumpeters. Of course, the comforts of the job decreased dramatically when the 'big boys' had a difference of opinion. Al Capone ran the Cotton Club and this place and that in Chicago; his brother Ralph controlled a club or two in Cicero; there were sundry gangs in charge of different territories; but ultimately Al Capone was overlord. Another fallout between rival mobs was imprinted on trombonist Preston Jackson's memory, and it illustrates another side of Louis' coolness under fire. A scuffle broke out one night at the Showboat. Guns began firing and Jackson described the reaction on the stand: 'Tubby Hall hid under the piano, Armstrong continued playing, but all the rest of the band dived.'

144

'In Chicago,' Louis said years later, 'all I wanted was a little elbow room. Every time you looked round it seemed there was a gun in your side.' He followed that up with what is largely a corroboration of Goffin's gangster passage. One night when he went into his room (he did not name the Showboat), he found a 'big cat' who instructed him: 'You're going to New York. I want you should be on the first train in the morning.' The trumpeter was about to reply 'What the...' when he looked up at his visitor. 'I saw I was looking right down the wrong end of a forty-five, so I changed my mind and says, "Well, maybe I will go to New York for a change." My manager straightened it out, but I thought it best to leave town next morning.'

Another cutting has bearing on this hassle between competing managers and club operators. Datelined New Orleans, 27 June, it reads: 'Members of Louis Armstrong's Orchestra have been expelled from the American Federation of Musicians for continuing to play with Armstrong after he had been expelled for not fulfilling a contract with a New York night club.'

The language here is of special importance because when GAC president Thomas Rockwell threatened the publishers of *Horn Of Plenty* with libel suit, in March 1947, it was reported by *Down Beat* that the portion of the book to which Rockwell objected was that in which Frankie Foster was alleged to have waved a gun at Armstrong and told him he was 'leaving to fulfil a contract at Connie's Inn in New York'. Nowhere in Goffin's account does the phrase 'leaving to fulfil a contract' occur, and it sounds very much like an agent's or booker's phrase. Goffin had implicated Rockwell in his story and the latter was talking to his attorney about court action. But in the *Down Beat* report Rockwell explained the true story. He was in Chicago with Dave Kapp of Decca and, in his hotel, was told by four men that he had four hours to get out of town. This, said Rockwell, made him mad, so calling up several friends he went down to the Showboat to try to see Louis. According to *Down Beat*, 'He says the friends accompanied him only

145

for support in case the four previously mentioned gentlemen showed up. Unable to see Louis, he says he caught the Century back to New York the next day. The incidents involving Frankie Foster concerned Connie's Inn and Foster himself, and did not involve him directly, Rockwell added.'

Almost anything may be guessed from these various reports and statements. Unquestionably Armstrong was in strong demand, and probably earning quite heavy money. But if he was being threatened with a gun, what was the union (the AFM) doing expelling him and then his musicians? A postscript to the Rockwell affair was supplied by *Down Beat* the next month: he would not sue Goffin and the publishers but insisted his name be deleted from all future issues of the book. Probably the publishers agreed to that. We don't remember seeing any edition beyond the first of *Horn Of Plenty*, and the book is today exceedingly rare.

What happened next was that Armstrong's ten-man band pulled out of Chicago (perhaps some time in May) and played one-nighters on the way to New Orleans. They covered the mid-west and much of the south and southwest. In all, going down to New Orleans and back up north via St Louis, where they played for the whole of September, the band stopped in perhaps fifty or sixty towns. Preston Jackson takes up the story again.

We left Chicago, and picked up Zilner Randolph, the writer of *Ole Man Mose*, who's the arranger and in charge of the band in the absence of Louis. We did one-nighters in Michigan, Ohio and Kentucky on the way to this job at the Suburban Gardens, and we was drawing nice crowds. Finally we left Louisville for New Orleans on the L&N, and that's the time all these bands met us at the station – it was a regular parade. Before we open at the Suburban Gardens, this Rockwell, he's on Louis. Louis' broken a contract. So we're called down to the local union and questioned. There wasn't anything done about it, but then they started making announcements over the air about 'the niggers coming down to New Orleans and taking the white musicians' jobs.' After that we were followed every night by a car with three or four guys in it. And while we were there at the Suburban we had some more trouble, as you may have heard. We didn't know how these people would take it, and it frightened me because my teeth begin to chatter, although I was born in that section. But it still was the South. However they took it in good part.

Armstrong tales from this strange southern saga are legion. By this time he had a man called Sherman Cook, known as Professor Cook, who was his valet, personal secretary and sometime Master of Ceremonies. Cook, appointing himself publicity director too, drummed up interest in the return of the prodigal son to New Orleans by sending telegrams from various stopping-places on the way, and by getting into town ahead of the band to see that a riotous reception was laid on. How much he had to do with it, no one can tell. But when Louis reached his birthplace – his first visit in nine years – he was met at the L&N station by the Zulu Club band and several more brass bands, a huge crowd of whites and blacks, and a contingent of police to keep the peace. And the Professor, of course, with his reception party. Louis was driven in a parade of honour along Canal Street and around the city, past some of the haunts of his childhood, to his hotel. He met old friends, those who had not left town to make good, and characters from his younger days, including his first wife, Daisy. He was reunited with his family, and invited to return to the Waifs' Home.

It was an unforgettable homecoming, and from his account the opening at the Suburban Gardens was no less memorable. Louis was the new King of Perdido, and the local newspapers all ran stories about the former reform-school inmate and newsboy who had come home from the north a jazz hero. Ironically, the people whose hero he was were not admitted to the premises where Satchmo was booked – New Orleans was, after all, a Jim Crow town – and another aspect of racialism was rapidly to be observed. The Suburban Gardens was on the air, and from June to

August Louis and the band broadcast nightly. Radio had played a large part in creating his nation-wide success. Armstrong, reflecting that there had been no radio when he left in 1922, looked forward to his first-ever broadcast from down home. A white man, naturally, would be doing the announcing before a white audience. However one viewed it, this opening night was a big occasion for Little Louis, even though a segregated one.

Some ten thousand black citizens lined the levee where the Suburban was situated, on the outskirts of town. 'Well, they wasn't allowed in there,' said Satch,

so quite naturally they gathered outside right along the levee, hoping to catch the music through the open windows. I'll never forget that sight. And the club was just as packed inside, five thousand people or more they said. And among them was people I'd grown up with, white boys you understand, I used to play games with on the empty lots after school, and they were there calling me by name, you know, pleased to see me again.

Louis had been a little worried about the reception he'd get, and his management had been worried too. The time came for the band to start playing and the broadcast to begin. Louis and his 'fine bunch of cats' were ready to go into their theme, and a packed house was waiting expectantly. The announcer appeared and commenced his 'Welcome to the Suburban Gardens' speech. Then he broke off, and explained to the listeners, 'I just haven't the heart to announce that nigger on the radio.' And he left.

Pandemonium, of course, reigned everywhere, except in Louis' place behind the curtain. He realized that for white men to announce blacks over the southern air was unusual; for a black to announce himself was probably unheard of. But the show had to go on, or the 'sonafabitches' he was working for would require to know why. The club's manager told him that the announcer refused to introduce him. Louis made up the rest of his mind quickly. 'Don't bother,' he told the manager, 'I'll handle it myself.' He

148

asked the band for a chord ('and hold it') and walked out to the microphone. The ovation was such that minutes passed before he could utter a word. Then he thanked the nice folks, and to loud shouts of 'Louis' and 'Hey, Dipper' waved the orchestra into *Sleepy Time Down South*.

'Like I said, it was murder – one of my happiest days,' Armstrong summed it up. 'For the rest of that night and the rest of that gig I did my own radio announcing. That other announcer? They threw him out the same night ... ain't that something?'

In New Orleans, where he was now a figure of comparative distinction, Louis sponsored one of the local baseball teams, supplying them with new caps and suits and gear. The shirts proclaimed 'Armstrong' across the front, and the team became known as Armstrong's Secret Nine. Already a cigar was being marketed as the Louis Armstrong Special. If you listen to Louis introducing the members of his 'congregation' on the November 1931 recording of *Lonesome Road*, you'll hear him say 'Here's two little songwriters, little Louis Dunlap and Charles Carpenter, and what do you think about that? They're smoking a Louis Armstrong Special cigar.' Dunlap and Carpenter – who wrote *You Can Depend On Me*, which Louis had recorded the previous day – happened to be in the studio, and Louis' recording methods were nothing if not informal. On the same title he also introduces Sherman Cook: 'He's looking all prosperous; he's a New Orleans boy, too.'

The engagement at the Suburban was an unqualified success, and Armstrong enjoyed his stay in the Crescent City until right at the end. His marriage went from bad to worse, and Lil told him: 'You don't need me now you're earning a thousand dollars a week. We'll call it a day.' She left, and returned to Chicago.

An informant swore that Lil had once gone after her husband with a .38. This sounded out of character, so we asked her if there was any truth in the allegation.

I never owned, used or carried a gun (.38) in my life. I don't

149

know who started that wild lie. I can tell you now that if I had used one, the whole world would have known beyond a doubt (I wouldn't have missed my target. Dig?)

Was she aware of the Alpha situation during the mid-'20s in Chicago? 'Don't know when or how long Louis had an affair with Alpha,' was her reply. 'I can assure you she was not the only one, so I didn't worry too much about it.' For some while, Lil had been trying to bring about a reconciliation, but that now seemed out of the question. Louis was after a divorce so he could marry Alpha. He and Lil were finally separated in this year, but the expected divorce took seven years to come through. What bitter feelings there were did not survive for long. Lil says her basic regard for Louis never changed, and he said that his marriage to her 'went through some good years, then we disagreed'.

Some of the compositions from Hot Five days were later a bone of contention, and this had to be settled in court. In 1967, while she was in Britain on holiday, Lil spoke about these old tunes, claiming that many of them belonged to her. Looking at the record labels, it was never clear if the 'L. Armstrong' or 'Armstrong' composer-credit referred to Louis or Lil. I don't suppose it was clear to them. At those OKeh sessions, the band was paid a flat rate of $50 a man per date. Presumably the composers received more, but not much. 'When we wrote those, forty years or so ago,' said Lil, 'we didn't think it important to get them copyrighted. We just put our names on them and thought of the immediate cash. Now I live off them. But it only happened after a big law suit, you know, over *Barbecue*. It had Lillian Armstrong's name on it, though, so I got that straight.'

Struttin' With Some Barbecue, Got No Blues, Two Deuces, Hotter Than That, I'm Not Rough are some of the tunes she claimed; also *Pencil Papa* and *Perdido Street Blues*. Talking of her early arranging experiments, Lil explained:

I helped with the arrangements in Oliver's band, scarcely wrote out anything on paper. Most of them were what we

150

call 'head arrangements'. *Perdido Street Blues* is the first one written out in full for the band. I got so many requests to make arrangements after that from other bands that I had to study arranging.

According to Spencer Williams, 'Pencil Papa' was a nickname for the then-famous pianist and entertainer Tony Jackson, who was in Chicago in the '20s. Others of the Armstrong-credited tunes belong to Lil, too. *You're Next, Jazz Lips, Knee Drops, King of the Zulus* and *My Heart* – the Hot Five's first recorded title, on 12 November 1925.

Lil, with her superior learning, must have been extremely useful to the Hot Five. That's not always easy to forgive, and we asked how Louis felt about her in later years. She laughed at the question and replied, ' 'Course he's not quite so friendly since that law suit. But you know Louis ... he's all right.' As for Louis, he once said:

Four women I married and none of them ain't hurt me yet. They must have loved me. They all proved something, said something, and they all gave me a lot of experience you couldn't get nowhere else. All my wives got the best that's in me.

The awkward announcer did not provide the only racial incident to disturb the general friendliness of Louis' welcome in New Orleans. Louis had been asked to play a farewell date for the city's black population at the end of the Suburban run, and agreed tó do it without a fee. But somewhere behind the scenes the plan was blocked. The dance was to be held in a US Army base on the evening after closing night at the Suburban Gardens. On the day, the area round the base filled with black Louisianians, drawn together to see the returned jazz hero. The band was ready to go to work, and Louis was feeling a glow of self-esteem at the realization that this multitude had gathered to hear the local wonder-boy perform. But as he came close to the base he saw the crowd moving away. The gates were locked; the dance was off. No one seemed to know exactly

151

why, but it was said that dancing wasn't allowed on Army premises.

Many of the crowd had come into town in cars, horse carts and even ox-drawn wagons, and they numbered several thousands. Understandably they felt furious at being turned away, and some of the anger was directed against Louis. It increased his growing disillusionment with the way the white bosses ran the city. Early next morning he left for Houston and other Texas towns, making up his mind to give New Orleans a miss for a while. On the way back north the band played Memphis, and this was when they landed in jail. Preston Jackson explains:

> When we leave New Orleans we goes to Texas, plays six weeks there, then into Tulsa, Oklahoma and Oklahoma City. Then we doubles back over the same territory and that's when we ran into Joe Oliver with his band. Anyhow this was when we had trouble in Memphis. It was somewhere around 7.30 or 8 o'clock when we hit Memphis, and there this superintendent say: 'Well, get them niggers out of here; I have to put them in another bus.' Now the other bus was much smaller and more inconvenient, so Mrs Collins told them she'd paid 50 dollars difference in these buses so the boys could enjoy themselves. After a hassle, he told the driver to go on round to the terminal, which he did, and it looked like half the Memphis police force met us around there. 'All right you niggers,' they said. 'You're in Memphis now, and we need some cotton-pickers, too.' They put us in jail, all except Mike McKendrick, and all them boys had pistols which they shedded, 'cos they didn't want to be caught with them. On Rampart Street then you could buy a pistol just as easy as a loaf of bread.
>
> They put us all in one big cell [Jackson continued]. A guy came through: 'Louis, I heard you fellers in Houston last week, you know.' Well, we didn't care where he heard us; we wanted to get out of jail and make Little Rock.

In his self-portrait, Louis makes the reasons clear. So does Mezz Mezzrow in his account of the same occurrence.

Mrs Collins, the manager's wife, was in charge of their

transportation, and she had chartered a big shiny new Grey-hound bus so they could get through the Murder Belt without riding in dirty spine-cracking Jim Crow coaches. She always sat up front with Mike McKendrick ...
When that bus pulled into Memphis the pecks all crowded around goggle-eyed, staring at the well-dressed coloured boys ... and especially at the one coloured boy up front who was, God forbid, sitting there actually talking to a white woman cool as pie, just like he was human. They couldn't let that go down.

Louis' story also records that, after Collins secured their release, they broadcast from Memphis and he laid a tune on the local police chief. It is not a tall story. Mezzrow assured us that all the vipers who hung round New York's Lafayette Theater heard the radio programme. Halfway through it, said Mezz, Louis dedicated his next number to the Chief of Police of Memphis. 'Dig this, Mezzeerola,' Satch is said to have announced over the air before sailing into his vocal on *I'll Be Glad When You're Dead You Rascal You*.

A date can be set for this particular southern interlude because the arrest, investigation, harassment, call it what you will, made the newspapers. On 10 October 1931 the Chicago *Defender* reported that the following were detained for failing to change to another bus at Memphis to make a date at Little Rock, Arkansas, 6 October: Mary Collins, manager, Randolph, Hall, Cook, Jackson, Alexander, Washington, James, Boone and Armstrong – 'all of Chicago'. No mention of Big Mike McKendrick, who kept on moving, just as Louis said.

It appears more than odd, considering the name he was building for himself in New York and Chicago, that Armstrong should have absented himself so long from those places to go gallivanting round the country. The only explanation which makes sense is that Louis or Collins, more likely both, thought it expedient to steer well clear of New York and, for several months, Chicago as well.

Since Louis immediately thought of New Orleans whenever either of the authors brought up the gangster story, it is possible that he instinctively returned 'home' when danger threatened. In spite of its own murky associations with crime and poverty, New Orleans was for him perhaps the safest port in a storm. He had known gamblers, pimps and some of the toughest racketeers when he lived there; besides, he would be surrounded by friends and admirers, and would thus learn through the local grapevine if his life was in danger. In addition, the New Orleans hoodlums belonged to their own mobs. They would possibly have resented the appearance of northern 'muscle' on their territory.

After the months back home, when the band recommenced touring, its itinerary did not move too far north. Collins himself, who had been having trouble with the New York bookers, must certainly have been menaced. Was Mrs Collins' presence throughout the long tour necessitated by similar considerations of safety? It was, after all, a dicey trip for her. Preston Jackson and Mezz both referred to Mary Collins in their Memphis anecdotes. It would seem that an inter-state journey by band bus down south in 1931, with one white woman on board with a black band, was practically courting disaster. But it may have been healthier than the alternative.

Eventually Collins – or Louis – decided to chance New York. The band came into town in January 1932, and played dates at the Lafayette Theater in Harlem and, in the week of 22 January, at the Paramount. A New York musician recalls that all the posters advertising these appearances were torn down, which suggests that business disagreements had not been settled. A number of one-night engagements followed, then the band fell apart. Presumably work ran out. Louis and four or five of the men went back to Chicago; the rest remained to try their luck in the Big Apple.

Connie Immerman of Connie's Inn comes into the Armstrong drama some time during this act. John Hammond supplied a news item in December 1931 which said that the court case of Louis v. Immerman and Rockwell was due to be heard in New York on 15 December. No results of this case were published, and it may have been settled out of court.

A sinister aftermath of the gang activities on the music scene was briefly detailed in a New York paper, which reported that the prosperous inn-owner had been beaten up by persons unknown. Mezzrow, writing of the same period, when East Side mobsters were trying to increase their holdings, said 'Not long before they had tried to rub Connie Immerman out, and I knew they would give the same treatment to anybody else who stood in their way.' Not surprisingly, then, Armstrong left New York and, shortly afterwards, Chicago. He had no band, once more. But he had money and a manager. Collins could still find some work for him in California, and in March Louis travelled again to the west coast. He liked the climate there, and he wanted a holiday. For two or three months he relaxed, playing a few dates with Les Hite's band. He was not to play in New York again for a while. Meanwhile, he was to leave America for the first time.

If the account of the gangster episodes is sketchy, it is because quotations, data and facts are hard to come by. Once, when I [M.J.] was doing some British broadcasts with Spencer Williams, I received a message from a New York character whose connections went back to the roaring '20s. It was simple, if enigmatic. 'Tell Spencer when next you see him that Brownsuit Charlie said hello.' This duty I duly discharged. There was a considerable silence, then Williams observed that everyone from New Orleans was capable of being evil. Friendly with them and you'll be all right, was the gist of what he said, but 'don't cross them or they get real mean'. Spencer came from New Orleans. I didn't mention Brownsuit Charlie any more, but ever after I felt that Williams regarded me unfondly, though we met several times. Spencer never referred to Charlie once. The gangster chapter in this story conceivably has the shadow of a Brownsuit Charlie lurking over it still.

An interesting aspect of it all, hinted at in Louis' remarks about Joe Glaser, is that Pops plainly saw the evil as stemming from the white community. After discussing the dressing-room gun scene, and his having to leave town, he volunteered: 'It was all right, though, when I got with Joe Glaser as my manager. He protected me and I got along with the white folk all right.' That latter sentence could be the starting-point for a separate book about the influence of organized American crime in the affairs of jazzmen.

Louis in Britain

Why Louis went to Europe when he did is not known for sure. His only explanation about his rather sudden departure from the west coast, where he had been working and holidaying, comes in his first and heavily journalized book. 'I decided I needed a good rest and vacation, and that I would like to see Europe.' Robert Goffin adds, in *Horn Of Plenty*, that John Collins is said to have driven out to Los Angeles in his new car on the day that Louis bought himself a second-hand one. 'I've just signed us up for Europe,' says Collins. Louis replies, 'Swell. If I ain't got my divorce by the time we leave, I'll get it in France.' They left almost at once for Chicago, then by car for New York and England by liner.

Louis' account in *Swing That Music* differs only in details. 'I bought myself an old Buick and drove it east to Chicago. After seeing Lil and attending to some things there, I took a train to New York, said goodbye to my friends in Harlem and sailed on the *Majestic*.'

Ignorance about jazz matters was widespread in Britain at that time, although jazzmen had entered the country as early as 1919, when Sidney Bechet visited with the Southern Syncopated Orchestra, and there was a tour by the Original Dixieland Jazz Band. Red McKenzie's Mound City Blue Blowers followed in 1925 and England was host to numbers of Americans working in local bands – for example, Danny Polo, Sylvester Ahola, Adrian and Arthur Rollini, Chelsea Quealey, Henry Levine, Bobby Davis, Max Farley and Fud Livingston. These musicians could acquire no more than a limited reputation with record fans and people who danced in London's West End; the same can be said of Jimmy Dorsey and Bunny Berigan, who visited London in 1930 with Ted Lewis and Hal Kemp respectively. Armstrong's flaring brilliance, on records at first, was the fiercest beam to pierce the gloom of Britain's jazz dark ages.

In leaving the United States for the first time and with no knowledge of what to expect on the other side, Louis took a chance. Hopes and plans soon foundered and it would hardly have surprised the people close to him if he had retired hurt and returned home after the set-backs which followed his initial engagement. But he accepted the vicissitudes with good humour, shrugging off the disappointments and revelling in the successes. When he did return, after four months, he may not have been much richer than when he left; but he had a new concept of the importance of jazz, and increased confidence in his own musical status. For this and other reasons the visit was to prove a turning point in his career. Like most of his decisive moves it was made at the ideal moment, though this was not apparent for some time.

The timing of his arrival in Britain was favourable for several reasons. The hard core of enthusiasts among dance musicians and fans was numerically strong enough to support him. Earlier, Armstrong would have found Britain unprepared for him. A later descent might have clashed with Duke Ellington's band, with Fats Waller, Joe Venuti, Coleman Hawkins (their paths were to cross in any case) and Cab Calloway; not that he had to fear competition, but the impact could have been different. More important, an attempt to visit Britain only three years later would have run into the Ministry of Labour ban, which effectively kept foreign jazz musicians out of the country for more than 20 years.

Armstrong's playing was at a peak at the time. He set such high standards for so long that it is possible to argue he was in peak form at almost any period during a span of

158

12 or 15 years; but in 1932, all the physical parts of his technique were in miraculous working order. He was the possessor of lung-power and throat, jaw, teeth and lip formation which seemed to be ideally suited to the production of trumpet tone. With these natural attributes went a control of the instrument giving him ease of performance in every department of the art. His mastery was matched by superior stamina, also by an artistic adaptability which was to be thoroughly tested on his first British tour. As a jazz player he had it all; all, that is, except widespread recognition as a creative musician. That was something he picked up in Europe, and not overnight.

Already, Armstrong was generously represented in the British catalogues. A Parlophone 'New Rhythm Style Series' advertisement of July 1932 listed no fewer than 30 of his records: 38 different titles ranging from *Muggles* and *St James Infirmary* to *Mahogany Hall Stomp* and *Rockin' Chair*. Record collecting was becoming a recognized pursuit, and jazz collectors were soon to get together in circles or Rhythm Clubs. The *Melody Maker*, then a monthly magazine but on its way to going weekly, was the enthusiasts' bible. Other periodicals took some notice of jazz and dance music, and a book on the subject – R. W. Mendl's *The Appeal of Jazz* – had been published as early as 1927. A minority of Britons had seen the light, and these specialists included, as might be expected, a number of dance band players. Most fanatical of the Armstrong admirers in Britain was Nat Gonella, a trumpet man raised in the brass band world. He came across a Louis record in the '20s and found that 'his style and feeling hit me right between the eyes and I became a raving fan'. Nat started to copy both his playing and singing, and was given a spot in Billy Cotton's stage show for an impression of Louis. The strength of this attachment can be gauged from the *Bessie Couldn't Help It* Gonella recorded with Cotton in 1930.

The booking seemed to be unforeseen and under-publicized, and the *Melody Maker*, which had been pulling every accessible string to get Louis over to England, was able to give its readers only very brief notice of the great event. The paper's lead story of July 1932 said:

The Melody Maker (Dance Band News). July, 1932.

GROSVENOR HOUSE SENSATION—SEE PAGE 531

Dance Band News

Vol. VII   JULY, 1932   No. 79

LOUIS ARMSTRONG COMING TO LONDON

For some time past, idle rumours have been afoot that Louis Armstrong was coming to London. His name has been coupled with the Savoy Hotel, Café de Paris, Ciro's and other places. Each time the *Melody Maker* has investigated these reports it has discovered a mare's nest. Now that the visit is really to take place it will come as a complete surprise, for no such rumour has heralded the engagement.

The report had gone to press on 24 June, after delaying the deadline for 24 hours, in order to break the news exclusively to 'all those in this country who will be most interested'.

The London Palladium's George Black had booked 'the coloured phenomenon' for a fortnight commencing 18 July. Louis was arriving without a band. What he would do by way of a stage act, and whom he would employ for accompanists, were facts not known to the *Melody Maker* or, they implied, to anybody else at that moment. 'At the time of going to press he is not in England,' the story continued, adding pessimistically, 'Even if he arrives within the next few days he will not have much time to rehearse a stage act.'

There was, in addition, speculation on how 'the coloured phenomenon' would be received; not by the converted – that was a foregone conclusion – but by the general public.

We feel that they, once recovered from the stupefaction, will

160

take Louis to their hearts. Only at the Palladium is this possible, for this house has a more or less regular clientele which has been educated up to the unusual in entertainment. In the provinces, or even in the suburbs, we fear that Louis would be too much for the general public.

It appears that the journal credited the Palladium regulars with more tolerance than they could muster. Perhaps it under-estimated Armstrong's capacity to shock 'straight' audiences. In the event he was immensely popular with the initiated minority, but much less so with conventional theatregoers, who left their seats in some force. I [M.J.] don't remember any walk-out to speak of when I saw Louis; but I believe I attended one of the four matinées, at a reduced price for *Melody Maker* readers, which took place on the Wednesdays and Thursdays of the run. Audiences at these special shows naturally included a high proportion of musicians and fans.

The normal evening shows attracted a large number of regular patrons, and Palladium regulars were not noticeably hip. Nat Gonella remembers 20 or 30 disgruntled customers leaving on the opening night, more on subsequent evenings. 'The business for Armstrong's first visit to the Palladium was said to be a record for the theatre at that time,' he told us. 'So that every performance would be full at Louis' opening, but by the time he had to finish the theatre was half empty, and I was there every night.' Nat and his brother Bruts had front-row seats for the first performance, after that 'rover' tickets. They sat wherever they could and when protesters walked out, tried to trip them in the near-darkness. 'We used to do that every performance,' Nat admits. 'I know memories slip a bit but my remembrance of tripping people up as they left the theatre is vivid. Hallelujah.'

Why the exodus? Well, this was a strange presentation. Bands were common enough, but nothing like Louis and the Parisian club and café musicians he had engaged had been seen or heard in Argyll Street. Jazz was quite simply the underground music of the era. Armstrong was an extremely fervent exponent as well as an unbridled presence on stage. His band was wild and wilful too. Iain Lang, writing much later of the Palladium act, agrees that Armstrong in person came as a shock:

> The sweating, strutting figure in the spotlight hitting endless high notes had only a tenuous and intermittent connection with the creator of the intensely moving music of *West End Blues* and *Muggles*.

This pin-pointed an Armstrong dilemma: how to live up to the expectations of people reared on the greatest of his many fine creations. Like every other arrangement on this trip, the band seems to have been a last-minute improvisation, for engaging suitable accompanists had proved to be unexpectedly troublesome. Jack Hylton, who had close links with George Black and the *Melody Maker*, had been consulted first and even asked to furnish a band, but he was going to be out of town at the time. Rudolph Dunbar, clarinet-player and -teacher, was approached with a view to forming what was described as a band of 'English Negroes'. This turned out to be difficult in the England of that day, and Dunbar suggested importing a few black players from Paris. His idea was vetoed because of the expense, and a plan was then put forward to have Spike Hughes and a white combo. The problem was settled when it was learned that Harry Foster – the agent who booked Armstrong in the first place – had been in touch with manager Collins and agreed to recruit 'a complete band of coloured musicians from Paris'. This group duly arrived in London, but incomplete; two places had to be filled by locals. It was reported that Armstrong had scant time to rehearse his Paris brigade, but this may have been a British misinterpretation of the situation. Rehearsals began in a Poland Street hall soon after the men's arrival on Saturday afternoon, and continued on Sunday and part of Monday.

Belgian author Robert Goffin, who had dedicated his 1932 *Aux Frontières du Jazz* to Armstrong, made the trip to

London in order to see his hero in person. He witnessed the first rehearsal and, indeed, met the incoming band. At the Palladium Goffin was told that Louis was waiting for some musicians who were due in from Paris, so he made for Victoria Station and found him. Ten minutes later Armstrong was addressing him as 'Gate'. Given a copy of *Aux Frontières*, he was so moved by the dedication to 'Louis Armstrong, the true King of Jazz' that he promptly kissed it.

The bandsmen included trumpeter Charlie Johnson and saxophonist Joe Hayman, both known to Goffin from Paris. Others with them were tenorman Fletcher Allen, saxist-clarinettist Peter Du Conge, guitarist Maceo Jefferson and maybe one or two more. The identities of the British 'deps' are unknown. Goffin remained in the hall listening to Louis until late evening. 'It was unbelievable,' he wrote in his book *Jazz*. 'He shut his eyes, flourished his trumpet, twisted his handkerchief, sang in tears, climbed up to hit notes with neck and cheek so distended that I thought they would burst. What a revelation!' And this was only the first rehearsal!

Two days later, as the time for Armstrong's British debut drew near, the Belgian was one of many who converged on the Palladium in a state of excited anticipation. 'When his number went up on the indicator board,' wrote Dan Ingman of the *Melody Maker*, 'there was a terrific burst of applause.'

Louis popped out in front of the curtain and took his bow. And what applause there was. His first number was *Them There Eyes*, his second *When You're Smiling*, his third (dedicated 'to the musicians') *Chinatown, My Chinatown* and his last, *You Rascal, You*. Each one was received with tumult. The packed house absolutely rose to it. There is no doubt, of course, that musicians preponderated in the house – familiar faces were everywhere.

But it was not record business all the time. 'It wasn't a failure,' says Ingman now, 'but not all of the 28 houses were full by any means. And every time I was there, which was often. I saw people walking out, some grumbling about "this hell music", or whatever it was they called it.'

Behind such a star attraction, the band received little attention. Ingman wrote at the time: 'The band? Beyond noticing that it was painfully under-rehearsed (naturally) and had very little of anything, I didn't notice it. He should have had – and could have had – much better support.' Surprisingly, Goffin paid no heed to it either:

> Monday at the Palladium was a sensation. Never have I experienced such an emotion ... The place was rocking like a steamship in heavy weather ... I went to join Louis in his box. Jack Johnson, the old world's heavyweight champion, was there; so were Nat Gonella and some other British musicians who could scarcely believe their eyes and ears. Some young trumpeters asked to examine Louis' mouthpiece; they couldn't believe that anyone could achieve such power without some mechanical aid.

I [M.J.] still remember reacting favourably to a few tricky clarinet solos and breaks, also some tenor stuff (Allen?) which I thought dashing enough then; but I was soon informed that the group was ragged and inferior. Probably it was the former, and certainly the latter by Louis' standards. What I *can* call to mind is an image of the man out front – a lithe, smallish but power-packed figure prowling the stage restlessly, menacingly almost, and growling and gesticulating when he was not playing, singing or talking into the microphone. He addressed his trumpet as though it had life of its own (Speak to 'em, Satchmouth), and controlled the band with faintly alien instructions like 'Way down, way down', 'Keep muggin' ... lightly, lightly and politely', and 'Swing, swing, swing, you cats'. Each tune was climaxed with outbursts of prodigious bravura trumpet. I think he played *Them There Eyes, Confessin'* and either *Chinatown* or *You Rascal*; and certainly a brisk and exceedingly energetic *Tiger Rag*. I remember doubting if he was in full control of himself. Reviewers everywhere pulled out the stops to describe Louis' act, and a great deal was made of him 'striding and sweating all over the stage' and mopping up with a succession of handkerchiefs. The *Melody Maker* reviewer pointed out that

top Fs bubble about all over the place, and never once does he miss one. He is enormously fond of the lip-trill, which he accomplishes by shaking the instrument wildly with his right hand ... He works with a microphone and loud speakers – except for his trumpet playing which varies from a veritable whisper to roof-raising strength, mostly the latter.

After praising Armstrong's showmanship and good humour, he concluded:

All the time he is singing he carries a handkerchief in his hand and mops his face – perspiration positively drops off him. He puts enough energy in his half-hour's performance to last the average man several years. He is, in short, a unique phenomenon, an electric personality – easily the greatest America has sent us so far.

A batch of 20 (or was it 40?) freshly laundered white handkerchiefs was on hand for each performance, and Louis made lavish use of them. It is uncertain when this routine began. Possibly it was when he started his career as actor–showman–musician in the 1926–7 period; it was certainly in evidence by 1929, because Mezz Mezzrow tells this of the days when Armstrong was in New York, doubling at Connie's Inn and the Hudson Theater on 46th Street:

Louis always held a handkerchief in his hand because he perspired so much, on stage and off, and that started a real fad – before long all the kids on the Avenue were running up to him with white handkerchiefs in their hands too, to show how much they loved him.

By the following year, when he was starring at Sebas-

165

tian's Cotton Club in Culver City, there is an account of him changing handkerchiefs six times during the course of a number.

The white linen squares served a purpose besides the principal one – as a useful bit of stage business which worked in the spotlight and helped to keep the customers' eyes on Louis. (Maybe the handkerchief had taken on a symbolic meaning for him, as the white gardenia did for Billie Holiday.) Then again, long after Armstrong's early '30s adventures in Britain, a musician who worked in one of his bands claimed that the handkerchief in Louis' left hand could fulfil another function: used in a certain fashion towards the end of a number, it indicated which of two possible endings the trumpeter would choose.

Practical arrangements for this first foreign tour were unbelievably haphazard. No one knew he was coming – 'When we heard the news some weeks ago, we were rather inclined to discount it,' wrote the *Melody Maker* that August – and, when the story was found to be true, nobody knew where he would be staying or exactly where or when he would set foot in the country. Nevertheless plans went ahead to welcome him in fitting manner. Billy Cotton's manager, Dave Toff, thought of holding a dinner-reception in Armstrong's honour, given by top bandleaders and hot players. With the help of the *Melody Maker*, this was organized for Friday evening at the Ambassador Hotel in London's West End, and tidings were sent by radiogram to Louis' party on board the *Majestic* in mid-Atlantic. Preparations were made to meet them at Southampton around midday.

Meanwhile someone had telephoned Louis in mid-ocean and been unable to understand much except that his trumpet would need repairing immediately he arrived. A last-minute telegram from John Collins announced that the party would disembark at Plymouth, and get to London soon after midnight on Thursday. In the resultant panic only Dan Ingman was able to go to Paddington Station to meet the 12.25 am boat train from Plymouth.

I hardly expected to meet anyone, but eventually the train came in and out of one compartment stepped five people, obviously foreign. One, a large man with small moustache and a cigar in his mouth, was in fact Johnny Collins. He had his wife with him, and there was an older lady I later took to be Alpha's mother. The big surprise was the other couple, a young-looking and charming black girl and a small, slight fellow wearing an enormous white cap and long biscuit-coloured coat. I believe he had on a purple suit, too. For a moment I wondered where Armstrong was. 'This,' said the big man, who looked how I imagined a gangster to look, 'is Mr and Mrs Armstrong.' I nearly collapsed. From his photograph I had been expecting a six-footer, broad in proportion, with a moustache, and at least 35 years of age.

Asked how they came ashore without permits, Collins said he just talked them in. Had they anywhere to stay? No. Collins answered the questions; Louis never spoke a word. So there was work to be done; accommodation to be found in the early hours of the morning for five travellers, most of them flamboyantly dressed and some of them black. Ingman started telephoning the London hotels. He began with the most famous – Savoy, Dorchester, Mayfair and so on – and, having no luck, worked his way through the second-rankers. Sometimes there was simply no room for five guests. When he found acceptance he thought it wise to mention that some of the party were blacks. At that, a total close-down.

I did the lot; I can't remember how many hotels, but it was the same story. There were difficulties after I mentioned colour. Remember these people were still standing on the platform, surrounded by masses of luggage and wondering what was happening. All I could say from time to time was that I wouldn't be long. No wonder they were getting irritable. Then a name came to me, of a hotel in Norfolk Street off the Strand, someone had recommended. I finally reached it and to my relief a voice said yes. So we all piled into taxis at Paddington and away we went to the Howard. I believe that was the name. It was a very exclusive hotel and we were ushered in with the utmost courtesy in spite of the late hour.

I promised Louis I'd have a trumpet repairer round first thing in the morning; then we parted and I went home to bed, after alerting a few people to Armstrong's whereabouts. I was the first man in England to lay hands on this VIP, and up to that moment the only one who knew where he was. By the next day, after arranging for Louis' trumpet, I had moved out to run the paper. Musicians, newspapermen, including P. M. Brooks, the Palladium people, Ben Davis of Selmer, they all took over and the hotel realized it had a bombshell in the place. Enthusiasts were practically camping in the foyer and the next thing was, the hotel made noises. I don't know the details – Collins complained that the hotel was too expensive – but whether or not the reason was money, the fact is they moved out shortly after this.

The fault in Louis' horn, whatever it may have been, was not serious. Fittingly, though, it was the means of Nat Gonella's meeting his idol.

I first met Louis personally in 1932. I just happened to be in Boosey and Hawkes' store when it was mentioned that the great man's trumpet was in for cleaning and was to be returned that day. I begged to be allowed to deliver it to his hotel, refused to hand it over to anyone but Louis, and spent a half-hour talking to him in his room. This was undoubtedly one of the great moments of my young life.

After further emergencies – Armstrong's possessions were still at Paddington and the only suit he had in the hotel needed pressing; Gonella came to the rescue with an instant pressing service – the guest of honour was delivered safe and on time to the Ambassador Hotel. The location was well chosen for Louis' first taste of ambassadorial treatment. Jack Hylton, in Ireland, sent a message of welcome and best wishes for 'a terrific success at the Palladium on Monday'. Among musicians able to toast the American jazzman in person were Billy Cotton, Ray Noble, Phil Cardew, Roy Fox, Lew Davis, Billy Mason, Buddy Featherstonhaugh, Lew Stone, Peter Yorke, Vic Filmer, Nat and

Bruts Gonella, Henry Hall, Harry Hayes, Spike Hughes, Freddy Mann, Ray Starita, Harry Perritt, Arthur Roseberry and Maurice Winnick. Most were bandleaders, and in addition there were the journalists, including Tom Driberg, W. Macqueen-Pope, Edgar Jackson of the *Gramophone*, and the *Melody Maker* editors. A similar banquet was arranged for Pops by musicians and press during his second (1956) trip to Britain, when he came over for the Hungarian Relief Fund charity concert. Dave Toff and Buddy Featherstonhaugh were the only ones who managed to attend both parties, though Gonella sent a wire from the north of England expressing his regards and regrets at not being there.

At the end of the Palladium fortnight the band from France had to return home. Louis rested until two one-night engagements were negotiated for him by the *Melody Maker*, prior to a week's run, which Collins obtained on sharing terms, at the Glasgow Empire. Armstrong had done well enough at the Palladium – a highly speculative booking, it was agreed – but managements were wary of somebody who, in the words of critic 'Mike', 'must be enjoyed as a phenomenon, as something for the moment that will not be believed in years to come when you tell your grandchildren of the good old days at the Palladium in '32. A fresh band had to be organized for him, and inevitably Spike Hughes was approached. Since he was busy orchestrating, Billy Mason provided a ten-piece orchestra whose line-up resembled that which Hughes would have drawn upon.

This band did not appear on records with Armstrong, for he made none in Britain, but is said to have proved itself a 'formidable outfit', judged by the standards of British musicians. It merits a special place in the chronicles as Armstrong's very first white band. The full line-up was Mason (piano) with Freddy Mann and Bruts Gonella (trumpets), Lew Davis (trombone), Harry Hayes, Sid Owen (altos) and Buddy Featherstonhaugh (tenor), Bill White (bass), Len Bermon (drums) and Alan Ferguson (guitar). Perhaps Ben Davis played saxophone on some occasions, and sometimes

169

ROYAL FESTIVAL HALL

(General Manager: T. E. Bean)

Tuesday, December 18th, 1956

AN EVENING FOR HUNGARY
IN AID OF THE LORD MAYOR OF LONDON'S NATIONAL
HUNGARIAN AND CENTRAL EUROPEAN RELIEF FUND

LOUIS ARMSTRONG

ROYAL PHILHARMONIC ORCHESTRA
(*Leader:* Arthur Leavins)

NORMAN DEL MAR

PROGRAMME

God Save the Queen
The Hungarian National Anthem

Tragic Overture	*Brahms*
Suite, The Firebird	*Stravinsky*
St. Louis Blues.	*W. C. Handy*

SIR LAURENCE OLIVIER

INTERVAL

Háry János Suite	*Kodály*
Sleepy Time Down South	*Clarence Muse*

Three Spirituals:
    Nobody Knows the Trouble I've Seen
    The Lonesome Road
    Shadrach, Meshach and Abednego

Variations on Jazz Themes	*Louis Armstrong*
Hungarian Rhapsody No. 2	*Liszt*

THE RT. HON. THE LORD MAYOR OF LONDON SIR CULLUM WELCH

Management: S. A. GORLINSKY LTD

The audience is particularly requested *not* to applaud until the end of each item.

only one trumpet was used (apart, of course, from the star's). Later, it was reported, an inferior band replaced this one: 'a much cheaper collection', the *Melody Maker* termed it, 'which was subjected to cuts as it went the rounds ... neither of the bands was used in a way to produce the best results'.

With the first collection of 'white swing-men', the trumpeter travelled to the Nottingham Palais, where he was reported to have attracted nearly a thousand people on the hottest night of the year; to a *Melody Maker* dance band contest in York; thence to Glasgow; and back to London for the week commencing 22 August, doubling the Victoria Palace and Finsbury Park Empire. Other dates followed in London, Liverpool and Birmingham, and then Louis took 'a little rest in Paris' before boarding the *Majestic* for home. By his own account, he docked in New York on the day Roosevelt was elected President, 2 November 1932.

Louis the European

From New York, in November, Armstrong travelled to Chicago to stay with Alpha's mother. He then made theatre appearances out of town, and did one Victor record date, fronting Chick Webb's band. In December he recorded a *Medley Of Armstrong Hits* accompanied by a pick-up band organized by Charlie Gains. Issued on a 12″ 78, the selection was not well received by critics, and became a rare collectors' item.

No evidence exists to support Goffin's statement 'Louis was now a star of the first magnitude ... on his return to America he received fantastic offers.' On the contrary, he was still an obscure figure outside jazz circles. In England he had been wined and dined, made a fuss of, and given press coverage on a scale hitherto unknown to him. John Hammond met Armstrong on the night of his return 'looking better than I have seen him in years'. He said Louis had enthused about Billy Mason's band and his reception in Britain, and wished to return next year and also visit France, Belgium and Holland. But for the present, his plans were 'a bit indefinite'. He hoped to get together a new band in Chicago and go on tour with it. Hammond ended: 'I hope that soon he gets some of the recognition he deserves.'

Bill Mather wrote, also from New York, about Louis' homecoming – and with a new nickname. 'The one and only Louis (Musicmouth) Armstrong arrived on the SS *Majestic* last Wednesday, 9 November, at 2.30 pm and I was in touch with him two hours afterwards.' (Note that the date is a week later than that given by Louis.) Mather met

172

him at Connie's Inn, where Louis was introduced from the floor, and they went on to Big John's and another warm welcome *from musicians and show people.* Mather confirms Hammond's story that Louis' future was unsettled and ended: 'We all hope he will make arrangements to come back here.'

Armstrong could have done with a publicity agent at that time, as Hammond recognized in a dispatch published in the January 1933 *Melody Maker.*

Louis as a person is just without equal in charm and general good nature. It's all the more unfortunate then that he is given insufficient publicity. It is a fact that when he came back from Europe there was not one line in any paper about it. Although famous now in England, he is virtually unknown to the theatre public here.

Louis was then playing local theatres in 'a pretty poor revival of 'Hot Chocolates'', backed by the Webb band, which 'didn't know how to accompany him'; also he had 'regrettably lost his voice from over-exertion', and was in trouble with the record companies, 'both Victor and Columbia claiming him as their own'. Of course, he had no band of his own, and his lip was troubling him as well.

Mezz Mezzrow recounts how Johnny Collins asked him to be at the Camden, New Jersey, studios for Louis' first recordings under a new Victor contract. Armstrong had played five shows at the Lincoln Theater in Philadelphia, also two broadcasts, and was then to cut four titles in the small hours. He was dog-tired and suffering from a sore lip. 'They wouldn't let Chick Webb use his bass drum on this date,' writes Mezz 'mainly because Louis' lip was in such bad shape and without the bass he wouldn't be pushed so hard. The first number he recorded was *That's My Home.*'

At least two takes of that song were made (and released), as was the case with *I Hate To Leave You Now.* The solo trumpet, which never strays far from the themes, stands up well to the test of time although the cognoscenti of those days tended to frown on the entire enterprise. *Hobo, You Can't Ride This Train* was declared by Hammond to be not far from very good. But *Home* was 'an outright steal from *Sleepy Time Down South* and quite saccharine'. A month later he was saying that almost everybody had been discouraged by these Victors with Chick Webb. 'Louis' future discs should be made with a small group of virtuosi, as in the old Hines days.' In Britain, Spike Hughes greeted these new sides by Louis ('Fun Man') Armstrong with guarded approval, seemingly detecting the tired chops. According to Mezz, the damage rapidly worsened, until in Baltimore that New Year's Eve Louis finished a show with his lip bloody and mangled.

Early in the New Year Louis went home to Chicago and assembled a backing group under the direction of Zilner Randolph: a ten-piece orchestra of local players, including Keg Johnson (trombone), Scoville Brown and Budd Johnson (saxophones) and the young Teddy Wilson on piano. With this band Armstrong cut a dozen titles in January 1933, and though again the band was criticized the records – especially *Gotta Right To Sing The Blues* and *World On A String* – were acknowledged to offer marvellous trumpet. One-nighters and more record sessions carried leader and men through until June. Then an offer of a summer season at the Pabst Blue Ribbon Casino in Chicago fell through, and on 1 July Louis disbanded.

In the meantime something very odd had happened in England. The *Daily Express* ran on 31 March, in all its editions, a front-page story that Armstrong, 'the Iron-Lipped Trumpeter', had died from what was guessed to be over-exertion. Both the *Express* and the *Melody Maker* were inundated with letters and enquiries; then, next day, the story was denied in the *Daily Herald*, and on 4 April, the *Melody Maker* received a cable from Spike Hughes, then in New York, saying: 'Louis was bitten by a dog. I always thought man bites dog was news.' British fans were assured that Louis was in fine fettle, barnstorming in the mid-west.

174

When the Blue Ribbon deal collapsed, Armstrong's manager booked him into a Philadelphia theatre for two weeks, beginning 8 July. He was appearing with the Hardy Brothers' orchestra. Before the end of the engagement, however, the long arm of the lawless caught up with him again. Pressman and promoter Ernie Anderson filled in the details:

The syndicates were not making the easy money they'd made during Prohibition and there were a series of incidents in which important show business personalities were forced to pay gangsters. Now Louis wasn't playing much for white audiences but was a big draw in coloured variety houses. Sometimes I suppose they had to pay other acts out of his percentage, but there'd be a moment when somebody would bring him several thousand dollars.

One afternoon at this black vaudeville theatre in Philadelphia, where he'd do five or six shows a day, a couple of men came to Louis' dressing room and assured him they were there for his benefit. They were going to protect him, and obviously they were waiting for the money to arrive. Well, Pops, through some typically ingenious dialogue, conveyed something to his valet who went to the front of the house, got the money, and took it some place else. Louis then told these fellows he had to do his show and would be back, and assured them the money would be up a little later. He did his whole show and skipped straight out the stage door and off to the local police station, where he asked them to lock him up. He explained that a couple of men were after him and he was afraid they might damage his lip. Then he called up Johnny Collins, told him to get the scratch from the valet, and said: 'Get me out of here somehow.' He added that he couldn't work anywhere in America because the hoods would find him. So Collins called some people, and the next thing you know Louis Armstrong was on a boat for England without any musicians and with his library.

Louis hadn't forgotten the European atmosphere, as his letters to friends testified. 'How's dear ol' England and all my wonderful friends?' he would ask. 'You were oh so nice to me ... How's my other two little buddies, Nat and Bruts

175

Gonella? Youall's kindness shall never be forgotten.' Perhaps he appreciated the comparative freedom from racial tensions and the absence of gun rule in the entertainment business. People in the know swear that his management at the time of the first trip was unattractive in its methods. Armstrong and most of those who have written about him were, not surprisingly, reticent on this topic. Collins was probably incompetent, more than anything else; a small-time businessman, brash and out of his depth in the altered circumstances he encountered outside the United States. As Dan Ingman put it:

> Louis was lionized by writers and musicians, and of course by titled people. William Primrose, William Walton, Spike Hughes ... they were three of the enthusiasts I remember. Collins was bewildered by the acclaim. So far as I was concerned, and I was closely concerned, he was totally inefficient over here.

One view of the relationship between Armstrong and his manager, and of the two men's characters at that time, emerges from Ingman's story of an evening at a Midland palais.

> Here was this man, Louis Armstrong, just before the show was due to start, waiting silently. He was smartly dressed, in dinner jacket, and holding his Selmer trumpet. The band was ready – there had been no rehearsal – and he was about to perform. Then Collins suddenly said, 'Where's the dough? If I don't get the dough, Louis don't play.' The promoter had a huge crowd and there was no problem. He offered a cheque but Collins was adamant – no cash, no Louis. It must have been humiliating for Louis, though he showed no sign of it. He just looked at the floor and went on swinging his trumpet in his hand until such time as matters were settled. He seemed utterly detached as this pasty-faced man with the cigar in his mouth demanded the money there and then, or no show. I estimate they had some two thousand people in there, and the promoter went to his box office and came back with several bags of half-crowns, of silver any-

way, and put them down in front of Collins. 'There's your money,' he told Collins, and I remember thinking: he doesn't know how to count it.

However, an action had been taken and Collins, satisfied, said 'Okay, Louis' – he pronounced it Lewis – and I felt that he was telling his 'boy' to go on. And of course Louis went on and did his stuff, as he always did, magnificently. Two things impressed me about his attitude. He was docile, this world-famous musician, subservient in the presence of Collins. And he was the one in the party who behaved himself best. The grandson of a slave, as he used to tell me, and he was the gentleman. Everything he did was right in an embarrassing situation for which we were all responsible to a degree.

Armstrong was not one to talk much about earnings, so it is difficult to estimate how much spending money he may have had in those days. A comparison of band salaries was made by *Variety* in late 1932. While its accuracy cannot be vouched for, it is the nearest thing to a figure available for Louis and his band in the period under review. *Variety* stressed that it was quoting weekly salaries paid, 'not asking prices'. It graded the orchestras according to earning power thus: Paul Whiteman's Band, £1,700; Ted Lewis's Band, £1,500; and so on down through Ben Bernie, Waring's Pennsylvanians, Guy Lombardo (all over £1,000); Duke Ellington and Cab Calloway at £1,000; and finally Louis Armstrong's Band, twelfth out of 13 at £500 a week.

What Louis himself earned is anyone's guess. He seems to have had little to spare after catering for his own and Alpha's tastes in clothes and entertainment. On his second visit to Europe, though, his financial situation improved somewhat. Nat Gonella recalls:

We used to go to the Bag O' Nails or Jigs Club in Wardour Street where Pops could get the food he liked, red beans and stuff. We went out most nights when he was in town. He and Alpha were very matey. They came to the Monseigneur

177

in Piccadilly, as I remember, after his opening night. Louis earned plenty then but I understand his management kept most of it.

Jeff Aldam, London writer and collector, saw a little of Louis in 1932, and a good deal in succeeding years. He remembers that there were usually musicians and fans around Pops, who liked to play records and talk music by the hour.

Louis and Alpha took me for the first Chinese meal I ever ate. That was at the original Shanghai Restaurant in Greek Street, a few doors from the old Astoria Hotel where the Armstrongs were living. The Astoria really jumped, which was probably why they closed it down soon afterwards! On one memorable night pianist Garland Wilson, guitarist Slim Furness of the Three Keys and a Harlem dance team, the Four Hot Shots, all turned up in Louis' room.

Later, when he and Alpha stayed at the Heathfield Hotel in Guilford Street, Bloomsbury, Louis still 'held court' to his friends. I now realize that Louis, though always a generous host, was living quite modestly then. Years afterwards Billy Mason told me how embarrassed he had felt to discover that as leader of the band he was being paid more than Armstrong, the star.

But the star's baggage held plenty of clothes, and he and Alpha went shopping in London. 'Louis was always a sharp dresser,' said Gonella, 'smart and a bit loud.'

Ingman recalls:

Louis came to my flat in Maida Vale for that English institution, afternoon tea. He never talked about money or discussed his associates, and normally I wouldn't have dreamed of asking him. But by now I distrusted what was going on, so I said that he must be worth a lot of money. He replied that he wasn't. I asked about the records he had made, the theatre and club dates, and he said (as near as I can recall it) that he had 75 suits. 'Go on,' I told him, and he indicated that he had pocket money and all the clothes he wanted, that was the lot. It is all a long time ago, so I may not remember the words exactly; but his income wasn't high. I felt that here was an artist of stunning gifts who had fallen into the wrong hands. It moved me to speak to Irving Mills, to see if he could do anything about it, but I don't know what happened.

Something did transpire, in Europe and afterwards, and managers began to 'have trouble' with the hitherto tractable Satchmo. Perhaps Alpha wielded stirring influences, as Lil Hardin had previously done. She didn't seem the indomitable type but Louis was to speak in later years of her extravagance and, significantly, modern outlook. 'Alpha was young and polished and her views were modern,' he wrote in *Ebony*. 'She was all right but her mind was on furs, diamonds and other flashy luxuries.' Opinions of her differ; one musician recalls her simply as pleasant-looking and vivacious, happy to go everywhere with Louis during the British engagement. According to Gonella she was quiet, and let Louis do all the talking. 'Did she dig music? I don't really know. I remember she loved to walk home from the theatre, to see the West End at night. Not expensive, I'd say.' But Iain Lang saw another side of the couple when he met them in a Paris *boîte*. 'Of course, Armstrong at the age of 32 was a very different man from the sober and circumspect elder statesman of jazz today,' he wrote. 'He spent himself prodigally, enthusiastically encouraged by his third wife, Alpha, who had an insatiable appetite for bright lights and late nights.'

Louis arrived in England at the end of July, to open at London's Holborn Empire. Collins was still described as his inseparable companion – but not for long. The *Melody Maker* of 19 August 1933 headlined a story 'Armstrong And His Manager To Part', explaining that the association would be severed at the end of the tour. The tour, in any case, had got off to a tragi-comic start. Some pressmen thought Louis was over-playing the sensationalism. 'Amazing Reception For Armstrong – Frenzied Applause for Meaningless Performance,' blared the *Melody Maker*'s front-page top story. He was deliberately commercial, the

179

paper lamented, and must have caused his most enlightened supporters to sorrow for him. His act was castigated as 50 per cent showmanship, 50 per cent instrumental cleverness, but 'about nought per cent music'. Still, it was conceded that the younger element had cheered him – 'wildly, unreasoningly, unjustifiably, out of sheer loyalty' – until the national anthem brought things to a halt. The band, from Paris again and with some of the same men on board, was dismissed as sounding unprepared, subdued and laboured.

Louis must have been surprised by this onslaught from friendly quarters. At home, for some years past, he had been 'sending' his listeners with a hundred or more high Cs on *Tiger Rag*. At the Holborn Empire the journalists complained of a *Shine* which afforded him the opportunity of whipping out, 'unaccompanied and ad lib a series of 70 high Cs culminating in a top F'. It was alleged the following week that he had noted the well-meant criticism and mended his ways. In all probability he did his best to cut down the fireworks and play 'properly' while making sure his presentation remained palatable to the paying customers.

Armstrong was plagued by management troubles as well during this year or so. He must have thought about going home, but instead John Collins returned to the United States, and late in September Jack Hylton was put forward as the likeliest man to take over his role. In spite of the headaches brought about by Collins' abrupt departure, Louis was showing every intention of carrying on. He even considered settling in Britain, where 'a greater percentage of the general public than in the USA appear to appreciate him'. He played more dates round England; then on 19 October he crossed the Channel to make his first appearances in Scandinavia. In mid-November he again left Britain, for a tour of Holland, and the year closed with him booked for a week at the Holborn Empire. His lip troubled him again and he eventually withdrew from the bill.

From Holland, Louis had broadcast; a programme, reviewed in this country, tells something of his repertoire then and of the form he attained between bouts of split lip. His material included *Black And Blue, You Rascal, You, Confessin', Dear Old Southland* and *Nobody's Sweetheart.* There were encores, an unrecognized number, and non-vocal versions of *How Am I To Know* and *Ring Dem Bells.* The reviewer commented that Louis' health and playing had improved now that he was free from managerial problems.

The enjoyment of new-found freedom (and possibly of greater prosperity) was reflected in an interview conducted by Bettie Edwards in January 1934. She stated that he cherished his independence and, 'when it was apparent that managerial exploitation was divorcing him from his true public, he severed the relationship with the happiest results'. Also, having worked without much of a break for ten years, he desired a rest. 'I'll go about two years, then I'm off on vacation. My new car wants exercise.' Already he was able to boast that he got a good time almost anywhere and had friends all over the world, especially in London. On the surface, this was a different person from the subservient one described earlier, and it may be that Louis was keeping the shutters down in 1932. 'I was nervous as a kitten,' he told Miss Edwards. 'But last year it was like coming home.' He had taken the first steps to becoming a world citizen.

Johnny Collins re-entered the picture at this stage, almost for the last time. A telegram was delivered to Pops at a band contest he was attending with his manager, Jack Hylton. 'Still all for you,' Collins had written, and, after offering lucrative engagements in New York, 'Telegraph time of your arrival.' The recipient crushed it and dropped it on the floor with the words 'Never, never, never.'

Satch was nearing the end of his second stay in Britain, and nearing the end of his road with Hylton, too. His new manager had sensational plans to present Armstrong in an entirely new way. For once 'sensational' was scarcely an exaggeration. Coleman Hawkins, among the most highly regarded tenor-players in jazz, was coming to London to partner Louis in a new act dreamed up by Hylton. The *Melody Maker*, then mixed up with Hylton behind the scenes, spoke of staging 'a special musicians' recital with Louis and Coleman together'. On 31 March, with Hawkins in the country, arrangements were disclosed to introduce the American tenor star at a Sunday afternoon concert in the West End 'under the mentorship of Louis'. The Hawk was said to be preparing for this great recital, fixed for the London Hippodrome on 22 April, and Louis was stated to have sent him a greetings message: 'Welcome to our country.'

Then came the blow: Louis refused to play. Weekly news flashes outline the swift course of events – 'Special Concert At West End Theatre' (31 March); 'Hawkins Fine Welcome ... Wild Rush For Seats' (7 April); 'Louis Quits: Concert Wrecked ... Armstrong's Amazing Last Minute Decision ... Hawkins Rushed Into Palladium Bill ... Bewildered' (14 April); 'Hawkins' Triumph' (21 April). A sole ray of humour in this stormy incident was furnished by the Palladium backstage, where the Call Board showed that dressing room number 7 was allotted to 'Coleman and Hawkins'.

Blame for the cancellation was laid firmly at Louis' feet, and perhaps he deserved the larger share of it. Seized with an acute attack of artistic temperament, he had walked out on Hawk after acquiescing in the arrangements, and he was not explicit about his reasons for doing so. Louis, it was allowed, was worried about his reputation. His own Hot Rhythm group was to accompany both soloists, and with very little time to prepare and new orchestrations needed, he felt doubtful of his ability either to provide good enough support for Hawk or to do himself justice. Furthermore, he was engaged until the Saturday night at Plymouth and would therefore have had to travel through the night to be ready for a 2.30 pm start. Soon, a few correspondents rose to Armstrong's defence, questioning whether he had been fairly treated. The subject of cash came up, and the *MM*'s editor wrote that the paper intended handing over all the net proceeds to Louis and his fellow recitalist.

Louis' reported threat to pack his bags and return to the States rather than play against his better judgement was untypical of a man who, as we have read, never permitted himself to miss an engagement for personal reasons. A statement later attributed to him was: 'I've figured it out and it seems it ain't going to do me any good.' Many years afterwards he wrote to us.

Concerning the concert in London Hawkins and I were sup-posed to be doing at the time we were both blowing there, everyone should remember why it didn't come off. Here's why – Hawkins was with Jack Hylton, a beeg man, and so was I. Seems Hawk didn't think I was big enough, to share a concert or billing etc. with me. He and his handlers, who ever they were, they did nothing more than mention the concert to me. That was all that happened. Later, when I ran across Hawkins in New York City, we were so glad to see each other – we didn't mention England at all. So you see it was all bullshit from the start.

It looks, in retrospect, as though this may have been a press-inflated non-event. Asked, some 36 years afterwards, to guess the reasons for Louis' behaviour, Dan Ingman thought behind-the-scenes management disputes were the most likely cause. Nat Gonella felt certain it 'had some-thing to do with the money'. Nat, who knew Armstrong perhaps better than anyone else in Britain, insisted that Louis always emphasized that his manager was looking after him – 'he got his own pocket money and the rest was put away for him; and he had that one thing about him that he would sooner trust a white manager than a coloured one, or that was my impression'.

What was his impression of Johnny Collins and, for that matter, the kind of management in general Armstrong re-ceived during those first visits to Britain?

Well, Collins was a typical Yank that you'd see in these gangster films, with a big cigar in the corner of his mouth;

183

tough guy, gangster I should think. Is he dead? If he's not, cut this out. I mean, I can't vouch for the story, but Armstrong was away from here for 22 years and they say that when he came back there was a tax bill waiting for him for ten thousand pounds from his visit in 1933. Of course you don't know, but I was told that when they wanted to bring him back in 1956 they had to pay the ten thousand because he'd sort of gone astray with his income tax, which his great managers of '32 and '33 should have settled. And of course he was easygoing about it; he knew where he had to go, and they'd take him there and he sat down and blew, and that's all he was worried about.

This acrimonious episode made an unhappy ending to Pops' stay in Britain – his last visit, as it turned out, for more than two decades. He decamped for Paris with Alpha, and the group of French-based and British black musicians which had served him for nearly a year was disbanded. 'When I left London that summer and went to Paris I needed a rest,' Louis remembered. 'My bookings were finished in England so I just lazied around Paris for three or four months, had lots of fun with musicians from the States – French cats too. And I'd do a concert now and then.'

The first two French concerts – Louis had been to the country the previous year but had not been heard – were held on 9 and 10 November at the renowned Salle Pleyel in Paris. The month before, he had reorganized his band for a Paris recording session at which six sides were cut – his first since he left the United States in 1933. For a year, it appears, he was unable to record in London despite offers, 'owing to the difficulties of coming to an agreement with Victor'. These five French titles – *Sunny Side Of The Street* was a double-sided effort – are therefore unique in making known to us the sound of Louis' horn and European band during 1934.* One coupling, *Will You, Won't You Be My Baby* and *Song Of The Vipers*, was deleted within a few

* Some concert recordings and air-checks from 1933 have since been released on the Musicmonth LP, 'European Tour 1933–1934'.

184

days of its release, possibly when the record company directors found out what vipers were. *St Louis* and *Tiger Rag* are fully representative of Armstrong's exuberant skill and drive as these were made manifest to theatre, concert and dance hall audiences at the time. *Sunny Side*, a logically constructed five-minute vocal and trumpet treatment of a popular song which remained in his repertoire, points very clearly to the more temperate and lofty style he was to favour in the coming months.

With Armstrong on these records were Pete Du Conge, Henry Tyree and Alfred Pratt (reeds), Jack Hamilton, Leslie Thompson, Lionel Guimaraes (brass), Herman Chittison (piano), Maceo Jefferson (guitar), German Arago (bass) and Oliver Tines (drums). Most, if not all, of them accompanied him at his Paris debut. In Louis' words, his first Salle Pleyel concert was a real gasser. 'I had to take so many bows until I wound up taking 'em in my bath robe. Nice?'

The exact date of this Paris recording session has not been determined more closely than October. It must have been late that month, because in a longish letter of 20 October Armstrong makes no reference to it, though he does mention 'my boys' and says, 'We will start back to work real soon.' They were started back by an agent named N. J. Canetti, who booked them through Belgium, France, Holland, Italy and Switzerland. Louis' reappearance was a surprise to the *Melody Maker* which ran a story: 'Where's Louis? All the fans are asking. He's touring the Continent.' Tenorman Alfred Pratt now left for Rio de Janeiro and was replaced by Castor McCord, who had come over to Britain with the 'Blackbirds Of 1934' revue. He left the show to join Louis and there was talk at that time of Garland Wilson going to Paris for the same purpose. However, the idea came to nothing and Chittison remained in the piano chair. Armstrong recalled (in *Swing That Music*) playing for the Crown Princess of Italy in Turin, and spending that New Year's Eve in Lausanne after crossing the Alps by 'bus into Switzerland.

During his lay-off in Paris Louis made the acquaintance of many more European musicians and critics and renewed friendships with those he already knew. Robert Goffin saw him again and noted that he was 'received with great pomp at the home of the president of the Bar Association in Brussels'. That all this made an impression on Armstrong can be gathered from his references, after the European tours, to music critics calling on him and talking for hours. 'That had never happened to me before in America,' he said.

One rising star whose path he crossed was Django Reinhardt. 'I met Django, he knocked me out. And I met Panassié and Delaunay and they listened to records.' Charles Delaunay evokes a somewhat different scene in his book *Django Reinhardt*, when writing about the guitarist's five months' stint at a place called the Stage B. 'Armstrong came in several times during the few months he stayed in Paris. Django, who never asked anyone the slightest favour, asked Louis to play for him. But Louis refused. It seems that he has never played except on stage.' Before this, Django and his brother had played for Louis at his flat without claiming his attention, according to Delaunay. One evening, though, the chance arrived.

> Bricktop, the famous cabaret hostess, telephoned to say that Louis was at her place. Naturally, Django and I set off at once, and for the only time in my life I heard Louis sing, accompanied only by Django's guitar. There were no discussions to decide what key they'd play in or what tunes they'd choose. Louis began and Django followed him in the twinkling of an eye. It was a revelation for me, and all of us were entranced.

Before 1934 was out, there was an explosive disagreement between Louis and Canetti. Louis suddenly left for home but the dispute rumbled on. Canetti threatened breach of contract, claiming an exclusive signing (though Satch had signed a 12-month contract with English agent Audrey Thacker), and suggested the trumpeter had quit be-

cause Chittison stole the applause. All but one of Louis'
accompanying bandsmen rallied to his side in a vitriolic
issue of France's *Jazz Hot.*

So Armstrong sailed into New York in late January 1935,
after an absence of 18 months, beset still by perplexities
about bookings but buoyed up by the knowledge that he
was a musical celebrity.

Swing That Music

On his return he set about fronting Chick Webb's band once more, only to have the plan scotched by John Collins. As he had done before in rough water, Armstrong retreated to his second hometown, Chicago, to rest and take stock of the situation. He needed somebody to look after a band for him, take care of bills and fees, and organize the workaday details. Managers he'd had; he wanted a closer working relationship with someone who understood and sympathized with him. Soon he found what he was looking for in Joe Glaser. Louis established an instant rapport with the sharp-tongued wheeler and dealer back in the Sunset days. Glaser gave him plenty of advice, and it worked. That, for Louis, was enough.

But before Glaser became his full-time right-hand man, other pressures made themselves felt. Lil Armstrong filed suit for $6,000 back maintenance. Louis' lip was in poor shape and doctors advised six months' lay-off. In March that year a British magazine reported that Louis was going to be managed by Mezzrow, a proposition dwelt upon in Mezz's book. Meantime, Pops sang with the Ellington band one evening in Chicago, and at an AFM reception in his honour. The bands at this affair were Jimmie Noone's Gang, the Johnny Long band, Tiny Parham's Savoy Band and 'youngster Raymond Nance's Band'.

Summer came and Louis, relaxing in his South Parkway apartment, nursed his lip, romped with his two dogs, and knocked around with his old friend Zutty Singleton. In June he resumed work, organizing a 13-piece band. Most biographies refer to him returning to the road with Luis Russell's orchestra, but the band was led and directed by Zilner Randolph. With Randolph among the brass were Milton Fletcher, Gene Prince (trumpets) and Eddie Fant and Dick Dunlap (trombones). The saxophonists were Shrod Smith, Leon Washington, George Oldham and Scoville Browne; the rhythm Prentice McCarrie (piano), Bill Oldham (bass), James Thomas (guitar) and Richard Barnet (drums). This outfit opened in Indianapolis on 1 July and toured the middle west and south, reaching New Orleans by August. Louis remembered 'a bigger welcome than ever' on this trip, which included the inevitable street parade in New Orleans. After turning north, the band barnstormed to New York where, at the Apollo Theater, it is said to have broken attendance records and been paid the highest sum ever given at that time to a black orchestra.

By now, Joe Glaser was at the helm. The when and how of his taking over are not on record. He himself, though he tended to backdate events in which he'd been involved, probably came close to relating how the deal came about.

In 1931 Louis came back from England, he was broke and very sick. He said, 'I don't want to be with nobody but you. Please Mr. Glaser, just you and I. You understand me, I understand you.' And I said, 'Louis, you're me and I'm you.' I insured his life and mine for $100,000 apiece. Louis didn't even know it. I gave up all my other business and we went on the road together.

In September 1935, Louis had to break up his band again. The musicians could not get union cards to play New York and returned to Chicago. It was then Armstrong joined forces with Luis Russell. 'In the first week of October I opened at Connie's Inn on Broadway with Luis Russell's band behind me,' he wrote in his first book, which must have been put together during this long New York engagement. 'Joe Glaser had decided we would take over the management of this fine band.' The stint at Connie's Inn lasted until spring the next year, and Louis was heard often at this period over the CBS radio network. His vision of a better regulated life, if not a quiet one, looked like becoming a reality. He had his ideal partner, a permanent band with its own director, work in plenty and, once more, an agreement to record at regular intervals. He was now able to concentrate on playing, and tend to his physical well-being so that he remained strong enough to cope with the strain of road life. For a large part of his career he had either worked for other leaders or left the running of his band to a straw-boss. This new set-up perfectly suited the course of action now proposed.

The Russell band had a fair reputation; it was a swinging orchestra which included several good soloists. It used arrangements based on New Orleans jazz techniques, and its leader and many of the men were well known to Armstrong, who had worked with Russell and recorded with him on a few occasions during 1929 and 1930. This band, a nine- or ten-piece in its heyday, had grown to 13 by the time Louis started fronting it. Russell managed the band, took rehearsals and for a while did most of the arranging. Louis' vocals and trumpet solos were what sold the band on theatre dates and one-nighters all over the country. There was an interruption one summer while he had his tonsils removed; Louis often gave the date as 1940, but we have a press report of 1936 which even mentions the cost of the operation – $400.

Records are vitally important to any jazzman's popularity, and Armstrong had a new Decca contract and was again recording frequently. The first session took place on 3 October, with the line-up that supported him at Connie's. The band, besides Russell at the piano, comprised Leonard Davis, Gus Aitken, Louis Bacon (trumpets), Harry White, Jimmy Archey (trombones), Henry Jones, Charlie Holmes, Bingie Madison, Greely Walton (saxophones), Lee Blair (guitar), Pops Foster (bass) and Paul Barbarin (drums). With one alteration only, this personnel recorded some two dozen titles between October 1935 and May the following year. Decca, whose policy it was to ring the changes on its popular artists' recording images, also had Louis accompanied by a white studio orchestra (with Bunny Berigan on trumpet), by Jimmy Dorsey's band, and (in August 1936) by a five-piece group, the Polynesians. Many of the tunes selected for these sessions were current popular songs; *I'm In The Mood For Love, You Are My Lucky Star, On Treasure Island, Thanks A Million, All My Eggs In One Basket* and *I Double Dare You* are pleasant enough and make agreeable vehicles for Armstrong's playing and singing.

Of course they were not like Louis' classics of the Chicago period, nor his earliest ballad recordings such as *Blue Turning Grey Over You*. But, from 1930 on, his recording showed ever more clearly the way his approach to popular songs was developing. In its use of a big band (ten counting Louis) and repertoire of pops-of-the-day seasoned with a few standards, and even in the layout of the arrangement and introduction of comic touches, the final OKeh output of 1931–2 was not unlike this new Decca series. The Victors, too, fit snugly into the evolving pattern which marks his improvement as a singer of love songs. There is little doubt that if Armstrong had not been away from the studios for such long stretches in 1933–5 we should be able to follow a clearly defined line of development in his trumpet method and musical policy. Whether he was 'right' to work the vein of Tin Pan Alley songs, with its high proportion of dross, instead of clinging to tried standards and breaking in original jazz compositions, is far from easy to decide. In the case of an Ellington or a Morton it was logical to ask for original orchestrations of their own or traditional material, for this was the work at which they excelled. Louis, however, was a supreme interpreter, with rare creative gifts, who poured his feeling and musical intelligence into any tune he picked up. He wasn't a composer, except in the instinctive manner, and he always had broad tastes. At first most of the tunes he learned may have fallen into what we would now call the jazz category, even though some of them were popular tunes. Later, as he read more music, a wider range of material came within his grasp.

In the spring of 1937 the orchestra was revamped to accommodate three of the old guard – Red Allen, Albert Nicholas and J. C. Higginbotham – and other replacements. There were extensive rehearsals in readiness for the exposure Louis was to receive at a Paramont, New York, theatre date in April and in a series of broadcasts (the first 'all-coloured radio series', the station said) due to open on 9 April.

Louis was no revivalist by temperament, but in 1936 he embarked on a policy of remaking a number of his 'good old good ones'. A reinterpretation usually lacks the freshness of the original, but these new big band readings contained pleasing surprises. The trumpet-playing, powerfully moving in its simplicity and highly finished tone, in some respects improved on the quality of the earlier versions. Attention should be drawn to *Mahogany Hall Stomp* and *Dippermouth* (1936), *Sunny Side Of The Street* (1937), *Struttin' With Some Barbecue, I Can't Give You Anything* and *Ain't Misbehavin'* (1938), *Save It Pretty Mama, Monday Date, Confessin', Savoy Blues, West End Blues* and *Heah Me Talkin' To Ya* (1939), *Wolverine Blues* (1940) and *Sleepy Time Down South* and *You Rascal, You* (1941). All of these contain trumpet on the grand scale, as do *The Saints, Swing That Music* (recorded in April 1936 as a companion to Louis' first book), *Planter From Havana, Jubilee, Ev'ntide* and several others from that era.

Critics have complained that his style had long since set – that his ideas were 'formula-ridden' already in the 1929 – 31 period, as Gunther Schuller insists in *Early Jazz* – but the charge is hard to substantiate in the face of the small but telling alterations evident on these recordings. As Albert McCarthy notes, the reaction of one critic at the time these first Deccas were released in Britain was favourable. Unable to colour his judgement with hindsight, the reviewer discerned that Louis was 'playing trumpet in a way that we have never heard before. His tone is different; his ideas are new; only his method is the same.' The slight modifications continued through the '30s – no critic would expect a great musician to jettison overnight an approach which had been maturing for 20 years – and hints of Louis' interest in the band sounds of the late-swing period emerge in *Groovin'*. Moreover, there are some Armstrong airshots with a big band from *c.* 1944/5, which riddles the theory advanced by some writers that no stylistic change in his playing could be observed over 30 years. Unquestionably he worked out a fairly set approach during the first years of the All Stars, but a number of impassioned performances on his musical autobiography *Satchmo* proved that he could still devise choruses which sometimes bettered the originals.

The playing of the Russell orchestra on records was uneven, listless at times and poor in intonation, and at its brightest it could never reproduce the form the band achieved during 1929–31. Its new role may have been partly responsible for this deterioration; it was now a hard-worked, hard-travelling outfit used chiefly as a support for Armstrong's trumpet and vocals. Record dates had to be fitted in between tours, theatre calls, filming and broadcasting, so opportunities for rehearsal must have been severely limited. Too often the band sounded tired or uninspired, but there were pleasing moments of Holmes, Higgy and company as well as excruciating ones like the out-of-tune clarinet solo on *Barbecue*, taken by Bingie Madison because arranger Chappie Willet had put it on his part, while clarinettist Albert Nicholas sat idle in the next tenor chair.

In the matter of style, too, the Russell band was undergoing an overhaul. The New Orleans spirit lurked, and was unleashed for numbers such as *Jubilee*, but swing music was influencing orchestras and writers alike. Louis, a born believer in swing bands before they had the name, would have approved of the swing formula as a setting for his solo outings on appropriate material. After all, he moved with the music, just as Bechet advised, until bop became the fashion in jazz. He could never have felt comfortable work-

I have played with quite a few musicians who weren't so good. But as long as they could hold their instruments correct, and display their willingness to play as best they could, I would look over their shoulders and see Joe Oliver and several other great masters from my home town. So I shall now close and be just like the little boy who sat on a block of ice—

My Tale is Told.

Tell all the Fans and all Musicians, I love Em madly.

Swiss Krissly Yours
Louis Armstrong
Satchmo

ing in a bop setting; and he was susceptible to the air of comfort or discomfort emanating from his accompaniment. Not that he was fussy about niceties of technique or style. Quite the contrary; he had the reputation of a man who could surmount virtually any obstruction when the mood was upon him. 'Louis Armstrong never bothers about what the other fellow is playing, etc. A musician is a musician with me.' He had the useful knack, when musicians were below par, of looking over their shoulders and seeing 'Joe Oliver and several other great masters from my home town.' He also said that it made little difference to him 'as long as the boys behind me are playing right'. Russell's personnel contained enough men who could meet that requirement.

'I enjoyed all the moments I spent with Luis and his band, maybe because the boys were mostly from my home,' said Armstrong, looking back. 'The warmth, the feeling, the beat ... the everything was there. They were all down to earth also in that band. I loved them, regardless what the critics said about us.'

Jimmy Archey, Red Allen and Albert Nicholas have all told us that the band could charge, roar, do whatever a solid big band was supposed to do, if the circumstances were right. When those three trumpets, with the unbeatable Shelton 'Scad' Hemphill leading, tore into a big finale and built and built, higher and higher with Louis soaring over the top, then the total effect was something to shout about even in those shouting days. A little of this force comes over on *You Rascal*, *Barbecue* and *Jubilee*, and most convincingly on the record of *Swing That Music*.

Nicholas, a conservative speaker on jazz topics, said he thought his happiest memories of all were of these late '30s experiences.

We had a hell of a fine band. Russell was the leader, and we had Pops Foster on bass and Paul Barbarin on drums – he was replaced by Big Sid Catlett in 1938. There were nothing but good sounds in the '30s ... Artie Shaw, Benny Goodman, Casa Loma, Duke, Basie, Fletcher Henderson, Chick Webb, Mills Blue Rhythm. They were tough bands, and they all had their own distinctive sound. But Louis really put the Russell band way out front.

It may be that recordings have told less than the truth, as so often before, and that Nick was putting the band back in its rightful place – a place, at any rate, it held with the public that paid to hear bands in clubs, theatres and dance halls.

All this time, Armstrong was consolidating his position as entertainer, bandleader and recording artist; and he was establishing a fresh reputation in films. His first shorts were made in 1931 and 1932, but *Pennies From Heaven* (1936), with Bing Crosby and the Jimmy Dorsey band, was his real movie break. He starred in the 'Skeleton In The Closet' sequence, with a group which included Lionel Hampton on drums. Next came *Everyday's A Holiday*, a 1938 picture with Mae West in which Louis played 'Jubilee' at the head of a parade band. Some of the musicians were from Eddie Barefield's band, and saxophonist Barefield was seen in the film playing trombone – a logical occurrence by Hollywood's jazz standards. *Doctor Rhythm* (1938), with Bing Crosby, followed *Artists And Models Abroad* (with Jack Benny), though in both of these Louis' scenes were cut from the versions seen in many countries. The way of a jazzman never was easy in filmland, especially if he was black, and so Pops' effort in *Doctor Rhythm* fell to the cutting-room floor. It led to rumours of race prejudice and Crosby is reputed to have tried to get Louis reinserted. Bing's brother, Larry, issued a statement denying discrimination and stressing that such scissor work was common practice in Hollywood, which indeed it was. And Bing quite recently told a BBC interviewer that the scene was probably cut because of footage problems: 'They always shot more film than they needed in musicals ... and they sometimes had to make a deeper cut rather than take snips out here and there. They probably would take a whole sequence out; I'm sure that was the reason for it.'

Thus the filming went on – from the 1943 *Cabin In The Sky* and *Jam Session* (with Ann Miller in 1945) to *Hello Dolly* in 1969. A new string to Louis' bow, it helped to shoot him to world-wide fame, although few of the movies did much of a public relations job for jazz. He also made great numbers of records, many of them in unlikely company. He collaborated with Frances Langford and Bing Crosby, with Andy Iona and his Islanders, the Mills Brothers, a mixed choir, the Casa Loma Band, Ella Fitzgerald, Billie Holiday, Louis Jordan, Bing Crosby again, Gary Crosby, Nina and Frederik, Gabriele Clonisch, Duke Ellington, the Dukes of Dixieland and numerous others. These strange associations have not generally proved fruitful, but the balance is redressed by several very choice tracks among the 17 recorded with Ellington in 1961.

For a time, Armstrong's marital affairs continued unsettled. Finally divorced in 1938 by Lil Hardin (who has kept the name Armstrong in private and professional life), he was able to marry Alpha Smith that October. Pops Foster was at the wedding in Houston and may have been best man. The couple took a somewhat delayed honeymoon in New Orleans before Louis had to journey to the west coast for more filming. This third marriage was not to last long. There were arguments, probably over money, and Alpha left.

In 1937, Armstrong was in Georgia one day when he met Joe Oliver. Talking about this with Richard Meryman, Louis explained how he and the other New Orleanians in his band clubbed up all they could spare for Oliver, then down on his luck and running a fruit and vegetable stand in Savannah. 'I didn't have too much myself. Wasn't making but $75 dollars a night. And I always had a wife to take care of and her desire for diamonds. She always wanted to signify with the chorus girls – new fur all the time, so they'd say, "Damn, what kind of fur is that?"' Another habit she had, in the early days of their marriage, was that of fining him $5 every time he came home late. 'But she was cute,' he admitted. Alpha finally bowed out of his life in 1942 by applying for a separation at $250 a month. She is now dead.

In the autumn of that year he married Lucille Wilson, a dancer who visited London with the 'Blackbirds' revue during the '30s. She is the wife who lasted and 'straightened out' his home life, who travelled almost everywhere with him and made notes of people and places that should be noted. 'She knows all the bigwigs by name,' as her husband put it, 'All I have to say is "Who's this cat?" and before I look around she's answered "Oh, Vouty-vouty", sumpn like that. Beautiful memory, Lucille.' The fourth Mrs Armstrong also mastered the art of living with his trumpet. 'That's why I married four times,' Pops once explained. 'The chicks didn't live with the horn. They got too carried away, all but the last.' And again, 'That trumpet comes before everything – even before my wife, Lucille. Had to be that way. I mean, I love her because she understands that. She's on my side.'

Lucille admits that an element of sacrifice is called for from the woman in such a marriage. She devoted herself to Satchmo's well-being, at home and abroad, displaying uncommon tact in her approach to every facet of his work.

'Let's say the eye sees what it wants to see,' she once said in an interview with Barbara Coleman Fox. 'There are all sorts of women in the entertainment field. They throw their arms around Louis. I have partial vision on purpose.' She never believed in surprising him either. 'I call Louis when I am going to join him while he is on tour,' she admitted.

She first met him while she was singing and dancing in the Cotton Club floor show in New York. Armstrong had told Luis Russell: 'I like that little chick, put a good word in for me,' which he did. Said Lucille:

Naturally I was thrilled. I told Russell, 'Just make believe that you didn't say anything.' He said, 'What'll I tell him?' I said, 'Well, just say you haven't had the chance to say anything to me.' A few days later Louis came to me himself and said, 'See here little girl, I know all the cats are sharking after you; I just want you to know I'm in the running too.'

After that he'd start sending little gifts up to the dressing room. Finally he asked me out to dinner with him and I went. I've been going to dinner with him ever since. We have so many wonderful moments in our lives together, he's just wonderful, great personality, great musician and fabulous person. Everyone loves Pops.

Going Back Home

Ever since the film *New Orleans* (1946), rightly advertised as a musical extravaganza, had featured Louis in traditionally instrumented small group settings, there had been rumours about him reclaiming, so to speak, his musical heritage. The time, and the portents, looked right. A New Orleans Revival was under way, bop was on the march, and boom days for big swing outfits were definitely over. Armstrong's own band had been making the kind of back-breaking one-nighter tours he was so familiar with, but bookings were falling off and the band was being panned by the critics fairly regularly. In the spring of 1947 it broke up. Joe Glaser gave Louis' 'suspected ulcer' as the reason, and Armstrong certainly had an extensive check-up.

There had been several signs of revolutionary thought in the Armstrong camp. As far back as January 1945 he played with a small all-star line-up. In 1946, after the making of *New Orleans*, it was suggested that he might take out the band shown in it as a regular unit. This would have included Barney Bigard, who ultimately joined the All Stars. Kid Ory maintains that he was approached, then and later, as a replacement for Teagarden, but declined the job for financial reasons. As Ory paid Red Allen $1,000 a week to work with him in 1959, it is understandable that he would turn down offers which he claimed reached no higher than $650. What finally caused the small-band break-through has not been agreed, but plans were formalized after the hugely successful New York Town Hall concert of 17 May 1947, parts of which make up the outstanding 'Town

199

Hall' album. Having Teagarden in that band undoubtedly delighted Pops. Ernest Anderson was responsible for that concert, and he remembers:

I'd been trying to get Glaser to put Louis in with a small group after seeing him at a Carnegie Hall benefit earlier that year. You see he was playing one-nighters then for as little as $350 to $650 – with a 16-piece band. They paid the $650 for Saturday nights. And through 1945–6, that period, he did nothing but those one-night stands. I told Joe, but he was hurt. So I talked to Louis and he agreed, but I could do nothing without Glaser. You know, their lives were so entwined. Then I went to the bank in the ground floor of the building where Joe's office is, and had a draft made out to him for $1,000. A cashier's cheque, just the same as money. I took it upstairs to his reception room and got the switch-board girl to go in and hand him the cheque. Next thing, the door opened and Joe was demanding, 'What's this?' and so on. I said that to explain it I'd have to come in. He said he'd give me five minutes.

Well, I talked about the 350 for Louis and the whole band, and the thousand bucks, and told him I had a date on the Town Hall for a Saturday night. 'Give me Louis for the evening and leave the 16 men behind,' I asked. Today it seems a ridiculously small sum, but then it was different. And if you put a thousand dollars in Glaser's hand, you'd never get that back. So I got Louis for a thousand. Next I fixed up Bobby Hackett as MD – we'd been hanging out with Louis, and Bobby lived near him – and we laid out an ideal programme. Then it was off to Philadelphia where Louis and the big band were working for a week, four or five shows a night in the Earle Theater. It took about an hour with Louis to do it, but we arranged everything and then fixed up Tea for $75 the night. Hackett got 50. The rest you know: Peanuts Hucko, Wettling and Catlett for drummers, Bob Haggart and Dick Cary. Dick knew everything Louis ever played, and he rehearsed the musicians a day or two before the concert, with Hackett playing Louis' parts. Pops wanted to rehearse and said he would, but had no time. He came at six on the evening of the concert, though, and jived with the guys and looked at the routines. One we hired who didn't turn up was Sidney Bechet. He said he was sick but later I heard he played Jimmy Ryan's. But we didn't mind when we saw the house. I put the whole thing on and paid for everything. I could have lost a lot but I didn't, not that night. All the musicians were thrilled about it, you know, and everybody was cold sober when it started. It went great – George Wettling for the first half on drums, Big Sid the second. The hall sold out on the night, no question about that, and all kinds of press and musicians were present. The music was marvellous and so were the notices. Glaser was there, of course, and he was absolutely thrilled. Later I took Jack Teagarden up to see him. So Louis finished his dates and never went out with a big band again.

The reviews, many of which were ecstatic, and the full, enthusiastic house, undoubtedly influenced the office, and Louis too, perhaps. Fred Robbins said that Armstrong gave Town Hall 'its biggest SRO sell-out of recent years on six days' notice with the lowest priced seat at $2.40.' Robert Sylvester's glowing review ended: 'He did just about everything ... no less than 27 straight songs, ranging from early jazz to modern film tunes.' It noted *Back O'Town Blues* and a wonderful, slow *Southland* with only Cary's piano for background. Wilder Hobson spoke of 'superb hot music, showing this art form at its best'.

This was the kind of music, 'contemporary-traditional', that was heard in February 1948 at the Nice International Jazz Festival from Louis, Tea, Bigard, Catlett, bassist Arvell Shaw and the brilliant Earl Hines, who had rejoined his old sidekick in the meantime. Armstrong's playing was as good as ever, his rhythm section excellent, and in Hines he had a showman partner worthy of his talents.

I was particularly struck [wrote Humphrey Lyttelton] by the almost puritanical simplicity of his playing; all the old trappings and ornaments which were such familiar characteristics of his earlier phases have been swept away ... and there was left a music which, with its purity and serenity, brought us perhaps nearer to the fountain-head of his genius than we have ever been before.

This simplicity, the musical paring to the bone, was a continuing part of the stylistic evolution which, in the 1935 Decca period, was observed to be a modification towards a more sober method of expression. Without question, the impact of the All Stars was considerable. This change back to a traditional format must be judged as another turning point in Louis' career. At Nice, he agreed he was happy to return to a small combo ('We started out with six or seven back home'); there was 'more room to move around'.

Years later, thinking over the All Stars' emergence, Satch remembered:

It was Joe's idea. After all he's the man who has guided me all through my career. Coming from the man I love, who I knew was in my corner, it was no problem for me to change. I didn't care who liked it or disliked it. Joe Glaser gave the orders and nobody else mattered to me. You see, I knew he was concerned about my life in music. He proved it in many ways. The film called *New Orleans* didn't have anything to do with the change to small combo. Nor did the concert in 1945 with Bechet, Higgy, etc. That was just another 'gig'. When we finished it we split and went to different directions. I went on a tour of one-nighters that would make your head twirl, that is if you are a weakling (Tee Hee). And the same thing with the 1947 Carnegie Hall concert with Edmond Hall sextet. I enjoyed doing it very much. I had always enjoyed Edmond's playing and he had some fine musicians in his band whom I knew from the good old Harlem days. They were (to me) the best on their instruments. They could all blow their ass off. Yeah. But always remember this one thing. Anything that I have done musically since I signed up with Joe Glaser at the Sunset, it was his suggestions. Or orders, whatever you may call it. With me, Joe's words were law. I only signed but one contract with him, and that was forty years ago. And that still stands. Of course, I am still with the Office, and everybody that is still in his office feels the same about us.

Arkansas and Africa

In 1960 Armstrong returned to Ghana, as the first stop on a very wide-ranging tour. This time, he had the help and blessing of the State Department. It was the first occasion on which he had their sponsorship; in spite of all the musical missions accomplished in the '50s, he – or rather his advisers, for Armstrong was not a man to 'mess with them diplomats' – had not been able to find a really sympathetic governmental ear. In 1950, it is true, the chief of the International Broadcasting Division sent a letter congratulating him on his contribution to the 'Voice of America' programmes. The letter stated: 'We have watched with interest the enthusiastic response given your tour through various countries to which the "Voice" broadcasts. We feel that you have succeeded in demonstrating to European audiences an important facet of the American musical scene.' It went on to wish him success, but if the Department was paying attention to Satch's overseas expeditions, no further signs of it were observed by his representatives, one of whom maintained that he did everything feasible to stir up some action in Washington during the following decade. The results were not encouraging.

Late in 1957, shortly before the All Stars' ground-breaking South American trip, the band played a week in the capital. Aides arranged to get Louis invited to the White House for lunch, and it was assumed (on Louis' side) that this would be taken with Eisenhower. 'But he never appeared,' said our informant. 'Sherman Adams came and shook hands with Louis and then walked away. Finally I said, "God damn it, I'll get Nixon." He was Vice-President, so we went to the Senate. Nixon greeted Louis and Lucille there, and some photographs were taken.'

The same man asserted that when Armstrong arrived at Washington Airport there was a good turn-out to meet his plane. 'I'd done the White House bit, you know, and the ambassadors from Brazil and Ghana, among others, came along. But no one from the US State Department was present.'

By this time, though, Satch had delivered his unexpected blast against the Government for its handling of the schools desegregation issue in Arkansas. During the September of 1957, while the All Stars were engaged in a string of cross-country one-nighters, he woke up one day in a hotel room in Grand Fork, North Dakota, where the band had stopped for a concert date. He switched on the television and watched casually as he got ready. Then his attention was riveted by pictures transmitted from Little Rock, where the situation had grown extremely tense. A few black pupils were attempting to assert their rights to a desegregated education in accordance with a Supreme Court ruling, and one child was shown walking timidly up to the school building. As Louis watched her passing the line of jeering whites, a man moved forward and spat in the girl's face. It was a moment of shock for the viewer, too, like a blow in his own face. He got mad and stayed mad.

A young reporter came to call at the hotel, presumably after the kind of story small-town newspapers usually seek from visiting celebrities. He was still at high school, he explained when Armstrong saw him, but worked on the side for the local paper. Could he have an interview, please? He was in luck. He could and he did. Louis let fly with an angry denunciation of Eisenhower, Faubus, the Government and the whole southern shooting match.

President Eisenhower had 'no guts' and was described as two-faced for allowing Governor Faubus 'to run the country'. The Arkansas governor was dismissed as 'an uneducated ploughboy', and Louis added that his use of the National

Guards to prevent integration in the schools was a publicity stunt 'led by the greatest of all publicity hounds'. For good measure he threw in the advice that 'because of the way they are treating my people in the south, the Government can go to hell'.

This was dynamite, and the boy put the story through as fast as he knew how. Soon his paper was on the telephone asking Armstrong to confirm the quoted remarks. He confirmed them. Would he sign the story based on his quotes? The answer was yes. In a short time the editor was with him. Satchmo was shaving when he arrived. Stopping to take the document held out to him, he read quickly through it and put it up against the wall to sign it. 'That's just fine,' he agreed. 'Don't take nothin' out of that story. That's just what I said and still say.' He wrote the word 'solid' at the end of the story, added his signature, and went on shaving.

When Armstrong's comments went out on the wire service they created a sensation. The integration controversy was highly inflammable, and his outburst added fuel and also publicized the struggle still further around the globe. Overnight, it seemed, he had become a protester. Because of his reputation for indifference to political issues, and the timing of his slams, the attack had maximum effect. The Government was forced to act almost immediately, and the consensus of gossip is that Eisenhower never forgave him.

Eartha Kitt was among the first to come forward and cry that Louis was absolutely right. Satch cabled his thanks and offered to kiss her next time they met. Less gratifying was the response of another black entertainer who was reported as declaring that Armstrong didn't understand civic events. Louis' reply was swift and pithy. 'Tell so-and-so,' he snapped, 'I understand lynching, and that's a civic event.'

Satch's blitz, and his refusal of a Government-sponsored tour of Russia then being discussed, were the talk of the entertainment business for a while. Leonard Feather cancelled a jazz package tour of the south, and Dave Brubeck and Norman Granz's 'Jazz At The Philharmonic' scrubbed out southern dates and certain Texas engagements where auditorium managements banned desegregated seating. Max Kaminsky, trumpet-player with the Jack Teagarden band, which was touring Britain at the time, supported Louis in a *Melody Maker* interview.

I think it was what Louis said that got Ike up off his rear over this Little Rock business. That episode is one hell of a smear over America, and it takes a hell of a lot of guts for Louis to stand up and say the things he said. Louis is not an Uncle Tom. He's a great man, apart from the fact that he's the greatest jazz trumpet player that ever lived.

The 'Tom' reference needs explaining. Armstrong had suffered in the preceding years from repeated attacks on his stage 'mugging' and what was thought of as his subservient attitude to the whole Jim Crow structure. Louis often protested that he was non-political, that he never employed the music medium to make overt political gestures, and his stand on this subject earned him the enmity of many musicians and followers involved in the modern jazz of the '40s and '50s. Albert McCarthy wrote of the insidious campaign against Louis: 'The young musicians who took up bop so enthusiastically had none of the background of the pioneers of the form, and tolerance of older musicians and styles was almost completely absent...' Pointing out that the 'modern' movement arose during a period when black Americans were fighting for and achieving some notable advances on the social and economic fronts, he continued: 'Naturally, the younger Negroes had no intention of allowing the position to deteriorate after the war was over and there grew up a demand for equality in all fields.' Though sympathetic to such ideals, McCarthy could see that with the militancy there developed a 'resentment against the past which found expression in a curious hostility to any characteristics which could be typed as essentially Negroid ... To the "new" Negroes any suggestion of southern Negro speech was tantamount to the worst sort of "Uncle Tomming".'

The sniping war waged by 'progressive' critics against

206

Louis' music and personality must be without parallel in the story of jazz. He was a figurehead and a kind of hero, and therefore a fitting target. It was inevitable but unfair. His stage bearing (the rolling of eyes, showing of teeth, joking and grimacing), came in for a great deal of touchy, superficial criticism, which made no allowance for the fact that he was a product of a community and an era in which entertainers of 'the race' all tended to conform to the vaudeville image. Most early jazzmen danced or sang, clowned or otherwise put on an act if they reached the spotlight of cabaret or theatre, and Armstrong grew up a natural performer. It is not as though he suddenly put on the merry-maker's mask. 'You don't pose, never, that's the last thing you do,' he once advised, 'because the minute you pose you're through as a jazzman. Jazz is only what you are.'

People of Louis' race view his character and stage manner in a more charitable or balanced light than those partisan critics did. Billie Holiday, for example, said after watching Satch on television, 'I love Pops, he "Toms" from the heart.' Billy Eckstine, who knew Pops well, looked at the question from both positions and summed up: 'He's really a great humanitarian, though he doesn't go about things like the young black militants today. They don't understand Louis' behaviour, but I know he's more humanitarian than Tom.'

Louis' stage presentation, which came in for bitter criticism during the '50s, should be weighed – even by those who found it distasteful – against his stature, and the hugeness of his contribution; but it is often no longer a case of 'it's what you play that counts'.

If they [the business men] decide they don't like you, they go gunning for you. The accusations they've been making about Louis ... There's four or five of these big guys been spreading stories about Louis being 'Uncle Tom' and Louis playing the same two choruses on a number for the last two years, and so on. To say these things about a man of Louis' calibre is the grossest stupidity and insult. Suppose he had been playing these choruses the same way for some time – there isn't anybody else could make them sound that way, anyhow. It's like calling Tchaikovsky a bum because his piano concerto sounds the same way each time you hear it.

Thus Max Kaminsky to Steve Voce in October 1957, shortly after the Little Rock furore. At about that time, writing a vindication of Armstrong in the *Melody Maker, I* [M.J.] ended with this sentence: 'Now that Louis has spoken out so angrily about Little Rock we hope his attackers will praise as readily as they condemned.' If they did, I saw nothing of it. His critics, after years of belittling him for suffering discrimination in silence, were themselves silent. Louis, however, learned early in his career not to worry about other people's opinions. He was gratified, though, when the lift boy in his hotel told him confidently, 'Mister Armstrong, that will be in the history books.'

With jazz becoming a form of inter-political communication, however, it was inevitable that the US Government should one day be involved in Louis' globetrotting. They went into partnership for his 45-concert tour of Africa which began in Accra on 15 October 1960. There was another partner, for some of the tour at any rate – an American soft drinks firm. 'Pepsi Brings You Satchmo' were the words inscribed on banners and posters in Nigeria. When Louis and the band flew into London en route for Ghana, journalists were given handouts headed 'Pepsi Sponsor Satchmo's Jazz Tour Of Africa'.

The band was going to entertain West Africans at one-night stands in Accra, Kano, Ibadan, Kumasi, Lagos and Enegu – places where most of the stadiums housing the concerts would hold some 50,000 people. Tickets had been put on sale in advance, a novelty in those areas. After Nigeria, he was to visit the Congo, Uganda, Kenya, Rhodesia, Liberia, Guinea, Mali, Tanganyika and Zanzibar. The lengthy itinerary might have included South Africa had the authorities there not imposed a ban on Louis and the cast several weeks beforehand. Armstrong

Above   The Hawk in England
for the first time. Coleman
Hawkins, newly arrived in
London during 1934, tries a
local 'cuppa'.

Right   Albert Nicholas, New
Orleans-born clarinettist,
pictured in Germany during
the early '70s.

Above   Louis in London—between chores.

Opposite above   Hines, Teagarden, Cozy Cole, Barney Bigard, Arvell Shaw.

Opposite below   Louis at the piano.

Above Louis in London—at work.

Below Louis.

Above John Chilton (r.), bandleader at New Merlins Cave in Clerkenwell, with altoman Bruce Turner and visiting celebrity Bill Coleman, October 1971.
Below Max Jones greeting Louis at Victoria Station during the early '60s.

Left Louis and his second wife, Lil, meet again in Paris during the '50s.

Below Ghana welcomes the All Stars in 1956. The woman in the foreground reminded Louis of his mother.

Above 'Rocking Chair' . . . sung by Louis and Trummy Young.

Left Joe Glaser, Louis' manager.

Above Accompanied by Humphrey Lyttelton and Trummy Young, Louis sings one at a Humphrey Lyttelton Club party held in London in May of 1956.

Left Warming up.

Left Louis sings in concert.

Below Louis in pensive mood.

Left Louis with Bing Crosby, recording 'Pennies from Heaven', 1936.

Below Mr and Mrs (Lucille) Armstrong, on tour, arrive in Sweden.

Above Trombone team: New Orleans veteran Kid Ory runs into Tennessee-born Dicky Wells in London in 1959.

Left Pops off-stage.

Above Louis disciples:
Nat Gonella (l.) and
Humphrey Lyttelton
exchange valve lore at
the London press
showing of the film
Satchmo the Great.

Left Ernie Anderson
and Artie Shaw.

Opposite Louis'
funeral, 9 July 1971.

Gennett

5134-B   11386

I'M GOING AWAY TO WEAR YOU
OFF MY MIND
(Smith)
King Oliver's Creole
Jazz Band

DIVISION OF
THE STARR PIANO CO.
RICHMOND
IND.

OKeh

Reg. U.S. Pat. Off. Marca Ind. Deposta Num. 2298 de 23 de Mayo de 1923

RECORDED BY   **TRUETONE**   PROCESS

8396-A   FOR BEST RESULTS
USE *OKeh* NEEDLES

THE KING OF THE ZULU'S
(At A Chit' Lin' Rag)
(Hardin)
LOUIS ARMSTRONG AND
HIS HOT FIVE
Talk by Clarence Babcock
Recorded in Chicago
FOX TROT

GENERAL PHONOGRAPH CORPORATION NEW YORK

OKeh
REG. U.S. PAT. OFF.
ELECTRIC

NOT LICENSED
FOR RADIO
BROADCAST

8312-A

Contralto-With Piano
Accomp.-Richard M. Jones-
Trumpet-Louis Armstrong

TROUBLE IN MIND
(Jones)
BERTHA "CHIPPIE" HILL

MADE AND PAT'D. IN U.S.A. RE. 16588 AND 1702564
OKEH PHONOGRAPH CORPORATION NEW YORK

OKeh
REG. U.S. PAT. OFF.
ELECTRIC

NOT LICENSED
FOR RADIO
BROADCAST

8300-A

Fox Trot
Vocal Chorus By
Louis Armstrong.

HEEBIE JEEBIES
(Atkins)
LOUIS ARMSTRONG &
HIS HOT FIVE

MADE AND PAT'D. IN U.S.A. RE. 16588 AND 1702564
OKEH PHONOGRAPH CORPORATION NEW YORK

had been quoted as calling the trip the most important of his life, but when one of the authors interviewed him his comment was rather different. 'This is an important event, sure, but don't get me wrong – all dates are important. Whenever I play it's important to me. You still got to hit them notes.'

Once again Accra's airport was in the grip of a mob when the All Stars arrived. Musicians and fans numbering more than 2,000 surged around them, and Louis needed police to escort him to the lounge where a press conference had been set up. According to a local report, he managed to say 'It's a thrill to be back after four years' before his voice was drowned by the cheering and jazz-playing from outside the building. All the 50,000 seats in the sports ground, the report said, had already been sold for Satch's opening.

From Ghana the band went to Nigeria for five days. In Lagos's National Stadium, a crowd of several thousands responded lukewarmly, and one correspondent wrote that the music 'never left the ground'; indeed, he went so far as to say of Louis that 'Pepsi can take him back again'.

Louis fared better in Ibadan. When he came back to Lagos, the reporter was surprised at the difference. 'A Louis bubbling with enthusiasm whipped up the band ... his trumpet playing was as good as any I've heard over the past few years.' Armstrong was possibly the only jazzman then who could have drawn large numbers to these open-air arenas, for it poured with rain at one or two of the concerts. Even with such an attraction, it is said to have cost Pepsi-Cola International £100,000 ($240,000) to subsidize the good-will tour.

In the Congo, one writer hailed the booking of Louis' musicians as a welcome sign of sanity on the part of the new Republic. Newspapers reported that he had united the Congo, that the people briefly forgot their differences in the excitement of his arrival. 'They cheered and jived in the streets as Satchmo drove past behind a truckload of native dancers,' wrote one eye-witness, 'We heard an African song composed in his honour. "They call you Satchmo", the song went, "but to us you are Okuka Lokole." Okuka, he was told, is the jungle wizard who charms wild beasts with his music.'

In Kenya the welcome was again ear-warming. Carloads of admirers made the journey out to Nairobi Airport to greet him. Louis joined the crowd on the waving base where a band of oddly-assorted local musicians from groups such as the Jambo Boys, the Royal Inniskillings Band, the Bata Shoe Shine Band and the Goan Band was providing a raucous welcome with *When You're Smiling* and *The Saints*. The Nairobi concerts took place in the City Hall on two successive evenings, and there was an additional afternoon performance at the African Stadium. These were presented under the auspices of the US Information Service rather than Pepsi-Cola.

A packed house for the first show included Africans and Asians but was predominantly European. The end came all too soon for what was described as 'a deliriously happy and excited audience'. At the football stadium on Saturday, the band worked on an open stand in the centre of the pitch with the strong sun beating down. The stands were full and so were the rows of seats arranged around the bandstand. 'It seemed that everyone on these chairs had brought along a camera,' we were told, 'and it says much for the good humour of the musicians that they never objected to the antics of the photographers.' On all these travels, Satch evidently won people over in droves, not only with his music but with his exuberant vitality. A resident of Kenya said of his impact:

Nairobi has taken him to its heart, and when one observes the reactions of the audiences and general public it is brought home with force what a wonderful ambassador Louis is for his country. There is a fair amount of anti-American feeling in Kenya, much of it engendered by sections of the local press. Armstrong, more than any other visiting American, has helped to overcome prejudice and made friendship ... his audiences demonstrated that the appeal of jazz cuts through social and political distinctions.

This visit to Kenya has left a tremendous impression on the public, and its success more than justifies the expense involved in a continent-embracing tour of this kind.

There was reason enough, then, for the State Department – tardy though it was – to embrace this seemingly indestructible jazzman and call him one of America's finest envoys 'through the magic Esperanto of his music'.

South Africa was supposed to have banned Louis' visit 'because it would not be in the interests of the country at this stage'. (Louis was leading a racially mixed group which even included one Hawaiian.) He looked puzzled when asked about the ban. 'I don't know nothin' about that,' he rumbled, shaking his head. 'You'll have to ask the office.' On the subject of playing to segregated audiences there, which is what the engagement would have meant, his reply was similarly unequivocal. He was prepared to do so if Joe Glaser sent him. 'He does my thinking,' Louis said mildly, 'I just play.' The man who did the thinking dismissed the entire incident with some curt remarks about Armstrong being busier than at any time in his life.

To prove he was not prejudiced one way or the other, Armstrong hoped the State Department would include the USSR in a future tour. In 1959 he had expressed willingness to take his band to Russia and Poland on an unsponsored visit. At that time he said the tour 'wouldn't be a peace mission', that he just played his horn for the cats and it made no difference to him 'if they're Russian cats'. A film of Louis in action had been sent ahead, but the plan came to nothing. In 1960 he said, 'Those cats don't seem to get anywhere with their summit conferences. Perhaps Satch might get somewhere havin' a basement conference. I'd like to go there.' He didn't go then, or later when further attempts were made. Regularly, after the mid-'50s, reports appeared that the Russian trip was on, off, on again.

Louis did, however, manage to forge links between opposing sides on other occasions. When he stepped off the

Congo River ferry from Brazzaville, the rival forces of Joseph Mobutu and those loyal to Patrice Lumumba combined to escort him. He felt uneasy among the rifles but they didn't go off. Then his spirits rose at the sight of a banner in the procession of cars and welcoming dancers. It proclaimed, 'The black man from overseas is at home in the Congo.' It was a compliment the Congolese could not have paid to many Americans.

'Louisiana'-1:
The Man

The period at the Batley Variety Club, Yorkshire, where Satchmo and the All Stars played a two-week season in June 1968, was memorable for a number of reasons. It was, to begin with, a major event – his first cabaret engagement in Britain, to be followed by concerts. It offered him a chance to stay in one place for a fortnight, which meant recreation and relaxation as well as work. He even found time to read a jazz book, an uncommon luxury for Pops then; it was *Ain't Misbehavin'*, the story of his old friend Fats Waller. But he also maintained a busy social life, receiving musicians and fans and pressmen by the dozen. 'I've been trying to follow you for 20 years,' one trumpet-player told him. Louis raised his head from the book he was autographing and smiled. 'Me and you both,' he replied. Edwin Hinchcliffe, a lifelong admirer, who had won the *Melody Maker*'s recent Armstrong Contest, showed Pops a card signed by him and members of the band when he first saw them at Harrogate in 1932. Louis, impressed, asked after the old musicians.

People filed into his dressing-room, young as well as middle-aged, some bringing records, some photographs or programmes to be signed. Most of them simply wanted to meet Louis and have a few words, a chance to compliment him. Locals from Batley and beyond were all represented. One girl said to him, 'Eeh, you were woonderful,' adding, rather surprisingly, 'you cannot get away from what you got, can you?'

Louis always took personal trouble over his fans. Of

course, he must have known that admirers wanted to see him, shake his hand, kiss or embrace him. The amount of affection around and about him really was warming. Greeting and signing sessions, like the hours he spent autographing pictures to send to letter-writers, were part of his world for years. Though they used up a good deal of time, he undertook them conscientiously, as he did all his public relations. Very occasionally – and rather more on the 1968 visit than before – we noticed a trace of asperity when the questions became more than normally idiotic. In particular he disliked those aimed at tempting him to say something controversial for 'good copy'. At such times his answers might sound a bit mulish. He also, necessarily, built a defence mechanism against questions of the 'how do you define jazz?' variety – which is why, if you asked him to explain the secret of his success, you would probably be told, 'rhythm, boy, just plain rhythm'. Without these answers, and most of his funnies, Armstrong would have either gone mad or grown into a pretentious bore.

At an informal press reception before the Batley run began, Louis allowed himself a rare flash of irritation, when pestered by a persistent and somewhat racist-sounding drunk. 'Do you know who I am?' asked this pest aggressively. He looked like a prototype American business tycoon. Louis rasped back, 'All you white folks look alike to me, Pops.' This was unusual behaviour for Armstrong, at a semi-public gathering, though it was clear he stood very little nonsense at work. At rehearsals, on stage and in television studios, he did what had to be done in a businesslike manner. He hated rehearsing, in fact, as most full-time jazzmen do. If it could not be avoided, he saw it through with minimum fuss and maximum good humour. It was an impressive sight to see him saving time and trouble. With musicians he knew, 'rehearsals' generally boiled down to a quick talk over the keys and the chorus routine. On TV, a little more is required because of the camera and sound men. Here, when Louis emerged to play his part, he often had the studio 'breaking up'. If he was pushed too hard,

though, he could produce an unbeatable streak of stub-
bornness. When he said 'that's enough', the producer could
forget about just one more for the lighting crew.

This antagonism towards rehearsals didn't stem from
laziness, since he was a persistent worker. We believe it was
connected with a fear of disrupting the flow of Armstrong
magic. 'I don't go through that and never will,' he protested.
'All these cats can blow and we don't need arrangements.'
According to him, all that was needed was agreement on
choice of tune and key. Then 'I say "follow me" and you got
the best arrangement you ever heard.' Louis was determined
not to be dragged down by what seemed to him unneces-
sarily complicated arrangements, musical or social.

His own living routine was fairly simple, once you allowed for pills and aperients, ointments and his careful
attention to the diet sheet, and he followed a set of rules
made long ago. Details were determined by whether he was
at home, on the road or on location for a week or more; but
in essence his habits were unchanging, and he wasn't easily
pressured into breaking his own rules. Sometimes this led
to unfair criticism. One of the more publicized 'scream-ups'
around the Louis camp took place at the Newport Festival
of July 1957. It started, they say, because he would not
change his regular concert programme. The organizers requested, officially through Joe Glaser, that Velma Middleton be excluded and that the band open with something
other than *Indiana*. A birthday cake was on hand – this
was a tribute concert to honour Armstrong's 57th birthday
– and Johnny Mercer was coming into Newport to sing
Happy Birthday to Pops. Old-timers such as Kid Ory,
Henry Allen and, of course, Teagarden were present to
appear with him, and there was some talk of Ella Fitzgerald doing a set with Louis.

A little gentle pressure and it might have worked, but self-
important 'wheels' were jumping around telling Louis what
to do. He was told, 'You do two numbers, then bring on
Ory.' It was hardly the way to treat him. Teagarden said it
was not Louis' fault, and that 'some of these people seem to

be trying to crucify Pops'. The first spark was lit when Satch didn't attend the dinner given by the Lorillards, hosts of the festival. Columnist Murray Kempton reported next morning that the guest of honour was in his hotel the evening before 'wondering about his duty to history' while unspecified friends telephoned to ask why he wasn't at the dinner. Kempton quoted what sounds like an eminently reasonable excuse. 'A long time ago I stopped going to dinner before I have to work. You go, you get full of that whisky and you sound bad, and the people who asked you to dinner are the first to complain. I gotta work.' It was a clear statement of a professional jazzman's creed, and Louis always lived up to it.

At Newport Louis had apparently not told Velma she was *persona non grata*. Joe Glaser, making a rare personal appearance, turned up to persuade his artist to implement the 'requests'. Glaser and the organizers then, apparently, forbade Velma to go on. Louis, his temper shredding under the repeated attempts to push him around (as he saw it), found his vocalist in tears and, according to Teagarden, went more or less berserk. Velma went on and Louis did his show. Mercer sang too, and Kempton recorded that the man whose birthday it was fell into the accompaniment 'out of ancient habit'. Towards the end it was pointed out to a still-furious Armstrong that Ory, Teagarden and several more veterans were waiting on him for a concerted finale. That was when he exploded with his reported reply, 'No one hangs on my coat-tails.'

It doesn't sound like the old eager-to-please Satchmo of legend, but it does illustrate what happened when his routine was too violently disrupted. By the following summer, all had been forgiven down Newport way. Pops guested with an International Band and augmented his All Stars with Teagarden and Bobby Hackett, both men he loved.

In Batley in 1968, however, the course of his life ran smoothly. There were daily shows to contend with, but that was his life. Only the first one was tough for him, because he was exhausted by days of travelling (hindered by a strike) and many press calls. But he declared that he would be all right 'because this woman travels with me' – he indicated Lucille who looked indignant – 'when we do long trips like this, a week or more in one place. But on those one-nighters Mama stops home. She takes good care of me and I take care of her. We look after each other. Of course, I take care of my insides with a laxative every day, and my chops with this Franz Schuritz lip salve. And if I forget that for any reason' – here Louis gestured towards the bottle and winked – 'she's got it.' Lucille, who kept a benevolent watch over her husband's solid and liquid intake, had an enduring respect for his stamina. 'He's got a lot more than I have, and I'm a good few years younger,' she said fondly.

Louis used to travel with a portable record player and about 20 LPs, mostly of his own music. His other essential piece of equipment was a tiny pocket radio. 'That's my kicks,' he said of the transistor set. 'Mama gave it to me for those sad-assed dressing-rooms.' Showing us a few of the albums, he explained, 'Whenever I want to reach back for one of them fine old tunes I got 'em here to refresh my memory. But I've also got Barbra Streisand – she can sing awhile, can't she? – and the Beatles. It's music, and they swing. I know them boys pretty well. Ask them what they think of Satch.' He played an acetate of the *Hello, Dolly* film sequence which featured him with Barbra Streisand. They had lately filmed the scene and he was massively enthusiastic, telling us how they learned the lines and just how the scene had been done with Barbra here and the chorus there – Louis playing all the parts, of course, in incredible pantomine. 'Sings her ass off,' Louis said approvingly. 'On the screen I have about twelve Negro boys with me. Sixty pieces made the soundtrack, with Lennie Hayton as MD. Sing it, baby.' The last remark was an admiring aside elicited by the Streisand voice. 'Say what you like, daddy, but she's outswinging every ass this year,' Louis stated with finality. Lucille smiled indulgently and reminded him of his entry to a poll run by *Playboy* to find out who were the musicians' favourites. 'Yeah, on the three places on the poll form for singers, first, second and third, I wrote on mine "Barbra Streisand" and "Ditto" and "Ditto".'

Louis believed in creating goodwill between the American and British peoples, and tried to do something positive in this direction. He found time to tape several messages of this nature, as well as to record programmes for BBC radio shows. 'We did a tape for the Royal Air Force, another for the US Army,' said manager Ira Mangel. 'He likes to let the Americans know about the English. Then the other evening we made a tape for use in the hospitals. Yes, he's kept pretty busy.'

Another part of Pops' leisure was devoted to trumpets – talking about them, cleaning them, guarding them from harm. In Batley one night he was telling Humphrey Lyttelton and me [M.J.] about his first Selmer, presented in 1932, and laughing uproariously at the memory.

That Ben Davis came down with this nice new horn and asked if I thought I could use it. I told him if he was giving it to me I could play it all right. Up to that time, back home, I'd paid for all my new horns. So I took it straight out on stage that night and played my show on it, and I been using one like it ever since. Yes, they were clever, those Davis boys. Made a lot of loot out of musical instruments? Fine: I'll tell you something. They could both play good, too.

On the question of mouthpieces, so often raised, Satch had no trade secrets and frequently relied on 'whatever came with the horn'. On this particular night there were two in his trumpet case; they looked as if they belonged to the K-Modified Selmer. Asked what type he preferred, he reached in his back pocket and produced a mouthpiece in its leather pouch.

I keep my favourite right here, always carry it with me, and from time to time I'll blow on it. It doesn't do to leave a mouthpiece lying about, picking up germs and all sorts of dirt. Trumpets likewise. I give my horns about five years. Of course I look after them, run hot water through the instrument every night so you know it's going to percolate. It will last for ever if you keep it cleaned out, like your stomach. So I could keep my trumpets longer, but I use a horn a lot and that's how long I usually give 'em.

There was a strongly fatalistic streak in Armstrong's make-up. He believed that music, and more specifically the trumpet, controlled his destiny. 'That horn is my boss,' he claimed, 'because it is my life.' The Selmer was seldom far away from him for long. At home or in a hotel room it was customarily nearby, in the open case on a table or desk, or at his feet, perhaps, where he could look down and see it. It was the centrepiece of sundry small rituals: the pouring through of hot water, the drying and oiling, the fingering of valves, and renewing of acquaintance each day. Louis practised of course, warmed up and so on, but his regular blowing and handling of the trumpet was more than a routine work-out – which, playing so much in his life, he scarcely needed. It was because 'you got to live with that horn, keep close to it'. So he and the trumpet were twin souls. He knew it intimately and looked after it, so that it would look after him. Anyone who saw him busy at his dressing table realized that Louis took the same pains with the instrument as he did with himself. He would sit there applying lip salve or Sweet Spirits of Nitre, using his gauze and pads of cotton wool, and from time to time stop to pick up the trumpet and concentrate on it silently while fingering the pistons. And when he had an opportunity, day or night, he would warm up with a few scales or long notes, even a passage from *Cavalleria Rusticana*, which he used to perform back in the Vendome era.

In a way, I feel sure, the trumpet ablutions were a part of Louis' own inner cleanliness operations. Speaking of one reminded him of the other. At Batley he was happy with the stringent diet, which he said had reduced him from over 200 lb to under 140, and happy about the new Armstrong outline and sharp, expensive wardrobe that went with it. 'These suits, shirt, shoes are all new. There's $4,000 worth of new clothes here, so you know I got to keep slim.' Many hours of his life were spent contentedly extolling the virtues of his pet laxative, Swiss Kriss. Clearly he regarded the entire process, from filling station to slipway, as a kind of secret life force. The belief may have been a blend of common sense and folklore, but Armstrong was in earnest about it, in spite of his eliminatory pleasantries.

Musicians who worked with him found themselves in the firing line, as you might say. A certain trumpet player, on first receiving a gift packet of the herbal 'remedy', was ungallant enough to try the contents on his wife. 'How did she react?' he was asked later. 'Can't say,' was his bland answer. 'I didn't see her for two days and then she wasn't speaking to me.'

On the Batley journey Louis was accompanied by Tyree Glenn (trombone), Joe Muranyi (clarinet), Marty Napoleon (piano), Buddy Catlett (bass), Danny Barcelona (drums) and the girl singer Jewel Brown. The leader's eye fell on Glenn's ample figure. 'I've got him on Swiss Kriss,' Louis said, 'and told him he'll soon be feeling the benefit. If he doesn't lose 25 lb I'll kiss your ass and not notice it. Fact is, Tyree's already benefiting. He told me, "Pops, the trouble is I hardly have time to take my jacket off."' Louis slapped his thigh and roared with laughter at the picture. 'I said, "Never mind that; it ain't your jacket you got to worry about, daddy."' He recovered sufficiently to deliver the pay-off he must have known was expected. 'And I shouldn't say "ain't" because it ain't right.'

But he was serious, too. Parrying the inevitable question from a fan about retirement, he promised, 'Oh, we're going to be a long time round here on this earth. I take my Swiss Kriss, man, they keep you rollin'. Old Methuselah, he'd have been here with us if he had known about *them*.' Others, closer to Pops' heart, might have gained time, in his opinion, had they followed stricter dietary regimens. We spoke of colleagues departed since our previous meeting, and among them were Billy Kyle, Buster Bailey, George

Wettling, Edmond Hall, Henry Allen and Rex Stewart. Armstrong looked suddenly grave.

Yeah, so many died. Red and all them cats. Some of 'em needn't have gone. They didn't take proper care of their insides. Money won't look after that. It's the food you eat, that's what counts. You have to cut down your food to stay healthy. Two meals a day is all you need. It's all I have and I never felt better.

Armstrong was an optimist about his health, and in general the optimism was justified. The most publicized bout, until the illnesses which put him in Beth Israel Hospital in September 1968 and again in 1969 and 1971, was the pneumonia he suffered in Italy in June 1959. Stories of blood clots and heart attacks spread alarm and despondency through the jazz world, even though the patient kept up a barrage of reassuring bulletins about his progress.

But Louis refused to accept the fact of chronic illness and repelled the notion of mortality. On the occasion of his Italian illness he was up and off home and back on the road while the obituary writers were still revising their copy. Back in Corona, Long Island, before his brithday, he first took in the Jack Teagarden band ('We were surprised to see him up,' said Jack, 'and even more surprised when he sat in with us'), then made an unexpected appearance at New York's Fourth Annual Jazz Jamboree, where thousands of concert-goers serenaded him – it was 4 July – with *Happy Birthday To You*. Borrowing a horn from one of Johnny Dankworth's brassmen, he played a couple of numbers with the Dankworth band. This was within a week or two of his reported 'near to death' fight with pneumonia.

Not a man to withhold a perky comment about his health, Louis assured *Down Beat* then that he had never felt better. He suggested Bix had tried to get him for the lead chair in Gabriel's band, but added, 'I couldn't make the gig. It hadn't been cleared with Joe Glaser, the union, or the State Department.' In Leeds, nine years later, he told

221

Lionel Crane, 'They gave me a beautiful little chick to nurse me and I started getting better the first day she come in.'

So it went on. Louis was dubbed by one writer 'the cat with nine lives'. He fought his way back from one crisis after another during his last two-and-a-half years, protesting that he'd 'heard no bugles', was getting stronger every day, and would 'soon be back in the salt mines'. And back he came, every time, until the illness which put him into the intensive care unit of New York's Beth Israel Hospital, in March 1971.

Even then he spoke optimistically of 'getting back on the mound' as soon as the doctors allowed it. People who saw him perform, during the new phase of his career which he embarked upon in 1970, had no doubt that he would return to his lifelong profession or perish in the attempt.

Louis was always so obviously happy to be at work. When he travelled to Britain in October 1970 to play on behalf of the National Playing Fields Association, his health gave concern to his friends; but his spirit was as indomitable as ever, and he had manifestly lost none of his love of the spot-light, nor his instinctive knowledge of what people wanted to hear. Lucille said music kept Louis alive and happy. She had no hang-ups about that, and seldom opposed his musical plans. 'Besides,' she admitted during Louis' last illness, 'when his mind's made up there's no use arguing.'

Armstrong's decision to play two weeks at the Waldorf Astoria, immediately before his mid-March collapse, must have been a mistake in his condition. But it was what he longed to do, and in spite of medical warnings he forced himself to finish the engagement. He was in hospital for seven weeks, near to death from a heart ailment, complicated by pneumonia and kidney trouble. As soon as he felt a slight improvement he begged Lucille to take him back home where he could taste once more the red beans and rice she had learned to cook in southern style.

Home was the detached house on 107th Street, in the

somewhat tumble-down Corona district of Long Island, where he and Lucille had lived since 1942. She had been the one to buy the house, because 'Louis didn't live anywhere then, and didn't want to.' When she told him about the down payment, he said 'Honey, we ain't never going to be there; what do we need a house for?' She went ahead with the purchase just the same, furnished the house and one day handed him a key – 'this is for your new home'. He had to take a taxi to find the house, but when he got inside he liked it.

As Lucille said, 'He came around, and it's given him a stability and a happiness he never had before.' Pops was heard to say that it was their pad, it was paid for, and he wasn't ever going to move. He didn't, for early in the morning of Tuesday, 6 July 1971, he died peacefully in his sleep. He was found by Lucille at 5.30 am and pronounced dead by Dr Alexander Schiff.

Two days earlier Louis had passed his 71st birthday quietly at home with Lucille and Ira Mangel. Typically, he and his manager were planning an appearance-schedule for late summer. In an interview a week or two before Satch had announced that he was 'an old cat you can't lose'. Complaining of weakness in his legs, he added that he would be back at work 'as soon as my treaders get in as good shape as my chops'.

His body was on view first at the funeral home in Corona, then at the Seventh Regiment's armoury in Manhattan. Services were held on Friday, 9 July, at Corona's Congregational church, where Peggy Lee and Al Hibbler sang, and the burial took place at Flushing Cemetery. Dozens of jazzmen and thousands of Armstrong's 'ordinary people' paid their last respects. Crowds gathered outside Louis' house and later outside the armoury and the church. It was estimated at one stage that 25,000 mourners visited the armoury. Spectators lined the funeral route. As the procession passed near the Armstrongs' home, two boys held up a notice. It read: 'We all loved you, Louie'.

223

'Louisiana'-2:
The Legends

For most of his working life Louis Armstrong was known and loved as much for his stagecraft and humour as for his musicality. He in fact possessed immense personal charm and a special kind of courtesy which enabled him to get on well with people of almost every type and nationality. Clearly, from the profundity of his finest musical creations, he was not merely the sunny, outgoing, kidding figure he usually appeared on stage or screen. He may have been a natural actor, but he was a showman for all that. Everyone who came into contact with him realized that the personal and professional stances were by no means identical.

That acknowledged, we venture the opinion that Louis was at heart a good-humoured man who was rightly valued – and occasionally feared – as an intrepid, extrovert storyteller. Nobody enjoyed a joke more than he; no one derived more pleasure from telling stories, or hearing tales about himself. He took delight in calling others by nicknames – 'Gate', 'Pops' or, in the case of one of the authors, 'Max the Knife' – and loved all his own too, as well as all the humorous allusions to his voice and other attributes.

Everyone had a pet name for everyone else in New Orleans down around those years. It was a pleasure to nickname someone and be named yourself. Fellers would greet each other, 'Hello, Gate' or 'Face' or whatever it was. Characters were called Nicodemus, Slippers, Sweet Child, Bo' Hog, so many more names. They'd be calling me Dipper, Gate-mouth, Satchelmouth, all kind of things, you know, Shadmouth, any kind of name for a laugh. We had so much fun. Nobody'd get angry about a nickname, and I had a million of 'em. Then I got Satchmo and I'm stuck with it. I like it. I went to all of them countries in Africa and they got that word 'Satchee-mo' down there. 'Old Satcheemo' all through them jungles, man, and in Leopold[ville] where they carried me high on this chair. I got pictures of all that stuff.

Armstrong is still fondly remembered throughout Kenya, where he is known in Swahili as 'Satchee-moo'.

There was a time he telephoned Billy Eckstine, who had a 'strep throat' which had rendered him almost voiceless. 'This is me, Pops; I heard you had trouble with your pipes.' Louis recommended one of his many medicaments and added that he'd suffered from the same trouble. 'I took this and I been clear ever since,' he said. Eckstine roared with laughter when he recounted the story. 'Here's this guy, calling long distance, gonna help me clear my pipes, and he sounds like he's singing in a gravel pit.'

Then there's the divorce story. It concerns the vocal timbre which Louis acquired, he said, directly his tenor voice broke.

It got me a divorce from my third wife, you know. I've had three divorces but never had to go into court but once. When I was up in the box and the judge heard my sawmill voice, he asked, 'Have you got a cold, Mr Armstrong?' I said, 'No, that's my ordinary voice.' The judge rocked for about five minutes, then announced, 'Divorce granted.'

Any time of day or night, any place and any company was right for an Armstrong riposte. Asked why he'd never had any children, he was known to reply, 'Well, daddy, I've always travelled so much.' But in 1949, when he first 'had an audience with the Pope in Rome, Italy', the answer was different. The Pope concerned – 'the little bitty feller I liked so well, the first one I met. You know he died' – was Pius XII, who spoke some English; Louis remembers 'flooring him with a couple of good belly laughs'. He asked Louis about his music and said he was glad the Italian people liked it. Finally he enquired whether Louis and Mrs Armstrong, who was present, had any children. Speaking slowly and distinctly, for the benefit of one grappling with a foreign language, Louis informed him, 'Not yet, but we're having a lot of fun trying.' The Pontiff took a good laugh before signifying that the audience was at an end.

Other favourite Louis stories concerned members of various European royal families – he played for several crowned heads – and especially British royalty. In the '30s, performing, he claimed, before King George V, he looked up towards the Royal Box and announced: 'This one's for you, Rex.' The number was *You Rascal, You.*

An early Louis story concerned the making of *Drop That Sack* in 1926, under another name for another record company while he was under contract to OKeh. When the disc came out, Louis was summoned to the OKeh president's office. *Drop That Sack* was played to him and he was asked point blank 'Louis, who played cornet on that?' 'I dunno, but I won't do it again' is the answer that went into the legends.

There were also mildly medicinal anecdotes, which showed Louis' wonderment in the face of anything laxative or indeed remotely effective on the human plumbing. Once a young mother, recently in childbirth, explained that she had advanced the birth by taking castor oil so that she could be up in time to catch this Armstrong concert. It was a moving compliment, especially since she had been afraid to laugh loudly for fear of breaking her new stitches. His comment, after her departure, was that the experience had given him 'a new respect for castor oil'.

And take the extravagant welcoming ceremonies in Ghana during the Pepsi tour. Bands played, colourfully dressed dancers leaped and shouted, and the Lord Mayor of Accra poured some spirits on the ground in traditional fashion to propitiate the gods. He chanted 'Akwaaba', 'welcome'. Not to be outdone in the courtesies, Satch unshipped a fifth of his Scotch and tipped it out to join the other libation. He did his little ritual dance on the spot and the Mayor said 'Akwaaba' some more. A *New York Times* reporter says that Louis replied 'Yeah.'

Hailing from Louisiana, Armstrong must have had some childhood knowledge of alligators in the swamps around New Orleans. And he had a standard joke about his mother sending him to get water from a pool. He returns trembling, the bucket empty, saying there's a 'gator in the pool and he's scared to go near. His mother tells him the reptile is more frightened than he is. 'If he's more scared of me than I am of him, Mama, that water ain't fit to drink.'

Satchmo's humour, like his music and his most vivid memories, always led back to home.

After a funeral the mourners would gather round a keg of beer and some food and they'd all rejoice. You got a lot of humour at some of them wakes, you know. When the body's laid out in the front room, and you all go in the house, you lead off with a hymn and then walk right back to where they got coffee, ham and cheese sandwiches and plenty liquor. So this fellow, who was a brother in the Elks club one time, was viewing the body of brother Jones. He touched the dead man on his forehead, and it seemed to him to be warm. So he went to the kitchen and told the widow: 'Mrs Jones, I just touched Brother Jones's forehead and he seemed a little warm to me.' Now she's crying, and all of a sudden she wipes her eyes and looks right at him, and says: 'Hot or cold, he's going out of here tomorrow.' Everybody's livin', you know, and he's gotta go.

These social clubs played an important part in the lives of the jazz musicians. Besides the Elks, Louis spoke of the Bulls, the Jolly Boys, the Original Swells and 'the Swells this and the that'. He claimed that the parades were beautiful: 'And that band would be blowin', you know, you could always hear that Onward Band.'

Speaking of the cutting, or carving, contests, Louis said: 'A band might come up on the corner, and another would come up and they were both swingin', and they just chained the wheels so neither could leave that corner. They'd jam and fight for hours. And they had a little tune they'd play when they'd beaten you,' he told the BBC's Geoffrey Haydon. Here Armstrong sang the phrase and explained: 'Played it when they were leaving and the crowd would just roar. That's a little thing, you know, means so-and-so. I can't tell you.' He laughed, and Haydon replied: 'Yes you can.' So Louis told him the title: ' "Kiss my fuckin' ass." And then the people just ... oh, god ... Like them old days down there were priceless.'

When he envisaged his own death it was in terms of a New Orleans-type wake. 'When I die, it's gonna be the prettiest funeral you've ever seen,' he told a newspaperman 'I just wish I could watch it.'

It seems curious, and a little sad, that his own departure was marked by no jazz parade, and only a few moments of music. New Orleans, the following Sunday, provided the traditional send-off for the greatest of all its sons. There, elderly musicians marched and blew for the absent friend who, in days long gone, had played as many funerals as he was offered.

The tragedy of his mother's death was recalled in a *New York Times* interview. Louis and Mayann had been very close.

Down South the ice man was likely to be your father [Louis told Lionel Crane]. Or the mail man or any mother-lover. My mother and grandmother were the people who raised me, specially my mother ... She said, 'Son, you got a chance. Don't waste it.' I loved my mother. The only time I cried in my life was when they put the top on her coffin.

And talk of funerals often led Louis to recall King Oliver:

I've seen him break up a baseball game coming from the cemetery. The game'd be playing when the funeral passed, and you know they'd take off their caps in respect, but when they pulled that snare from the drum at the MacDonald Cemetery in Algiers and they got the pass to go to the levee, man, they was blowing ... 'Oh, when the Saints...' You can see 'em, can't you? Dropping baseball bats and every-thing to follow the parade, 'cos they know old Joe Oliver going to reach up and start hittin' them notes.

The young Louis accepted all the parade jobs he could fit in. As there were 'more clubs than you can count' in New Orleans, and as 'cats died like flies' at that time, he kept pretty busy.

This unbroken link with New Orleans and his fellow 'landsmen' provides most of what clues there are to Armstrong's musical thinking, to his inspiration, to his outlook on professionalism and audiences. To understand him, as he frequently remarked, you had to understand how he felt about music. Music was his life; everything else was secondary to it. Since his artistry was centred on New Orleans, his character and behaviour probably cannot be understood without constant reference to the city and the start it gave him. It isn't clear why, after that start, he didn't follow the path of crime, drunkenness or some spectacular debauchery. But genius cannot be explained; we are happy to agree with Humphrey Lyttelton, who said: 'It's something he's got. I've seen it come through, and I still don't know what it is.' Whatever it was it was rooted in his New Orleans heritage, and he never outgrew that upbringing. To adapt an Ellington maxim, it may be said of Armstrong that you could take the man out of New Orleans but you couldn't take New Orleans out of the man.

The trombonist Trummy Young elaborated on this point in a discussion with David Halberstam:

You can write down notes for me to play but you can't tell me what I did as a kid; you can't tell Louis Armstrong what it was like to be a little kid in New Orleans and what it was like for us to grow up. You can't put that down. When we're playing I'm always feeling Louis' mood. On *Ole Miss* I feel fired up, running hard, everything's out of my way, a clear road at last.

As Young sees it, jazz means something almost exclusive

229

to a band of musicians of a particular era and, perhaps, of a particular class and loosely defined area. Similarly, the drummer George Wettling wrote more than 25 years ago: 'Only a handful of musicians know how to play real jazz anyhow, and the majority of them are on the 40 side and still going strong.' Both statements are based on a purist view of jazz, of course, and neither of the musicians who made them felt narrowly about music. What they were doing, I imagine, is talking about the essence of jazz – the original black jazz. Louis, they would have agreed, personified that essence, an essence distilled in its purest form in the most impoverished parts of uptown New Orleans, early in this century. In other areas of the south too, but not in the educated communities and not, at first, up north. Of course they soon had music rather like it, and, as the first wave of jazzmen spread, music exactly like it. Today there is a mass of music rather like it, more fully developed and cleanly played. But the feeling isn't quite the same, because the players lead different lives.

Joe Bushkin, the pianist, once asked, 'Tell me, Pops, when you're improvising what do you think about? How do you get the feeling?' Louis replied, 'Joe, just close your eyes and remember the good times you had when you were a kid. Then you'll find music will just come out.' It was one of the many remarkable things about a remarkable man that in spite of the harshest poverty and deprivations he remembered and re-lived his youth with endless pleasure. The sweetshop on the corner, the 'poor boy' sandwiches (a loaf of bread with ham or some other meat in the middle), the sight of King Oliver through a crack in the wall of a honky tonk, the hustling women and young prostitutes who looked like schoolgirls, all these images contributed to his picture of the old well-loved days 'when you could hear a good band every night on every corner of the red light district'.

He didn't persistently re-live his past, of course, for in his repertoire he was no traditionalist. He enjoyed applying the know-how of a lifetime to an up-to-date song, but when he

230

went into musical action the spirit of New Orleans was ever-present, because the essence was always there in Louis' heart and mind. Jazz is what you are, and Louis didn't change much. His attitude to New Orleans was long an ambivalent one because of the city's race ordinances. For a period he refused to play there unless they would accept his white trombonist Jack Teagarden, though latterly the laws were relaxed in this respect. But in the matter of his jazz-craft, the old influences took over because Louis was completely absorbed in his playing, always remembering his early idols.

When I pick up that horn, the world's behind me and I don't concentrate on nothing but that horn ... I don't feel no different about it now than I did when I was playing in New Orleans. No, that's my living and my life.

'Life's always been good,' Louis wrote not long before he died. He could look back and account himself lucky. But, as Philip Larkin wrote in 1970, 'it is we who have been privileged to share this century with such a perpetual fountain of original excitement, beauty and good humour. It is we who are the lucky so-and-so's.' That excitement and beauty and humour made Louis recognized, in his lifetime, as jazz music's first giant and first truly popular figure. Perhaps, though, his full worth has yet to be recognized. Let Max Kaminsky have the last word.

Sure, Louis is famous now. But I still don't think he's got the appreciation he deserves. Maybe in a hundred or two years from now they'll know how great he really was. That purity that came out of him, that great classical playing; how many could have done that? It's pure genius.

231

Satchmo Says

I was brought up around music, can't see how I could have thought of anything else. My mother took me to church when I was ten, I sang in the choir. Before ever I played trumpet I was singing in a quartet, that was my hustle, we used to sing in the streets and pass the hat around. We always opened up with *My Brazilian Beauty,* I was singing tenor harmony, the bass voice would make them low notes.

I didn't play at all before I went into the Colored Waifs' Home for Boys. The discipline there could be tough at times, but I was so happy from the time I began the music that all my memories come from that.

After I'd been in the Waifs' Home for six months, Captain Jones and Mr Davis let me play the drums, they put me on alto-horn, trombone, I became the bugle-boy then played cornet in the band I learnt just that fast.

The Waifs' Band played for the people through the streets sometimes. Once up in the district I came from, round the third ward, we collected a whole hatful of money for new instruments. Black Benny, the great bass-drummer, was around that day making sure that all the money went into the hat – he was a tremendous character, tough, a nice bad cat, sort of god-father to all us boys, he had a great sense of humour and was only rough, but how rough, when he had to be. Not scared of anyone and so great on the bass-drum, a good heart – he was my star.

After I came out of the Home I stayed a while with my father Willie's other family – he had a wife named Gertrude, a nice woman, she thought quite a bit about me, and I kinda liked her too. She and my father had two boys and a girl. I stayed with them for a while, but I commenced getting a little lonesome for my mother and my sister. Before I realized it, I was back living with them again in that great big room where the three of us happily lived.

No luxuries you understand, we were poor people, but we were always dressed up and clean. No toilets where you pulled the chain, only one outside 'privy' for everyone to use and emptied once a week. My mother always believed in physics for me. Long before my Swiss Kriss days she'd go over the other side of the railway tracks and pick up what we'd call Pepper Grass. Little later, I'd dash to the outhouse and find that someone had left (a turd) on the seat that looked like a trombone. I remember my mother firmly believed in old-fashioned remedies, she always said never worry about things you can't get. We didn't know about cold cream and all that; in the winter time if you looked a bit ashy and scratched your legs Mum couldn't afford vaseline she'd put axle-grease on us. Wasn't gonna waste that food-money on cold cream, she'd go and grab one of those wheels and stick her fingers in the nuts and rub it off on your ankles. Of all my memories they were the choicest I think.

King Oliver was the one who taught me after I left the Home, I listened to the others, but he gave me the tuition – I used to run errands and things for his wife. In my days he was top man, Buddy Bolden was the great man when Joe was a kid. Joe was the most creative trumpet player I ever heard.

One night he sent me in his place at Pete Lala's, he was always a kind man. I'll never forget it, Pete Lala came over to me soon after I started and said, 'Put that bute in,' that's what he called a mute.

I played for a while at Henry Matranga's 'tonk', used to earn a dollar and a quarter a night, but in those days my mother could make a good meal for 15 cents, I could get a suit tailor-made for ten dollars. Matranga's could be full of tough sportin' people – we didn't even know the word gangsters, then we used the expression hoodlums. All those girls who kept their money in their stockings – they liked to hear me play the blues – but once trouble started between the bad cats someone would make sure I was safe.

I used to play in a few bands, they'd send someone down for Little Louie that's what they called me then. I'd substitute for various guys. One night I went with Sam Dutrey's Band at the Palm Gardens, he looked at me and said, 'What are you doing here boy?,' the rest of the band said leave him alone he's playing with us tonight, then Sam said 'I was only kidding son', but I was scared of him all night long.

In those days there were a hundred and six bands working outside of Storyville. A lot of musicians would go out balling all night then think they can give their best on the horn, but it catches up with them. I always noticed that old man Moret was blowing loud and strong long after some of the guys who'd been drinking at the Eagle Saloon had fallen out of the parade. I had a lot of respect for him.

I got to play pretty strong and worked with the Tuxedo Band and others, then in 1919 when Joe Oliver left for Chicago he got me his place with Kid Ory's band. I doubled with Ory's Band and the Tuxedo and gigged with bands for parades and funerals.

When I went on the Streckfus steamers, that was the first travelling I did, it could be hard work, but all good for you. Davey Jones, who played mellophone and sax, was with Fate Marable's Band, he helped me. When he got to know me he gave me lessons in reading music.

I think it was in the summer of 1920, that Joe Oliver came up to St Louis to visit me. He had a few days off from working in Chicago and came to find me at the place that I roomed at. That day I was playing a day-trip with Fate Marable on the boat, so as usual, I took along a packed meal – plenty of good food – enough for both of us. Well, Joe came on board with me for the day and sat there listening and smiling and he got around to start eating. When the time came to quit playing for a rest I found he'd eaten all

the food that I'd brought along. I just had to smile, he'd
been sitting there listening happy as could be dipping a
hand down for more food. I saw there was none left, nothing, but I was happy for him.

I left Fate Marable and went back to New Orleans, and I
was doing plenty of work. I got the message to join Joe in
Chicago, and as a matter of fact Joe Oliver was the only
one I would leave New Orleans for. When I got to Chicago
I was in my glory, but every chance the musicians got they
wanted to cut his throat. He could have hired good musicians out of Chicago, but he felt he couldn't play unless he
had boys from New Orleans. But to me, New Orleans
musicians for generations always had malice, they never
did stick as one.

I called him Papa Joe 'cause he was like a father to me –
I used to eat regular at his house in Chicago, his wife was a
good cook. So many breaks were originated by Joe, and I
had the second harmonies for all of them and they thought
I was marvellous – we were a team and nobody could catch
us. He used to kid me along that he really was my father,
but when my mother came up to Chicago he didn't know
her too well at all, and how we all laughed about that. I had
married Lil, and Lil with the better education and experience only did what any wife that's interested in her husband would do, her suggestions, etc., were all perfect I
appreciated them all. Joe Oliver made a statement to Lil
saying 'As long as little Louis is with me he can't hurt me.'
Right away Lil got behind me and that did it. With a
thought like that in King Oliver's mind, as much as you
idolize him, you must leave immediately, because King
Oliver and his ego and wounded vanities may hurt your
pride. Lil said, 'It's all indications that King Oliver is trying
to hold you back.' I didn't say a mumbling word I just
split.

After I left Joe, I auditioned for Sammy Stewart, but I
wasn't 'dicty' enough, regardless of how good I played, I
wasn't up to his society, as a matter of fact I didn't get to
play a note for him, he just passed me up and within a few

years he could have kicked himself into oblivion, but at the time I could have kicked him. Then I got the offer to join Fletcher Henderson, going to New York in those days was a big thing. Everything was fine when I got settled in. Coleman Hawkins, 'Long' Green, Kaiser Marshall, they were all there. While I was in New York I did the dates with Clarence Williams also made the records with Bessie Smith, she had a certain something in her voice no other blues singer could get. I like everything I did with her, but only in recent times have I finally got around to hearing the things I did with Maggie Jones all those years ago, and I think I like them as much as anything I did with the blues singers. I never worked with Bessie Smith outside of the recordings. No rehearsal. I was there to make the records, didn't get to talking to her too much, don't think we spoke the same kind of language. I do remember clearly that the stories about her carrying all her money in a big pouch under her dress were true – someone asked her if she'd got change of a hundred and she dived under the dress to find it.

Fletcher only let me play 3rd cornet in his band. The whole time I was in his band he'd only give me 16 bars to get-off with, but he'd let me hit those high notes that the big prima-donnas, first-chair men, couldn't hit. I stayed and tolerated those fellow-musicians cutting up on the bandstand instead of playing their music. The fellows had such big heads if they missed a note so what? Hmmm. When I talked to Lil on the 'phone and told her what was happening she immediately said 'come on home', Chicago was my home town then, Lil said 'I've got a good job for you playing first cornet in my band' which was an elevation for me. I gave Fletcher my notice and joined Lil at the Dreamland, oh, was I so much relieved and happy over that. As far as Fletcher was concerned he wouldn't even listen to me sing nothing. All the singing that I did before I joined Fletcher Henderson went down the drain so you can imagine how glad I was to join Lil and her fine band. She had a damned good band. To me, it was better than Fletcher's, other than all those big arrangements that Don Redman was making, I wasn't moved very much with them, too much airs, etc. Fletcher was so carried away with that society shit and his education he slipped by a small-timer and a young musician – me – who wanted to do everything for him musically. I personally didn't think Fletcher cared too much for me anyway. But no hard feelings, at Fletcher's funeral I sent a piano made of flowers, was real pretty. I changed from cornet to trumpet while I was with Erskine Tate at the Vendome, Jimmy Tate (Erskine's brother) played trumpet, and they figured that it would be better if I did too. We played some difficult shows with that orchestra, good for reading, you'd suddenly get the call to turn back five pages in the overture or something like that. I never tried to be a virtuoso or the greatest I just wanted to be good. I learned a lot playing under the direction of Erskine Tate, we played all kinds of music. I really did sharpen up on my reading there. We played the scores for the silent movies, and a big overture when the curtain would rise at the end of the film. I got a solo on stage, and my big thing was *Cavalleria Rusticana.* That always stayed with me, sometimes I used to warm-up with snatches from it. One day with the All Stars in Miami, Florida, a guy knocked at the dressing-room door and said he'd heard me playing it as he was walking by. He was a flute player from the Philadelphia Symphony Orchestra and he complimented me on my interpretation and phrasing – after all those years – I felt good about that and we talked for hours about music.

It was Joe Glaser at the Sunset who first put my name up, he had a big sign saying 'Louis Armstrong World's Greatest Trumpeter', he heard someone say 'Who put that up?,' 'I did,' he said, 'and I defy anyone to move it.' I was making regular records, the Hot Five and that, we'd work the tunes out in the studio, no trouble. Good atmosphere, so good that a trombonist, not Kid Ory, forgot himself and started blowing like hell into the wall instead of into the recording. A lot of those comments on the records were just as though we were talking to one another on a club date –

real natural. But when the recording man thought the idea good and asked everyone to do it sort of on cue, well that was a different thing. Johnny Dodds got nervous about talking on the record *Gut Bucket Blues*, I think it was. We had a go at it, but when it was Johnny's turn he started stuttering out what he'd got to say. I laughed, and Johnny said 'Alright then you say the mother-fucking thing yourself' – then all of us laughed, Johnny as well. Later on, Don Redman used to come down by train from Detroit and we'd have a few arrangements worked out. As to Jelly Roll Morton, I never had a conversation with him until about 1936, never could figure out how we wrote *Wild Man Blues* together, guess he was working for the publisher at the time.

When I took the band (Carroll Dickerson's) to New York there was a show 'Great Day' I took all the band but they just wanted me, I didn't work in the show. I went into Connie's Inn instead, my boy Mezzrow was around with me during my trip with Connie's 'Hot Chocolates' show, we took some pictures of Mezz with my movie camera, and I was the director. Later, I went to the Cotton Club, Culver City and Johnny Collins became my manager, he came to Europe with me in 1932, he wasn't a bad man, it's just a lot of people didn't understand Armstrong, I finally paid him 5,000 dollars for my contract. Haven't heard of him in a long time, I won't say anything happened to him (God forbid), last time I heard, about ten years ago, he was in Florida.

Before I came to Europe my own big band did a lot of touring, course we played in Chicago and did a summer in New Orleans, but that touring could be tough. Good spirit in the band, all drove together in a band-bus. Wasn't always the same vehicle, one company would be contracted to drive you for so many miles then another company took over and you hired another bus for the next series of dates. One day we arrived in Memphis and got ready to change buses. The man who was due to transport us took one look – you dig? – and said 'I'm not driving you anywhere.' We got out the contract and said, 'Look here, it says so-and-so to drive Louis Armstrong and his Orchestra from this date and so on.' 'I didn't know it was going to be like this,' says the man, remember, this was the Old South. Well now, one of the musicians was smoking a cigarette in a long fancy holder and this somehow didn't please the man, and he kept looking at my trumpet man Zilner Randolph who had some sort of French beret on. Zilner began to make it pretty clear that he wasn't standing for any of this shit. I said to Mike McKendrick 'go off and 'phone Mr Collins and he'll sort this mess out,' I'd seen this kind of scene before.

In no time at all one word had led to another and before we knew what was happening we all got arrested. Just as we're being hauled into the police wagons Mike McKendrick came running round the corner – I can see him now his coat all flapping. He was quick, but so were the rest of the band, nobody waved or shouted or did anything, and Big Mike kept on running just like all he wanted to do was catch a train and at least we had somebody on the outside.

By now, a few of the band were really worried, and so was I – for them. See I knew that one of the guys sometimes carried a .45 and another had a regular pimping scene going for him that didn't want too much questioning. They put us two to a cell, I shared with 'Professor Sherman Cook', a good old hustler, he was sort of a valet to me (kinda like 'Doc' Pugh later on), the 'Professor' also used to act as master of ceremonies for us. Anyway we're in this cell and he turns to me and says 'Now look Louis I've got something in my pocket that could mean trouble,' out he pulls a great big joint all neatly wrapped. 'Hey man,' I said, 'we can't be in any more trouble than we are in right now,' so we lit-up and smoked our way out of trouble. Now when the other cats in their cells caught the smell of the stuff they all started shouting out about passing it around, but old Cook and myself we demolished the evidence.

Soon after, Mr Collins got us out on some condition that we play a broadcast before we left town. The place was so crowded I had to climb over the floor to get to where I had to play, and do you know some of those crackers who'd given us all the trouble were sitting down there on the floor applauding louder than anyone, strange. It was there that I laid the one on the Police Chief by dedicating *I'll Be Glad When You're Dead You Rascal You* to him.

I'll never forget England and its people, so nice to me. Plenty of memories like Nat Gonella getting my pants pressed for me so that I could go and meet the press. Met Hugues Panassié and all those cats all over Europe, they had rhythm clubs from one end to the other, before I knew where I was, I'd done 13 command performances. I couldn't speak the language, but I always say a note's a note in any language if you hit it on the nose.

After I came back from Europe the second time, I stayed around Chicago then Joe Glaser who I'd worked for at the Sunset became my manager. Our first contract was for ten years, after that we didn't bother, don't know whether I was right or wrong, but I was happy. He stuck by me, the best friend that I ever had.

Big bands could be a headache, but I had Zilner Randolph, Mike McKendrick, Joe Garland, Luis Russell, Teddy McRae along with me at various times, but big bands, small bands, everyone's got to live the same music. Joe Garland was one of the greatest musicians I ever worked with – he used to rehearse my big band. Like me, he couldn't stand hearing wrong notes, and even in a big band arrangement he would immediately hear a single wrong note. He wouldn't bawl anyone out, but he'd make a funny noise in his throat like 'err-umpp' then he'd look at the guy who'd played the wrong note, and that cat didn't need telling again. Made the band sound nice. Like I said I never have liked a wrong harmony, going right back to my earliest days singing in the quartet, as a kid it just came natural. I never was one for going on and on about the changes of a tune, if I've got my horn in my hand then let's go, all I want to do is hear that chord. I started to go through all that business of studying them big chords and harmonies way back, but then I found out I'd been playing them all the time. To me, it was like the idea of learning to say a greeting in each country I visit. Man, with all that studying and thinking about what's going to come next I'd ended up saying pleased to meet you in German when I got off the plane in Italy. When I say 'Good Evening Everybody', they know I *mean* it – same with the music, just do what come natural.

People say to me what do I think of when I'm playing. Well, I just think about all my happy days and memories and the notes come out, always had been that way. To me jazz has always got to be a happy music, you've got to love it to play it, I can't vouch for anyone else.

The old days were priceless. I had many good times on the road with the big band, lot of tours, but I could sleep anywhere, buses, trains, planes, grab it when you can. I enjoyed all the moments that I spent with Luis Russell and his band. The warmth, the feeling, the swing, the beat, everything there. They were all down to earth also. Regardless of what the critics said about us – I loved them and still remember them. Last time I saw King Oliver alive was when I had the big band, we were in Savannah, Georgia, me and the boys laid it on him best we could, but he died of a broken heart. He ended up his days in that part of the world, and not in New Orleans. From 1931 onwards I made many return dates to play in New Orleans all through the years, and I must say I had some wonderful welcomes. Bands turning out to meet me, lots of beer being drunk, made me feel good, funny thing used to be that a couple of days later I'd get a bill for the bands *and* the beer, but I wouldn't part with those memories for anything.

In 1949, when I was crowned 'King of the Zulus' that was a great honour, and the Mayor said to me 'Louis, I've always heard it said that you felt you would die happy if you were made King of the Zulus.' 'That's true I said that always was my ambition, all I hope is that the Lord don't take me too literally.'

I heard all the guys in New Orleans: Manual Perez,

241

Freddy Keppard, Bunk Johnson, but Joe Oliver was my man. I hear things that are supposed to be new but I heard Joe Oliver play them years ago. When I got to New York, I listened to everyone, always used to catch that B. A. Rolfe, and Vic D'Ippolito – a great first-chair man. Joe Smith could do so much with a plunger – made it sound like a human voice, Bubber Miley was another great plunger man, and Cootie Williams too. Bunny Berigan I always admired for his tone, soul, technique, his sense of phrasing. Red Allen, he played in my big band for a long while, he was one of Joe Oliver's boys. Roy Eldridge has power and a pair of chops out of this world, and of course Dizzy can really blow. Bobby Hackett, always lovely to listen to, makes it come out so pretty. Rex Stewart used to fascinate me, first time I ever heard him he was in a New York club alongside Joe Garland that was in the 1920's, he always seemed to be pressing the wrong valve down but the right note came out and I thought to myself that cat's got something going for him. Too many good men to name who I like to hear, but besides the solo I always like to hear a good lead-trumpet in a big band – that first chair is so important. Scad Hemphill was a great lead. In my big band, whenever we had a new man coming in on first, I liked to try and make him feel at home – have a nice talk before he played his first date with us. Never forget the night that Fats Ford joined, he came into the room and we shook hands. 'Well Louis,' he says, 'I want you to know that I start out on top F.' Wump! but he could play all right.

As to the All Stars, forming that band from the big band was just like a rabbit in a briar patch – I started out in small combos. The All Stars opened up at Billy Berg's Club on the West Coast. Barney, Big Sid, Jack, they'll never be another Jack Teagarden, little later Earl came in for Dick Cary, then we had Cozy Cole, Billy Kyle. Clarinet men, Peanuts, Joe Darensbourg, Buster Bailey – on the road with me 40 years after we'd first played together – now wasn't that something – Ed Hall. We must have travelled oh so many thousand miles, some didn't want that much, to each his own. Joe Muranyi joined on clarinet, at first I used to get his name by thinking of it as Joe Ma-Rainey. Lucille was with me on most of the tours, she remembers it all so clearly. Trummy saw a lot of those miles too, Tyree Glenn came in when Trummy settled in Hawaii, that's where Danny Barcelona's from. But all that travelling doesn't wear a man out if he keeps in the right frame of mind, last time we heard Trummy in Hawaii he was still blowing his arse off. Velma was along as vocalist, and doing the show with me – that beautiful smile. The bass men, fine Morty Corb from the Coast, Jack Lesberg, Buddy Catlett, and Arvell Shaw for a long time.

Not too long ago, during my lay-off, I went to hear Arvell Shaw with his trio giving a show in aid of retarded children. We talked over all those one-nighters and touring days. Freezing cold sometimes, but making one-nighters so long got used to changing climates – no bother. Coldest I've ever been was once in North Dakota – seemed to be as cold as they tell me it is in Siberia. Funny how it turned out, that day it was so cold that I didn't even want to get up out of bed, there and then this tune came to me – I couldn't get it out of my head. I said to myself well if you don't get up now you'll never remember it. I got up and wrote the thing out – *Someday You'll Be Sorry*. Lucille called out, 'Hey Pops are you alright,' worried at seeing me jump straight out of bed and start writing music.

Music's my language, on all those trips all over the world, maybe the musicians can't speak with you, but play *Struttin' With Some Barbecue* and they'll know their parts and chime right in. All the trumpet players in Japan gave a dinner for me, I took off my shoes and sat down with them. I met the President of this country and that, travelled all over. When I was in Ghana I saw a lady who looked just like my mother.

I don't dive into politics, haven't voted since I've lived in New York, ain't no use messing with something you don't know anything about. A cat came up to me once and asked about the Big Four, I said I just hope that combo has

243

good time. As far as religion, I'm a Baptist *and* a good friend of the Pope, and I always wear a Jewish Star for luck. Those people who make the restrictions, they don't know nothing about music, it's no crime for cats of any colour to get together and blow. Race-conscious jazz musicians? Nobody could be who really knew their horns and loved the music. I hope that all my tours made people happy, and maybe helped· them to understand certain things a little more. I got used to people asking me all sorts of, well, crude questions – maybe I was the first of my kind that they'd ever talked to. Education's gonna sort out so many problems. We'd finished playing our shows in Japan, and someone got talking and saying how much he'd loved the music, and how sorry he was that we had to all go back to Alabama. He was being serious, not rude, he'd just been reading all the wrong books I guess. Serious, Alabama? Velma and me just cracked-up.

I feel the crowd with me when I get that first hand as I get up on the stand, then it's up to me to play. No use getting up there drunk. Once on a big spectacular with the All Stars we had a lot of time off before the finale. The trombone-man had played our set just fine, but then with a lot of time spare he'd been given a whole lot of gin by someone else in the band. When we got back on stage to sign-off with *Sleepy Time Down South*, man, you should have heard it – it was so rare that things got like that with us. And the musician who'd been filling the glasses full, he was the first one to criticize. 'What the hell's he doing with that slide' he said. 'I think I know the cause of the trouble' was all I said. Silence. I've been on the road too long for that kind of hassle, next night everything fine. Another time, we started a show, and while we're playing one of the men leaned across and said, 'Pops, I'm just too drunk to make it tonight, I've just downed four big Martinis.' All I said was 'Next time, stick to two.' No use exploding, carry on as though nothing has happened, the public don't want to share a hangover. Don't care what people do as long as they don't mess with my music. Joe Glaser selected the men, set their salaries and kept them happy, I don't know what they got, but they know I'm the leader, that way I've got a band at all times.

The public's ready to give you a hand for anything you play good, whatever you play – play it good. Ain't no such thing as getting tired of playing a number, Paul Robeson, when he got up to sing *Old Man River*, may have been a million times, but he sung it good. When I used to take a dozen or more choruses, I'd be playing for the musicians urging me on for one more chorus, but there's people all over the world, they like to hear that lead. Ain't no sense playing a hundred notes if one will do, Joe Oliver always used to say 'Think about that lead.'

You'll always get critics of showmanship. Critics in England say I was a clown, but a clown, that's hard. If you make people chuckle a little; it's happiness to me to see people happy, and most of the people who criticize don't know one note from another. I came off one night after playing *Tenderly* I think it was, and this man got all steamed up with me. He said 'I heard you playing that love song, and I'd hoped you were going to play some of the great old jazz tunes you did in the 1930's.' 'Hell,' I said, 'I recorded *Confessin'* about that time and that sure ain't a hate song.'

My illness meant I had the longest lay-off I'd ever had. Twice under intensive care in four months. I came within an inch of cutting out from the world so naturally everything to do with my 70th birthday was all happiness. People all over the world were just wonderful. I sang at the big celebration concert on the Coast, but I'd been warming up on trumpet for months every night before my dinner. All my biggest selling records have been singing but the singing and the horn have always gone together with me, so as soon as the doctor gave the word the All Stars came up to my home and we rehearsed there. In September we went to play for two weeks at the International, Las Vegas, Tyree and the guys back with me, and we enjoyed that, first time I'd ever worked with Pearl Bailey and she gassed me.

People ask me about the scars on my chops, after 56 years of playing, what do they think? I don't care how they look, that's my embouchure, put the mouthpiece in the groove. Take care of my chops, teeth and everything, I've gone through life trying to stay healthy. No regrets about not having children, travelling too much to raise a family as one. I never want to be anything more than I am, what I don't have I don't need. My home with Lucille is good, but you don't see me in no big estates and yachts, that ain't gonna play your horn for you. When the guys come from taking a walk around the estate they ain't got no breath to blow that horn.

I've got a million happy memories, and in my home, all the tapes of radio shows, records of everything I ever did. I'm satisfied with my work – I play music – you call it what you want to, I don't try to prove nothing.

Louis on Record

John Chilton

Legend is quick to attach itself to early jazz history. We are always being reminded of the superhuman prowess of musicians whose skills had faded or gone before the recording era began. Fortunately, Louis Armstrong's unique artistry is amply documented for posterity by a recording career spanning 47 years. But imagine if Louis had been born 50 years earlier, and the only indication of his talents was in the memories passed to our generation by word of mouth. Think of a worthy veteran recounting what had been told to him by his elders: 'Now, Louis Armstrong, well, he was the greatest jazz trumpeter who ever lived, absolutely the most skilful and creative improviser – he had range, power, tone – he was the finest soloist and the best lead, and don't forget that he was also the most influential jazz vocalist.' If this amalgamation of superlatives was presented only by hearsay, then even the most romantic jazz buff might be sceptical. Amazingly, all these assessments are true, and readily evident on many of the thousand and more records that feature Louis' playing and singing.

The man was undoubtedly the most important and influential figure in jazz. There can be few areas of human activity where an individual has had such a dominating role. His playing more than revolutionized jazz, it virtually established the whole structure and technique of jazz improvisation. Staccato solos, harmonically naive, and full of simple, jerky syncopations were the hallmarks of early 'hot' improvisations. They were superseded by the creative majesty of Louis' phrasing. Solos with undreamed-of emotional and technical range flowed effortlessly from his horn. His creativity and harmonic sense revealed new potentials to arrangers; his rhythmic phrasing influenced every jazz instrumentalist.

Many of the great jazz trumpeters have openly acknowledged their debt to Louis. Rex Stewart has told of his complete dedication to Armstrong – even trying to dress from head-to-toe like the great man. Henry 'Red' Allen recalled his youthful impatience when waiting for the original release of the Hot Five recordings, and Roy Eldridge has described his overwhelming emotions on first hearing Louis in person. Bunny Berigan decreed that the two essentials for a travelling jazz musician were a toothbrush and a photograph of Louis. Bix Beiderbecke said that Louis was a god, and Max Kaminsky echoed him: 'I'm very religious, I worship Louis.'

Louis began his recording career with King Oliver's Creole Jazz Band; on 31 March 1923 he waxed his first solo. In addition to the exquisite 24 bars on *Chimes Blues* we hear Louis revealing a concept and interpretation of improvised second-cornet parts that has never been equalled.

The solo on *Chimes Blues* is unmistakeably individual, but Louis' execution of it is not typical of his later work. There is an air of precision in the phrasing and articulation that suggests the solo was carefully worked out – understandable in that this was his recording debut. However, in the last two bars of the solo Louis relaxes, shifting the emphasis of the beat in a masterly fashion – and with this phrase emphatically places his calling card in the hall of fame.

The fact that the Creole Band was never adequately recorded is one of the greatest losses for the jazz listener. Admittedly the OKeh sessions are more clearly recorded than the Gennetts, but even so, we are only given hints of the full-blooded sound that this wonderful ensemble must have produced. The emphasis is on ensemble playing – usually on tunes that contain several different themes. Though careful rehearsal must have been responsible for the disciplined polyphony at which the band excels, the listener never hears anything that sounds stilted. Clarinettist Johnny Dodds plays superb counterpoint as well as creating solos full of intense feeling. Trombonist Honore Dutrey is sonorously effective, but on recorded evidence was not in the same class as the rest of the front line. His solo excursions are ponderous, and he occasionally plays alarmingly out of tune. At times the sturdy rhythm section is at odds over harmonic progressions, but it is carping to single out minor defects, for the factor that places this unit among the greatest of all jazz bands is the strength and inventiveness of its cornetists. The uniqueness of the duo is apparent both in ensemble and in their exciting shared breaks.

There isn't a trace of rigidity in Louis' playing of the second-cornet parts. Previously, when two cornets had played together, individual freedom was minimal, and the two parts moved like Siamese twins. Louis' intuitive musicianship enabled him to alter this procedure. He gave another voice to the traditional three-piece front line, but he did this without impairing the band's cohesion. Any example of Louis and King Oliver playing together is an object lesson in musical team-work. On *High Society Rag* (where Louis plays in the chorus preceding the bridge passage), and on *Riverside Blues*, we hear that Louis' concept of time is quite different from Oliver's. Yet he never tries to usurp his mentor by pulling the lead part away, nor does he attempt to superimpose his phrasing on Oliver's.

Louis is given a fair allocation of solo space, and on *Tears* is strongly featured in a long series of well-taken breaks. It is interesting to note that one of them recurs virtually unchanged in Louis' masterly *Potato Head Blues*, recorded four years later.

Louis' work with Fletcher Henderson proved that he

could fit into a more orthodox brass team with ease. He was unobtrusive in the section, but showed complete individuality in solos. If he was at all apprehensive of the celebrated musical company that he joined he shows no signs of it on his first recording with the band. On *Go 'Long Mule* (October 1924) he is in sparkling form. During the 7th and 8th bars of his solo he plays a perfect linking phrase, avoiding the rigidity that affected many soloists of that period, who stiffly marked time, awaiting the next 8-bar tune pattern before embarking on their follow-up phrase.

Elsewhere in this book, it is made clear that Louis' stay with Henderson was less joyous than jazz historians would have us believe. The only indication that he gives of being aware of Joe Smith's existence is on *Shanghai Shuffle*. Here the original arrangement was perhaps conceived to accommodate a Joe Smith solo. Don Redman may have suggested this to Louis, for he plays his chorus into a loosely-held plunger mute. For me, it is one of the least satisfying of Louis' solos. His entry after Redman's oboe passage is relaxed enough, but as the solo progresses one suspects that Louis feels miscast. In a rare spate of fidgety phrasing he lapses into a series of repetitive octave jumps. Muggsy Spanier was later to use this device regularly with telling effect, but in Louis' solo it seems inappropriate. During the last 8 bars, Louis mispitches several notes, through the plunger being held too close to the bell of the cornet. The inference is that Louis was proving a point, for on the previous day he had shown superb plunger control on Clarence Williams' *Everybody Loves My Baby*. The experiment was not repeated, and on all the other recordings with Henderson Louis fiercely maintains his own identity. His interpretation of *Meanest Kind of Blues* is completely dissimilar to Joe Smith's who had recorded the same tune with Henderson three months earlier. Both versions encapsulate fine jazz performances – each entirely different in concept.

The impact of Louis' style was to transform the New York jazz scene. It is fascinating to hear how his arrival

250

accelerated the development of Coleman Hawkins' tenor-saxophone playing. On *Naughty Man* Hawkins precedes Louis and one feels him groping for the poise and sense of form that distinguish Louis' solos.

Louis dominated almost every Henderson record of that period, *Bye And Bye, When You Do What You Do* and *One Of These Days* being supreme examples. On the last-named he plays a 32-bar chorus close to the melody; the tune itself is excellent but Louis' variations are superior music. On all these solos, the brilliance of his tone is high-lighted when his ill-matching colleagues Howard Scott and Elmer Chambers re-enter. When Joe Smith rejoined the band, to play alongside Louis, the section work greatly improves. But comparison between, *T.N.T.* (from Louis' final session with Henderson) and *Go 'Long Mule* fail to show that Louis' skills were dramatically improved by his 12 months in New York. The rhythmic freedom is more discernible, the technical assurance more obvious and the incisive vibrato more controlled; nevertheless, it seems that his year with Henderson favoured the New York musicians more than Louis.

No one had the foresight to record a vocal chorus by Louis during his early stay in the north, but from the short coda on Henderson's *Everybody Loves Mv Baby* (November 1924) we get an inkling of the singing style that was to be as influential among jazz vocalists as his playing was among instrumentalists.

About this time another facet of Louis' enormous musical talent became apparent – his skill as an accompanist. Throughout the year in New York, Louis had many opportunities to project his immense feeling for the blues on recordings with Bessie Smith, Ma Rainey, Alberta Hunter, Virginia Liston and others. This work falls into two categories: sessions where Louis shares the accompaniment with piano or organ, and others where he is joined by one or more front-line instrumentalists.

The duos consistently produce the most satisfying results, simply because Louis is able to establish a closer

251

link with the vocalist. There are magic moments in the larger ensembles, but the less cluttered sessions produce Louis' best work. Years with Oliver had developed his innate harmonic sense, and in larger accompanying groups we can hear him change his direction in mid-phrase as he realizes that the culmination of his intended line will double the same note being played by one of the other musicians. This problem doesn't arise on the sides with piano accompaniment, for Louis is free to give his full attention to the singer, and accordingly plays phrases that usually dovetail perfectly with the vocal performance.

On the Ma Rainey session for Paramount (October 1924) certain band passages have the semblance of a rehearsed arrangement, but there are several musical collisions during the 'free' ensembles. These failings, added to the indifferent recording, do less than justice to what was one of the outstanding unions of that era – the combination of Ma Rainey's superb voice and Louis' accompaniments. None of the cornetist's phrases obstruct the singer, but it's sad that Louis never had the opportunity to work with this great blues artiste in a less crowded studio.

In recent years, reviewers of reissues have criticized some of Louis' accompaniments to Bessie Smith. In one of her few printed pronouncements, Bessie praised the sides with Louis, but to the instant confusion of discographers gave a hefty back-handed compliment by saying that the playing was 'too pretty for Louis' and was actually by Joe Smith. It seems that Bessie, like Jelly Róll Morton and many others, took little interest in the documentary side of her recordings. The Bessie sessions fall almost evenly into the two categories mentioned: five titles have Fred Longshaw (piano or harmonium) sharing duties with Louis, while on the other four trombonist Charlie Green is added. *St Louis Blues* remains the masterpiece – if superior trumpet accompaniment exists, then I've missed out. Louis' rapport with the singer is peerless; it extends beyond the selection of notes and their rhythmic placement; the mood is in exact accord and Louis' use of dynamics skilfully highlights the

Empress of the Blues' magnificent voice.

At this period only two volume markings were usually observed when backing singers – loud and soft. But listen to the dozen or more shadings of volume that Louis puts into his performance. His introduction to *Sobbin' Hearted Blues* sets the mood perfectly. I suspect that the lesser moments on the session, where Louis (completely out of character) plays wa-wa effects on a Harmon-type mute, were incorporated on the advice of Bessie's musical director, Fred Longshaw.

The sessions shared with Charlie Green are less noteworthy, nevertheless they rank among the high spots of blues accompaniment. Green (a fine accompanist in his own right) and Louis find themselves in a situation where only telepathy or intensive rehearsals could have produced cohesion. Bessie's sessions were assembled with an informality that was casual to the point of being haphazard, as Demas Dean, who accompanied Bessie on a session made in February 1928, explained. On this particular day, Demas was whiling away time outside the Lafayette Theater when Charlie Green approached and asked if he'd seen Joe Smith. Demas replied no, whereupon Big Charlie said 'Well, there's a record date with Bessie Smith, go get your horn, you're on it.'

Doubtless the sessions with Louis were accorded more planning, but not much, as an alternate take of *Careless Love* reveals. In the last chorus, the instrumental routine has a different order – not, I suspect, by design. This explains an unusual phrase in one of Louis' answers to the singer; he ends the lead-in on a major third – not perfect for continuity but explicable if one thinks of Louis being suddenly pitchforked into a different part of the sequence.

As a blues singer, Maggie Jones can never be compared to Bessie Smith or Ma Rainey, yet one can understand why Louis had a soft spot for his work on his recordings with her. He puts implicit trust in spontaneity and his accompaniments are brimful of interesting experiments. His daring solo on *Anybody Here Want To Try My Cabbage?*

creates an anxious moment in Fletcher Henderson's usually firm but staid accompaniment – an indication that the pianist feels this time Louis has become inextricably entangled in his own complex syncopations. Louis, however, is in full command of the situation and emphasizes this with a perfectly played entry cue for the vocalist. In the last eight bars Louis shows just how relaxed he was on these sessions. He backs the vocal line with a quiet low-register phrase that is almost as fast as anything he ever played.

Much has been written about Louis' pioneering use of high notes in jazz improvisation, but he was also one of the first to improvise in the lowest register of the trumpet. The notes below C had been playable (and played) ever since the valved trumpet came into existence, but very few early instrumentalists used them except to play the lower notes of a melody. On many of the 1924–5 blues sides Louis shows the potential of low register playing by regularly improvising fat-toned phrases full of bottom Gs, A flats and As.

While in New York, Louis played on several sessions organized by Clarence Williams. Williams' musical skills were limited, but as a session-organizer he was as shrewd as they come; wise enough to capitalize on the fact that the two greatest improvisers of the era, Armstrong and Sidney Bechet (both working in New York), could be brought together in a recording studio. Realizing that there was more than a possibility of up-staging, Williams took fastidious care in allocating an even amount of solo space to the two giants. To hear the musical thrust and parry of these two men, both pioneering the same concept of swing, is one of the great jazz listening experiences. Both submerge individual aspiration during the ensembles, but come solo time and each is out to cap the other's performance. On *Texas Moaner Blues* (the first of the series) Louis plays a gem of a solo and brings it to conclusion with a downward run covering almost two octaves. Bechet, to combine power with invention, takes his chorus on soprano saxophone, and promptly inserts an ascending double octave glissando. He returns to clarinet for the final chorus, and again both masters pool their talents for a classic example of ensemble rapport.

Mandy Make Up Your Mind is remarkable from many aspects, not the least being that it contains the only sarrusophone performance in jazz. Bechet's musicianship enables him to be almost dextrous on this unwieldy double-reeded hybrid. The sight, let alone the sound, of the performance could have turned the record into a hokum offering. A lesser musician than Louis might have been tempted to 'cod' a solo alongside this instrumental rarity. But Louis, who throughout his career seemed incapable of playing corny phrases, turns in a delightful lilting obbligato to Bechet's low-note excursions.

Louis and Bechet recorded two versions of *Cake Walkin' Babies* in January 1925, both full of interest. For the Gennett recording, the tune is played in G concert, to assist the vocal ranges of 'Beatty and Todd'. Again, each man takes a rigidly allotted amount of solo space, but there is nothing rigid about the solos. Bechet plays a break in suspended time, so daring that it would have thrown most of his contemporaries off balance. However, Louis' perfect sense of rhythm picks up the lead at exactly the right tempo. He was a man born to swing; his amazing feel for the exact pulse of a tune never deserted him, but remained a constant source of wonderment to his colleagues. Years later, a drummer in the All Stars habitually played breaks at a speed that didn't quite relate to the piece being performed. Unperturbed, Louis always crackled in with an emphatic phrase that re-established the correct tempo.

Despite the absence of Bechet's stimulating presence, Louis continued to play with great inspiration on his last sessions with Clarence Williams (October 1925). On *Livin' High* (following a charming vocal by the musicianly Eva Taylor) Louis begins the last chorus with a fiercely played top C; then his masterful ensemble sense enables him to perceive that the band is beginning to lurch, so he plays the second half of the chorus an octave down and stomps the band into cohesion.

Two other Louis sessions from 1924–5 (recorded in vastly different musical surroundings) need mentioning. The Red Onion Jazz Babies' *Terrible Blues* and *Santa Claus Blues*, recorded for Gennett (with Lil Armstrong on piano), seem the prototypes of the Hot Five recordings, and as such would have served the rival OKeh company with a demonstration of the potential of a small group led by Louis. Both instrumentation and format are identical to the early Hot Fives (recorded a year later). Buster Bailey, Buddy Christian and Charlie Irvis do not measure up to Dodds, St Cyr and Ory as individualists, but Bailey plays particularly well; fresh from Chicago, he obviously has many of Johnny Dodds' phrases still ringing in his ears.

The differences in sound and style between the Red Onions and the Corona Dance Band are too many to enumerate. The circumstances behind Louis recording two numbers with the pseudonymous big band (rumoured to be a Sam Lanin outfit sprinkled with Henderson alumni) have never been established. The session affords little chance to identify individuals, but Louis' presence is indisputable. He doesn't play in the brass section and thus his entry in *I Miss My Swiss* is a perfect example of instant ignition. The 16-bar solo, played against solid off-beat drumming, is dramatically different from the music that precedes and follows it, proving that the young genius could create masterly solos regardless of musical company.

Within days of returning to Chicago, Louis recommenced his recording career, playing sessions with Blanche Calloway, Hociel Thomas and Chippie Hill. He was to record regularly with Chippie Hill (in company with Richard M. Jones) during the following 12 months, and an analysis of these sessions demolishes the theory that as Louis' technique increased so he paid less heed to his duties as an accompanist. On the earlier sessions he is poorly recorded and sounds less effective, but his phrases on *Trouble In Mind* (February 1926) repay attentive listening. On the November 1926 session, however, the balance problems have been overcome and we are able to hear Louis' fulsome tone to great effect. *Pleadin' For The Blues* ranks among his finest efforts, both in the call-and-answer phrases with the singer and in the beautifully constructed solo. His playing on *Pratt City Blues*, recorded immediately after *Pleadin'*, is less satisfying. Faced with providing another B-flat blues accompaniment in similar tempo, he seems determined not to repeat himself, and sets his sights on positive variations. However, he had just created an immortal solo, and on this occasion limits himself to one masterpiece.

The same trio recorded *Lovesick Blues*, notable for the exemplary way in which Louis matches his harmony part to the vibrato and timbre of Chippie Hill's humming. On *Lonesome Weary Blues*, from the same session, Louis starts his chorus with an uncomplicated series of phrases on a minor-third motif, yet each time he plays the blue note he inflects it in a fractionally different way, bending the notes exactly as though he were singing the solo.

Any changes that gave Louis extra prominence on the later blues accompaniments were part of the A & R man's plan. By May 1927 Louis' name was big business for OKeh, and the fact that he plays the final chorus on Sippie Wallace's *Lazy Man Blues* indicates that the company was trying to enhance the sales of the record by emphasizing Louis' presence.

OKeh was the first company to present Louis Armstrong as a bandleader. In late 1925 they contracted him to begin his famous series of Hot Five recordings. With the exception of Lillian Armstrong (née Hardin) all the musicians were from Louisiana. The initial session must have been something of a reunion, for Dodds, Johnny St Cyr and Armstrong had not worked with Kid Ory for over five years. The group only assembled for the recordings, and there is some supposition that Dodds and Ory were either intimidated by the leader's skills or wilfully given a backseat by Louis. Certainly Dodds usually played his best when he was in charge of a session, but he is close to top form on many of the Hot Fives.

The band was hand-picked and Louis had an obvious

respect for Dodds' skill; so much so that in the early Hot Five routines he gives more solo space to the clarinettist than to himself. On the very first title recorded, *My Heart* (originally written as a waltz), Dodds and Lil (the composer) share the 32-bar chorus; except when taking breaks, Louis contents himself in leading the ensemble. This is no isolated example. On *Yes I'm In The Barrel* Louis exhibits some superb plunger playing on the minor verse, then after a 12-bar ensemble gives Dodds two choruses, again restricting himself to breaks in the last eight bars. He takes a 12-bar solo on *Gut Bucket Blues*, as do Ory, Dodds and Lil, but on *Come Back Sweet Papa* he entrusts the main solo work to Dodds, who takes a whole chorus on alto saxophone. If anyone was shunning the limelight it was Louis, for although Dodds was a great jazz clarinettist his alto playing was poor, not only technically but also in jazz content. He seems so intent on mustering the right notes out of the instrument that the question of impassioned improvising never arises. Louis didn't need solo space to reveal his genius, for his lead playing abounds with fresh, startling ideas. He obviously revelled in working in an ensemble in which his front-line colleagues knew what to play and when to play it.

The group's February 1926 session produced six great jazz sides. On *Georgia Grind* Louis and Lil sing two choruses apiece, leaving the solo work to Ory. The solo space on *Heebie Jeebies* is given to Dodds. The next title recorded, *Cornet Chop Suey*, is the first of the Hot Fives on which Louis gives himself maximum solo room. It was one of the first jazz instrumental features ever recorded, and perhaps the first to be conceived, for Louis had composed (and copyrighted) the tune in February 1924 (while still with King Oliver). So much for those who contend that Louis' trip to New York served to polish up a very rough musical diamond. *Cornet Chop Suey* was originally marked for rejection, but OKeh was quick to alter its reservations about issuing the record when the success of Louis' first Hot Five recordings showed the sales potential of his name.

The three other titles from the morning's session were *Oriental Strut* (where Louis brings the piece to a mighty climax with a searing solo taken over stop-time breaks); *You're Next* (here he follows the incongruous piano introduction with a haunting interpretation of the minor verse); and the original version of *Muskrat Ramble*. The quality of performance on all six sides is remarkable, underlining Louis' powers of sustained creativity and lip-endurance.

Take into account the physical pressures that Louis worked under during this period. He often played four shows a day, yet managed to sound as fresh as a daisy on recording sessions. The scars on Louis' chops proved how wearing was the paying of these dues. Only on one occasion does the rigorous schedule take toll of the music. On 28 May 1926, he did two recording sessions, one with Erskine Tate's Vendome Orchestra, the other with Lil's Hot Shots (the Hot Five, renamed for contractual reasons). The Tate recording is revealing in that we hear Louis playing alongside his regular colleagues (including the outstanding pianist Teddy Weatherford) rather than recording with pick-up studio groups. Louis shows no restraint in his fiery breaks on *Static Strut*, and plays a dominating part in *Stomp Off Let's Go*. On the second session of the day, Louis gives out with some powerful blues hollering on *Georgia Bo-Bo*, but fatigue seems to overtake him on *Drop That Sack*. He muffs the introduction, and mispitches several notes in the ensemble. Nevertheless, by sheer determination and mouthpiece pressure he manages to produce a performance any other jazz trumpeter would be proud of. Louis settles an old score completely with his 1959 recording of the tune.

The Hot Five worked out their routines in the studio, and many of the tunes came to be organized in a markedly similar way: verse/chorus/solo/vocal/ensemble, with Louis taking the final breaks. *Dropping Shucks* is an example of this pattern. The companion title, *Who's It*, is in similar format, except that Louis plays the slide-whistle instead of singing. The jazz compensation for this novelty interlude is

259

the expressive chalumeau-register backing that Dodds gives to Louis. Louis' flexibility becomes increasingly apparent and some of the keys are chosen to allow him to project the melody with the full sonority of his upper register playing. How this strategy puts life into a 'dog' tune like *I'm Gonna Gitcha*!

The lack of variation in the band's routines didn't diminish the jazz content. Quite the contrary; the production number *King Of The Zulus*, with rehearsed introduction, backing figures and comic interjections from Clarence Babcock and Mr and Mrs Armstrong, is probably the Hot Five's poorest recording. Over-planning also mars *Jazz Lips*, in which there is a feeling of uncertainty within the group, and the glut of organized breaks impinges on the free-wheeling style at which the group excelled. Ory sounds ill at ease on *Jazz Lips* and *Skid-Dat-De-Dat*, but on *Big Butter And Egg Man*, from the same session, proves that he was the finest of all tail-gate trombonists.

On *Big Butter And Egg Man* we get some idea of what musicians mean when they say that everything about Louis is jazz. He literally swings the spoken word; his commentary following May Alix's vocal is so rhythmic that it becomes the perfect prelude for one of his greatest solos.

Ory is absent from the next Hot Five session (27 November 1926). His inadequate replacement (probably the late Hy Clark) begins his short stay with the group in a most inauspicious way, fluffing the very first note on the first title recorded, *You Made Me Love You When I Saw You Cry*. Throughout the session, the trombonist plays semi-breve notes wherever possible. This in itself would not have created serious problems, but unfortunately Johnny Dodds is poorly recorded, and, Louis' contributions apart, the session is unmemorable.

Four months elapsed before Louis recorded again. In April 1927, he made four titles with Jimmy Bertrand's Washboard Wizards (with Johnny Dodds as his front-line partner). Louis, having already been reprimanded for recording on Vocalion while under contract to OKeh, is said to have deliberately played quietly on this date in order to remain incognito. Certainly he restricts his volume on the lovely *I'm Goin' Huntin'*, but his individuality is so complete that a change of shoelaces would have been an equally effective disguise.

On the same day, Louis recorded under Johnny Dodds's leadership in the Black Bottom Stompers; within three weeks the two men were to swop leader roles and record three of the same titles. Both takes of *Wild Man Blues* from Dodds' session show Louis in a restrained, sombre mood; his own Hot Seven recording could aptly be called *Wilder Man Blues*. Although the arrangement is almost identical, Louis throws caution to the wind in a performance that is positively volcanic. The differences between the two groups' versions of *Melancholy* go beyond interpretation. The Dodds arrangement is more commerical, and Louis takes a solo close to the melody. For the Hot Seven session it becomes a vehicle for unrestrained improvising. *Weary Blues* was the other title that the groups shared; it is odd that Louis chose not to re-record his own composition *New Orleans Stomp*.

During a single week in May 1927 all but one of the Hot Seven recordings were made. Baby Dodds on drums and Pete Briggs on tuba were added to make the band into a septet. The group missed Ory's sturdy contrapuntal playing; trombonist John Thomas' performances were limp in comparison. But a week's recorded work by the colossus was enough to provide the jazz trumpeters of the world with dozens of musical phrases that have echoed and re-echoed ever since.

On *Potato Head Blues*, Louis makes a dramatic entry to what is consistently cited as the perfectly formed jazz solo. Musicologists look at the solo on paper and are enthralled, but no transcription can reveal the tonal beauty and the expressive vibrato that distinguishes Louis' rendering. There's a superb moment in the ninth and tenth bars where Louis emphasizes a phrase by reiterating the same note using alternate fingerings; thus poised he moves on and continues building the chorus to its climax.

Another session from the same week featured Louis with his own regular band – completely different in style and instrumentation from the studio-assembled Hot Seven. *Chicago Breakdown* gives us the only chance of hearing how Louis Armstrong's Stompers (then resident at the Sunset Café) sounded. Louis said that the band didn't rely on intricate arrangements, and this is borne out by the record. The line-up sounds unwieldy and the highspots are the solos by Earl Hines and Louis. This was a transitional period for Hines; there are only brief indications of the rhythmic independence that was to mark his later work. Louis takes two solos, one open and one muted, accompanied only by the guitar. Had the pianist shared the muted solo, we should have had a great opportunity to compare the respective developments of Earl's and Louis' playing in this pre-*Weather Bird* period.

During the fall of 1927, the original Hot Five recorded their last sessions together. By now there were discernible differences in Louis' approach, both instrumentally and vocally. His superb technique enabled him to project instantly the most complex ideas, much of the roughness had left his voice, and the new mellower qualities showed through on *Put 'Em Down Blues*.

Kid Ory was given the chance to re-record his famous *Creole Trombone* feature. Alas, the Kid was not in his sharpest form and it was left to Louis to whip up the excitement after the cumbrous trombone breaks. This title and *The Last Time* (which also contains minor 'goofs') were originally rejected, and remained in the vaults until George Avakian arranged for their issue in the early 1940s. There was no question of delaying the release of *Struttin' With Some Barbecue*, a fine tune by Lil which has deservedly become a jazz standard. Intro and coda were carefully arranged, in a manner akin to a white 'New York' session, but here the comparison ends, for the piece caught fire from the very first bar of the tune. The ensemble had a lovely, bright sound; Dodds and Ory share a chorus, then Louis soars into his stop-time solo with great panache and rhythmic assurance. *Got No Blues* lacked the same verve, but here Louis played his final phrases over a sustained chord, introducing an effect that was to feature on many of his later recordings.

Guitarist Lonnie Johnson 'guested' on three of the titles that the Hot Five recorded in December 1927, and his presence acted as a catalyst for Louis. Johnny Dodds plays superbly on *I'm Not Rough* but even this fine work is overshadowed by Lonnie's and Louis' solos. Neither Johnny St Cyr nor Lil adjust to Lonnie's concept of rhythm-playing, whereas Louis is stimulated by it. On *Hotter Than That* their kindred feel for the beat allows Louis to scat one of his most adventurous vocals, and inspires him to play one of his most oft-quoted solos. If the re-creation of a jazz phrase entitled the originator to a fee, then Louis would have made a cool million from *Hotter Than That* alone.

On the last title of the session, *Savoy Blues* (written by Kid Ory), the band follows the composer's chorus with a worked-out riff, then Louis zooms into a cluster of impassioned phrases that leave little room for Johnny Dodds to manoeuvre. Significantly, this recording marks the parting of the ways for these two. In retrospect, we hear that Louis' playing was constantly developing, rhythmically, harmonically and technically, during the two-year period in which the Hot Five recorded. In contrast, Dodds had already moulded his own completely individual style by 1925, and that style was to remain unchanged for the rest of his life.

Louis and Earl Hines had played together on several recordings (and residencies) prior to 1928, but from the summer of that year the linking of their talents was to be the chief factor in this phase of Louis' career. Earl plays on every recording that Louis made during the last six months of 1928. On the first session they play alongside Jimmie Noone and Mancy Carr accompanying Lillie Delk Christian, a singer whose vocals have a limited appeal. Her style, far removed from the blues, is well suited to the indifferent material she selected for her recording debut. Noone

263

usually worked in less robust company; he and Louis seem to have agreed to swap registers, for the clarinettist rarely plays harmonies above the trumpet. The same quartet backed Miss Christian on two later sessions and produced jazz performances that more than compensate for any vocal deficiencies.

The significance of the Armstrong–Hines partnership becomes clearly apparent on the first of the 'new' Hot Five sessions. The addition of the great drummer, Zutty Singleton, makes the group into a sextet. The other newcomers, Fred Robinson (trombone), Jimmy Strong (clarinet and tenor saxophone) and Mancy Carr (banjo and guitar), were all competent musicians but the immortal jazz comes from Louis and Earl. These two giants bring forth their innovations in a spirit of competitive co-operation, flamboyantly exploring previously untravelled musical paths, each out to surprise and inspire the other with rival daring.

Fireworks, the group's first recording, is aptly named. The tune is taken at a faster tempo than anything the previous Hot Five recorded. The sextet give a nod to tradition in the first 16 bars, then rely on a sketched-out arrangement with Louis' solo well showcased by crisply played off-beat figures. On *Skip The Gutter*, Louis and Earl started throwing ideas at each other in a manner that was new to jazz. Their colleagues wisely kept well out of the way, for many of the phrases are as explosive as hand-grenades. A day later, the group recorded a masterpiece, *West End Blues*. Louis' introduction is electrifying; judged solely on the basis of composition it is truly a great moment in 20th-century music. Louis plays every one of the twelve notes of the chromatic scale within the cadenza, but resolves them with such skill that the listener is in no doubt that the phrases are firmly introducing the key of E flat. Many jazz trumpeters have tried to meet the technical challenge of this cadenza, but even the most skilful imitators are never able to capture the nuances of timing that were Louis' and Louis' alone. In the opening low-register chorus his concept of form is again obvious; he ends the 12 bars with an ascending phrase that

264

provides the perfect link for the following solo. The last chorus is full of majestic blues stanzas that ring out as his phrases descend from top C.

In *Don't Jive Me* we have a perfect example of Hines' revolutionary technique. His attack on the single-note runs and the pulsating tremolos suggest the articulation and vibrato of a trumpeter, or rather *the* trumpeter.

In July 1928, all the members of the Hot Five recorded with Carroll Dickerson's Orchestra, the eleven-piece ensemble in which they earned their daily bread. On *Symphonic Raps* Hines plays a dazzling solo, then Louis, spurred on by the fervour of Zutty's drumming, takes over. The band hits a few clinkers in the last chorus, but overall it is in command of what was, for the period, a complex arrangement. The companion title, *Savoyagers Stomp*, is a streamlining (by Louis and Earl) of the first theme of *Muskrat Ramble*. Earl is again at his most adventurous; Louis is less daring, but the two men's achievements give a sense of direction to an arrangement that certainly wasn't conceived as a show-stopper.

The OKeh company's recording schedules seem to have been organized in a way that eliminated continuity. At times, Louis was in the studio on several consecutive days, then, despite being resident in Chicago, not called on to record for months on end. After one of these long gaps, the Hot Five (by now renamed The Savoy Ballroom Five) began their last series of recordings.

Don Redman is added (on alto and clarinet) for the last three sessions. He was never in the front-rank of jazz improvisers, but the inspiration of the company brings forth one of his best-ever solos on *Heah Me Talkin' To Ya*. The prime reason for bringing him down from Detroit was for him to provide arrangements for the group. However, the best arrangement of the series comes from the lesser-known Alex Hill. His artistic *Beau Koo Jack* prods Louis' musical intellect and the trumpeter responds with a lucid example of his powers of thematic development.

On one of the last sessions that Louis made before going

to New York, he again enhances Lillie Delk Christian's vocals. On *I Must Have That Man* (December 1928), he provides peerless accompaniment by playing a series of muted arpeggios that underline the harmonic changes of the tune – guiding the young vocaliste through her performance. When we realize that this was recorded just seven days after he'd waxed the incredibly technical *Weather Bird* duet with Earl Hines, we get some idea of the man's immense sensitivity and versatility.

During the following spring, Louis paid a brief visit to New York. On 5 March 1929 he was booked to record two titles with Luis Russell's band. All the previous night was spent celebrating with welcoming musicians, black and white. Louis, with his fellow-revellers still in tow, arrived at the studio early. The party's warm-up on the impromptu blues *Knockin' A Jug* was mercifully recorded for posterity by the enterprising studio engineer. It was Louis' first recording with Jack Teagarden, a man who was to become one of his favourite partners; their playing on the record reflects the mutual admiration.

The session with Russell's band was also an instant success. Louis' vocal on *I Can't Give You Anything But Love* is the epitome of tenderness, and he follows it with a series of rhapsodic variations of the tune before dramatically ascending to a high-note finale. The team then produced the definitive version of *Mahogany Hall Stomp*. Lonnie Johnson is present, and with Paul Barbarin on drums and 'Pops' Foster on string bass we hear Louis working happily with a 'home town' rhythm section. Doubtless, if Louis hadn't been tied to OKeh, he could have spent every available moment in various recording studios. He was fitted into a Seger Ellis date to good effect by the Dorsey Brothers – two of the many admirers that Louis had in New York's white musical fraternity.

Louis temporarily returned to Chicago, then moved back to New York with the full Carroll Dickerson unit as travelling companions. In July 1929, a contingent from the band backed Victoria Spivey. Louis' approach to the session is an example of his absolute professionalism. He makes no attempt to 'hog' the date, carefully avoiding spectacular phrases that might lessen the impact of the vocaliste's performance.

The success ratio of Louis' New York recordings with Carroll Dickerson's band is high. Many of the tunes were from contemporary shows, including *Ain't Misbehavin'*, where Louis ingeniously increases then decreases the sense of tension engendered during his playing of the middle eight. His ending phrase on *Black and Blue* is simple, but intensely poignant. Of both *Some Of These Days* and *When You're Smiling* we have two takes, vocal and non-vocal, each revealing multiple variations. On *When You're Smiling* he plays the last chorus close to the melody, but takes it up an octave, soaring effortlessly to his high F in the closing bars. The backing band is solid rather than sensational, but Louis benefits from the superior material. He could always make a poor tune sound good, but he could also make a good tune sound great.

Outside circumstances soon caused the break-up of the Dickerson orchestra and Louis found himself reunited with Luis Russell's band. Whereas the Dickerson arrangements were specially tailored to feature Louis, on many of the early recordings with Russell, Louis plays a 'guest' part in arrangements that were part of that band's regular repertoire. This produces exciting moments on *I Ain't Got Nobody*, where Louis and Henry 'Red' Allen indulge in some no-punches-pulled sparring. Though 'Red' was well on the way to his goal of complete individualism, on these dates he deliberately plays in the Louis manner. The initial release of *St Louis Blues* prompted one British critic to suggest half-heartedly that Louis played and sang at the same time, rather than concede that any other trumpeter could sound so much like Louis.

The shared vocal on *Rockin' Chair* was to become a perennial in Louis' future programmes. On Armstrong's first recording of the tune, the seated worthy's lines are sung (very melodramatically) by the composer, Hoagy Carmichael. The lusty sound of Higginbotham's trombone is heard on several titles from this series. His fiery inventiveness is in stark contrast to the doleful efforts of the three white violinists (enlisted from the local theatre orchestra) who augment the band for *Song Of The Islands*. Their unco-ordinated scrapings fail to distract Louis who scats an expressive chorus and plays a muted solo of delicate beauty.

In April 1930, Louis recorded another trumpet–piano duet, his partner being the able Buck Washington. Alas, *Dear Old Southland* has none of the magic of *Weather Bird*. The tune, composed in 1921 by Creamer and Layton, has all the ingredients of an age-old plantation song. Louis' tone is well recorded, but there's a quasi-dramatic feel about the whole performance. On the same day, accompanied by the Mills Blue Rhythm Band, he sang his most uncharacteristic vocal. Even geniuses are not immune to the influences of mass media, and I can never hear *My Sweet* without thinking that Louis was subconsciously affected – albeit temporarily – by Al Jolson's singing. This anomaly occurs only once. On *Exactly Like You*, recorded soon after with the same cast, Louis sings and phrases in his own inimitable manner.

Louis moved to the West Coast in the summer of 1930. His first session in Los Angeles was with the famous country singer Jimmie Rodgers. How this improbable partnership came into being remains one of jazz's unsolvable riddles. An unknown pianist is also present (definitely not Earl Hines or Lil Armstrong). Restrained authority marks Louis' solo; in the backings he sounds apprehensive while contending with the problem of following the singer's markedly individual concept of bar lines. The date was a semi-informal moment in Louis' crowded career. Understandably he could not recall the circumstances leading up to the session, but he clearly remembers making the record. In 1970, when Louis had just finished recording a country-and-western album, someone asked him if this was a change of policy on his part. 'No change for me, daddy,' said the great man, 'I was doing that same kind of work 40 years ago.'

Louis' engagements in California were at Sebastian's Cotton Club in Culver City. The Club's resident orchestra back him on the remainder of his West Coast recordings. The saxophone scoring on the arrangements (by Charlie Lawrence, Russ Morgan and others) is often dismissed as being Lombardo-ish and unhelpful to Louis. Certainly most of the adventure comes from Louis, but the unrestrained improvisations show how happy he felt about the backings. If one had to pick a dozen consecutive sides to depict Louis' amazing consistency they would be the twelve from this period.

Several of the young accompanying musicians had witnessed Louis' live performances in Chicago during the '20s. One of them was Lionel Hampton, and how Hamp responded to the stimulation of working with his boyhood hero! The band only boasted one major soloist, trombonist Lawrence Brown, but Louis and Hamp combine with a dynamism that gets everyone swinging, particularly on *I'm A Ding Dong Daddy From Dumas* where a series of scalding breaks cascades from Louis' trumpet. The medium-paced *You're Driving Me Crazy* also romps along in fine style, and a second take shows that the band's soloists – inspired by Louis' example – weren't content to rely on set solos. The informal start to this number gives us a memento of the good-humoured verbal introductions that Louis provided for the night-club clientele. Louis is at his most sublime on the slow ballads. His interpretations of *I'm Confessin'*, *One Hour*, *Just A Gigolo* and *Sweethearts On Parade* have given generations of jazz trumpeters ready-made features.

Louis returned to Chicago in the spring of 1931. A big band was assembled and rehearsed by trumpeter Zilner Randolph, and for the next year this was to be Louis' regular accompanying unit. Its personnel remained more stable than the level of its recorded performances. All the musicians were recruited in Chicago; three of them, Tubby Hall, Preston Jackson and Johnny Lindsey, were New Orleans expatriates. The work of these men in smaller

269

groups has justifiably been praised over the years, but no one except Louis plays anything memorable on the 1931–2 performances. Certainly few records in jazz convey a more joyful group-spirit than *Lonesome Road*; but the band's performances are remarkably uneven, considering they were a regularly working unit. They sound most effective on slow material, and we hear masterful performances from Louis on several tunes that were to become regulars in his future programmes: *Sleepy Time Down South, Georgia* and *Lazy River*.

Neither Louis nor the band was well served by the arrangements – except *Little Joe*, which is scored with care and attention. A series of good saxophone figures highlights Louis' muted playing, and allows him space to play telling double-time phrases unhampered. The arrangement comes off well in the studio. It provided Louis with a backing that did justice to his inventiveness, allowing him to interpret the theme exactly as he chose, without having to contend with a saxophone section staunchly pumping the straight melody into his ears.

Another arrangement that seems tailored for the recording studio is *You Can Depend On Me*. Here the only thing of merit is Louis' vocal, backed by the second trumpeter's pleasant obbligato. The pace is slow, yet still there's an abundance of wrong notes from the band, who sound very ragged and ill at ease in the last chorus. After a poorish middle eight by the saxophones, Louis is reduced to playing a series of incongruous siren-like effects before a walking bass figure fades out the recording. It is the nadir of the band's performances, and is analysed to emphasize that Louis didn't need elaborate arrangements to produce works of everlasting magnificence. On the previous day he had recorded one of his greatest solos on *Stardust*, where the band's backing duties consisted solely of playing percussively accented minims. All three takes are brilliant, take 3 being the masterpiece. The trumpet playing is impassioned, and the vocal purely improvisatory, scarcely touching Carmichael's melody – or, at times, the lyrics. The bold way in which Louis' vocals reshaped well-known tunes into personal musical statements was to inspire countless jazz singers.

Louis' last recordings with the group took place in March 1932, and the year spent together hadn't really improved the band. On *Love You Funny Thing* Louis hollers 'bring it out!' to the saxophones, and for once, it sounds as though he might not be kidding.

Louis changed record companies shortly after his triumphant 1932 tour of Europe. Victor was quick to underline Louis' potential 'star' quality by getting him to record 'A Medley of Armstrong Hits', in which he was cast primarily as a vocalist. His horn is silent on *You Rascal, You*; he sings (and plays) on *Sleepy Time*; a drum break then leads into a one-chorus tear-up on *Nobody's Sweetheart*. This tune is the odd one out in the selection, for Louis had never recorded it before; perhaps the unusual 40-bar melody fitted Victor's plan to give listeners maximum playing time. Louis doesn't play on *When You're Smiling*, but sings the lyrics in a very light-hearted fashion. The linking of this with *St James' Infirmary* gives him no chance to establish the elegiac mood. In consequence, he keeps on smiling right through the usually sombre theme.

The trumpet work behind Louis' vocals (played by the band's leader, Charlie Gaines) is interesting. Usually trumpeters who backed Louis were so overwhelmed by his presence that they tried, and usually failed, to play Louis-like phrases as accompaniment figures; but here Gaines plays in a very individual way. Louis takes the last two choruses on trumpet then modulates for the band to lunge into *Dinah*. Here he sings the choruses exactly as though he were improvising on trumpet, even injecting some of the horn quotes that he reserved for this sequence (ranging from *Lady Be Good* to *Pagliacci*). The band stick bravely to their written parts while Louis scats out an amazing stream of complex syncopations. His one chorus on trumpet is a brilliantly conceived miniature of the *tour de force* that he had recorded with the Mills Blue Rhythm Band.

271

The four titles made a week later, with Chick Webb's Band, are all of a high standard. On *That's My Home* a subdued vocal from Louis precedes his intense trumpet solo in which he brings forth vehement phrases that spark the entire band. Again an alternate take indicates that Louis' store of ideas seemed inexhaustible. Neatly-led saxes give Louis firm support during his lively vocal on *Hobo You Can't Ride This Train*. Elmer Williams plays a full-toned tenor-saxophone solo before Charlie Green, in driving form, gets the maximum effect from the minimum amount of notes. Louis isn't perfectly placed for balance, but still comes cutting through on every track, and in his solo on *Hobo* plays a virtuoso series of perfectly controlled lip trills. On *I Hate To Leave You Now*, Louis plays the melody with an unusual mute, probably borrowed from one of the brass section. His fine vocal is again aided by bright, in-tune saxophone playing, and by good trumpet fill-ins, and his last phrases create the perfect ending. The only inappropriate thing on the session is the unaccompanied trumpet introduction to *You'll Wish You'd Never Been Born* (*You Rascal, You* thinly disguised). Louis probably varied this for each performance, but the take caught on record doesn't seem to have much to do with the theme.

Shortly afterwards, Louis returned to Chicago where Zilner Randolph again assembled a band to back him. It was a better all-round unit than the 1931 band, and three of its soloists – Keg Johnson, Budd Johnson and Teddy Wilson – were able to take some of the brunt from Louis' shoulders.

The rhythm men work together with more cohesion. Banjoist–guitarist Mike McKendrick's style of playing high inversions – which left a gap in the overall sound of the earlier rhythm section – fits nicely with the young Teddy Wilson's chording. The saxophone team is consistently more impressive than the brass section.

The new band began by recording four consecutive slow tunes, all featuring Louis vocals. On *I've Got The World On A String* Louis takes a relaxed muted solo following

Wilson's succinct piano introduction. He stays close to the melody but adroitly weaves in unexpected notes that make the most of the tune's interesting harmonic sequence. In the middle eight he stretches out the time values of the melody and in doing so creates a subtle flow of suspensions that

273

enhances the tune. *I've Got A Right To Sing The Blues* is a breath-taking example of instant composition. Louis begins his solo by filling the break-space with a single low-register note, and this quiet beginning heralds the climactic improvising that follows.

On *Sittin' In The Dark* we get a clear indication of the immense gulf between Louis' phrasing and the work of his colleagues. The brass section sounds positively stilted in the four-bar passages that serve as introduction and bridge to Louis' solo. The master prefaces his solo by playing two notes on the beat – at least, that is how they would be presented in musical notation, but the impetus that Louis gives to these two notes defies transcription. Budd Johnson solos well. Though Louis' ending is technically impressive (descending and ascending glissandi) it is not this theatrical finale but the two clarion-like notes that are the quintessence of the man's genius.

The band goes into a faster tempo for its version of *High Society*. On this title Louis leads the brass section and the difference is immediately apparent. He sits out the penultimate chorus, and a colleague, plainly overawed by what has gone before, plays in a nervous manner. Louis then unleashes a chorus frantic enough to indicate that he had overstretched himself on the session. However, master of the unexpected, he unites stamina and skill on the last title of the day, *He's A Son Of The South*. He again takes the first trumpet part and tops a fine performance with a spine-tingling coda played over the saxophones' sustained chord.

In April 1933, the band made its last two recordings. Changes had taken place in the personnel and the style of the band had also altered; the brass section was relegated to a subsidiary role in the arrangements. (No great loss to the listener.) The improved saxophones make the most of their chances, and on *I Wonder Who* phrase their 16-bar passage in a manner almost worthy of a Benny Carter section. Louis sings (or talks) on all eleven titles recorded. One of them, *Laughin' Louis*, is a personality presentation rather than an inspired jazz offering. Aesthetes have criticized Louis for waxing this title; they fail to see the issue in perspective. It presented the general public with a recorded example of Louis' personal exuberance as a performer and bandleader. King Oliver had proved that the recording of great jazz performances alone didn't automatically ensure 'house-full' signs. This image-building was vital, for at that time Louis was the only jazz soloist regularly fronting a touring band. His versatility proved to the moguls of the entertainment world that a jazzman could tour with his own regular big band and survive. Thus he paved the way for the success that many band-leading jazz soloists were to enjoy later in the same decade.

Sweet Sue is also dismissed as hokum by those who like their jazz strait-laced. For me [J.C.], it contains one of the session's outstanding moments. At the beginning of Budd Johnson's 'viper-language' middle eight, Louis answers the 'muta mumblings' with some fantastically imaginative vocal phrases. Impromptu ideas fashioned for that particular moment, they remain a timeless example of Louis' supreme gift of spontaneity.

Louis' return to Europe meant a big break in his recording career. Excepting the Paris session of October 1934, he was absent from recording studios from April 1933 until October 1935. A private recording of early 1935, made at the Chicago home of trumpeter Bob Burnet (with Zutty Singleton, Joe Rushton and Charles LaVere), used to exist but was destroyed years ago.

In October 1935 Louis and Luis Russell's Orchestra renewed old ties and began working together regularly. From the first of these recordings we become aware of a new phase in Louis' development. His phrasing is sparser, the expressive vibrato broadens the impact of his notes; gone are the double-time flights that featured regularly in his earlier work. The economy of notes is deceptively simple, for if anything the subtleties of timing become even more intricate and awe-inspiring. His superb attack and range were unchanged, as he shows in the climb to high G in *Solitude.*

The masterful placement of notes in Louis' playing and singing gave a musical significance to what were only pop tunes of the day. His telling mixture of staccato and legato phrases on *Treasure Island*, and the full-toned impact of *Falling In Love With You*, make evanescent Tin Pan Alley themes unforgettable.

By the mid-'30s, Louis' harmonic approach was set, though his improvisations were as spontaneous and inventive as ever. During the 1935 recordings with Luis Russell he occasionally flirts with 'new' harmonies – the whole-tone-scale run on *I've Got My Fingers Crossed* – the vocal finish on *Old Man Mose*, where he hinges a phrase on the 13th note of the chord – but these are mere whims of the moment rather than the restless efforts of a musician set on an experimental course.

The big failing in the initial stages of the reunion is the band's performance. Time and time again Louis plays his heart out while the rest of the ensemble seems to be trundling its way through the parts. We hear brief solos from Charlie Holmes, Greely Walton, Bingie Madison and Jimmy Archey, but the excitement and intensity that were synonymous with Russell's earlier bands is missing. Many of the arrangements were second-rate and even the more thoughtfully scored *Got A Brand New Suit* falls away badly and it is left to Louis to make the record memorable.

Louis thought these were some of his happiest moments, and he stoutly defended all of the recordings with Luis Russell. Naturally, the band was delighted to share the stand with Louis, but the mutual joy doesn't come through on the 1935 recordings. On *Red Sails In The Sunset*, Louis plays 24 muted bars full of deep poignancy, but the band finishes off the chorus with eight bars of groan-worthy playing.

From 1936 until 1940 Louis played on many records without the Luis Russell Band. During this period he was featured with a wide variety of backings, most of the partnerships being brainchildren of Decca's Jack Kapp. At the time, the choice of company provoked the critics, but in

276

retrospect we hear some marvellous examples of Louis' versatility. Throughout his career, he smiled his way through many critical assaults; he answered them with music that made nonsense of the critics' contentions. At the time that his playing was being dismissed as a series of high-note frenzies he was recording some of his most restrained and plaintive work with the Mills Brothers.

With the exception of the regular sessions with the Mills Brothers (musically and commercially successful) all the ideas were one-shot try-outs. Louis' tasks ranged from singing and playing with Hawaiian bands to the resurrection of an age-old comedy monologue entitled *Elder Eatmore's Sermon*. Sessions with white studio groups produced a fine *I'm Putting All My Eggs In One Basket* (1936) and a superlative version of *Ain't Misbehavin'*. There was also one date with the Casa Loma Orchestra. In 1939, this unusual pairing produced two sides. On *Lazybones*, Louis is featured only as a vocalist (Grady Watts taking the trumpet solos), but on *Rockin' Chair* he had an expansive trumpet solo that is much more than a perfunctory re-creation of his earlier recordings. His vocal partner on this version is Pee Wee Hunt (singing the 'pappy role' *à la* Jack Teagarden).

In summer 1936, in connection with the film *Pennies From Heaven*, Louis made some records accompanied by Jimmy Dorsey's Orchestra. This band seemed determined to give its best for Louis, and in doing so tried hard, perhaps to hard, to swing. The two-beat feel on *Dippermouth Blues* isn't as relaxed as it might have been; nevertheless Louis rips out some interesting variants on the three 'classic' Oliver choruses. Here he shuns the mute and plays the choruses open, over shot-figures from the band. This was more than just another record date for Dorsey, and his groan of disappointment can be heard as the band goofs during Louis' last chorus. *The Skeleton In The Closet*, from the same session, is a feature for Louis. (For British release the Skeleton was prudishly placed in the Cupboard to avoid any suggestion of lavatorial necrophilia.) A longer version of the feature (taken from the film) is now available on LP and is the only instance of a sound-track version of a tune that is superior to Louis' record – simply because the film version is longer, allowing Louis, as ever, to make inventive use of the extended time. On the same LP we hear two versions of *Shine*, one from 1931, the other from 1941. They afford us a perfect chance to hear how the intervening years had changed Louis' approach to the tune. The earlier version is quite frenetic. People who have seen the film *Rhapsody In Black And Blue* will remember the sequence where Louis, dressed in a leopard-skin ensemble, looks for all the world like a lithe middleweight boxing champion. In the later film Louis' apparel and his playing are more dignified. Neither rendition matches up to the *Shine* that he recorded in California with Les Hite in 1931. The LP's best offering after *Skeleton* is an excerpt from the film *Jam Session* in which Louis plays and sings *I Can't Give You Anything But Love*; there's an unexpected twist at the end of his solo, when he rises to a top F, then floats up to a B flat above top C before the large studio-band engulfs him.

By the summer of 1937, the Luis Russell band had been greatly strengthened by the re-enlistment of three of the old guard – Henry Allen, Albert Nicholas and J. C. Higginbotham. Shelton Hemphill was brought in on lead trumpet and the huge improvement is immediately apparent on the revised personnel's first recordings, *Public Melody Number One* and *Yours And Mine*. The brass section at last sounds full and confident. When Louis swaps phrases with the band there isn't the dreadful drop in tension that blemishes so many of the earlier records.

At the end of the '30s, Louis re-recorded many of his earlier successes, and each new version revealed a fresh approach. *Struttin' With Some Barbecue* was one of the Hot Five's most brilliant recordings, yet on the 1938 version Louis gives the composition thrilling new dimensions. In the first of his choruses he punches out the melody with a prodigious swing, then rides out the final chorus with incredible vitality and invention. The chorus culminates with an astonishing series of phrases, in which a combina-

278

tion of lip flexibility and half-valving – and genius – produces an effect that neither Louis nor anyone else ever repeated.

By 1938, Louis was being featured on record as a vocalist, *sans* trumpet. The importance of his influence on vocalists has been stressed; there is no mystery about why his singing was such a decisive force, for all the qualities that distinguish his trumpet work are ever-present in his vocals.

Early in 1939, drummer Sid Catlett took Paul Barbarin's place in the Luis Russell band. This rhythmic whirlwind debuts with the band on the January 1939 session that produced *Jeepers Creepers* and *What Is This Thing Called Swing?* These releases were aimed at the general public rather than the jazz fans, but there isn't a single Louis record (*Eatmore's Sermon* apart) that isn't a jazz performance. When Louis phrases a tune like *Jeepers Creepers* he does so in his own inimitable manner, and no one else in the entire realms of jazz could communicate more with that melody. Three months later, he again re-recorded a batch of his 'good old good ones' and here Catlett really comes into his own. His presence and Joe Garland's direction of the band's phrasing and dynamics turn a good band into an excellent one. On *Heah Me Talkin' To Ya* Louis is obviously stimulated by Catlett's off-beat 'sock' phrasing and shares an exhilarating coda with him. The success of the new partnership is also apparent on the new versions of *Save It Pretty Mama, Savoy Blues* and *West End Blues.* The latter is based on the 1928 recording, complete with opening cadenza. Mid-way through the record, Louis follows a short piano interlude with a magnificently conceived blues chorus. A drum fill-in from Catlett leads him into a re-creation of the 1928 finale with the ending altered to accommodate a new coda.

On all the 1939–41 recordings the band is more flexible and versatile than before, and, except for some suspect intonation in the saxophone section on *Wolverine Blues,* plays consistently in tune. *Wolverine* is a minor triumph for Louis; he doesn't enter until the fourth chorus, but from that moment the record comes to life. Occasionally the band performs novelty chores like *Cain And Abel* and *You Run Your Mouth* (a piece seemingly devoid of melody), but records like the instrumental *When It's Sleepy Time Down South* and the driving *You Rascal, You* more than compensate. The sombre intensity that marks Louis' playing in the minor keys is perfectly featured in his brief solo on the 1941 recording of *Don't You Call That A Buddy*? On these 1941 recordings the old-established arranging format of introduction/vocal/solos/trumpet chorus was gradually disappearing. Occasionally the change is too drastic; *Leap Frog* is an ordinary 32-bar riff tune that could have come from any one of a dozen crotchet factories. The band makes the most of the material; there's an effective contrasting of tone-colours as Joe Garland on bass saxophone plays answers to the derby-muted brass section, but Louis only enters for the last eight bars, and for all the band's steadily acquired prowess it is still Louis' playing and singing that are the vital elements in the Decca recordings.

Purists still view the entire Decca period with suspicion. To them, Louis' proper place was in a three-piece front line of trumpet, trombone and clarinet. But, excepting recording sessions, less than 12 months of the first 40 years of his life were spent working with that instrumentation. Louis' unmistakable individuality precludes pseudonymity, but I conjecture that if any one of his Decca recordings could be convincingly put forward as the only example of the work of an anonymous trumpeter, then that mystery man would be hailed by all the detractors as a jazz genius.

Louis did some small-band recordings in the early '40s, notably those with Sidney Bechet. The partnership did not yield the exciting rapport that had marked the earlier shared recordings, but individually both giants were in great form.

The American Federation of Musicians' recording ban meant an enforced gap in everyone's recording career, but several of Louis' performances from 1944 have been reissued, taken either from V-Discs or from radio transcriptions. An example is the Esquire Metropolitan Opera House Concert (on which Louis shared a bill packed with great jazzmen, including Roy Eldridge and Barney Bigard). We hear the first version of *Back O' Town Blues* and more of Louis' variations on *I Can't Give You Anything But Love*. Unflustered by a false start he changes microphones, and, although this move places him further from the rhythm section, he plays a powerful chorus strongly supported by the indomitable Sid Catlett. Art Tatum provides Louis with ultra-attentive backing for his 16-bar solo on Jack Teagarden's feature *I've Got A Right To Sing The Blues*. On *Basin Street Blues,* Coleman Hawkins – reunited on record with Louis after 20 years – is in brilliant form. Louis follows Hawkins and for once almost sets out on the wrong foot, then plays a very positive solo that leads Jack Teagarden into the concluding verse.

Another airshot shows Louis' 1944 big band in action. The repertoire blends old favourites like *Lazy River* with hit tunes of the period such as *Blues In The Night*. One of these wartime favourites, *I've Got A Gal In Kalamazoo,* brings the best out of Louis. The strangest item is the swing-style revamping of *Dear Old Southland*. A modern approach is obvious in some of the sidesmen's solos, but Louis doesn't stint solo space to his younger colleagues. On *Perdido* (recorded at an army base in Pennsylvania in September 1944) he makes a point of featuring tenor-saxophonist Dexter Gordon. From the same date comes Louis' first record duet with Velma Middleton, *Is You Is Or Is You Ain't My Baby?* – it goes down well with the audience.

Superb relaxation marks Louis' 1945 studio recording of *I Wonder*. Here the fullness of his dynamic tone rings out over the low-register saxophone scoring. Somehow the popularity of this record deepened the schism between Louis' fans and others who bought his records. It was almost as though the fans couldn't bear to share Louis with the big wide world. Many said that Louis was 'too good' to be a popular artist – but they overlooked the fact that great

281

art can be enjoyed for all the 'wrong' reasons.

Louis continued to work with his own big band, but several 1946 sessions feature him with smaller line-ups. On the Esquire All Americans' date, organized by Leonard Feather, Louis takes a vocal on *Long Long Journey* then plays a mellow-toned blues chorus whose final phrases provide a perfect springboard for the next soloist – the great Johnny Hodges. Unfortunately this session is the only one that these two great exponents of blues-playing ever shared.

While filming on the West Coast, Louis headed two small studio groups: 'his Hot Seven' and 'his Dixieland Seven'. With the former he was ably assisted by the wry trombonist Vic Dickenson, his old comrade Zutty Singleton, and Barney Bigard. Dickenson and Bigard back Louis' vocals superbly and help produce a well-integrated ensemble sound. On the next date, Kid Ory, Minor Hall and Budd Scott replace Dickenson, Singleton and Allen Reuss. This is not the rugged Ory of 1926, or of 1956. Two of the tunes have 'New Orleans' in their titles. Conceivably, nostalgia for the Crescent City produced a lump in Ory's throat that made it impossible for him to play with any gusto. His fellow Louisianians seem unaffected; Louis and Minor Hall are outstanding. I maintain that Ory, at his best, was the finest of all ensemble trombonists, but I have to suspend my belief when listening to his maudlin efforts on this date.

The stage was gradually being set for Louis to work regularly with a small group. In February 1947 his concert date with Ed Hall's Sextet produced yet another fine version of *St Louis Blues*. Soon afterwards he was to take part in one of the most famous of all live recordings. The success of the New York Town Hall Concert meant that the planning of an all-star group became a reality. The happy atmosphere of this memorable jazz event comes through on every released track, and one regrets only that all the recordings made at this concert have not been issued.

The All Stars made their official debut in August 1947, and by the end of that year had recorded many titles. The music was superb, and for a time, all seemed well with critics, jazz fans and general audiences. But once the delight of seeing Louis on stage with such stellar talents as Earl Hines, Barney Bigard, Sid Catlett and Jack Teagarden had worn thin, a concert by the All Stars was almost guaranteed to produce either veiled or direct criticism. Personnel changes were inevitable in such a mobile unit. Trummy Young, Billy Kyle, Ed Hall, Peanuts Hucko, Arvell Shaw, Cozy Cole and others did great work with the group, but it was presentation rather than personnels that caused most of the snide remarks which nudged their way into reviews during the '50s.

Much of the adverse comment seemed based on the assumption that on each and every public performance Louis was duty bound to pack his programme with tunes he had recorded 25 years earlier. There was dismay when he included show tunes and popular ballads – yet this was no departure for Louis; he had always selected his repertoire that way.

The showmanship that had ever been a feature of Louis' stage work seemed suddenly to prevent critics from judging the performances aurally. Pundits said that Louis had lost the art of improvising. But the contention that a solo has to be spontaneous to be jazz was exploded long before Louis ever worked with the All Stars. Yet the same people who said that Louis' solos were musical gems, comparable to classical compositions, became petulant when he took them at their word and gave repeat performances in Hawaii and Hamburg. His solos do bear repetition; one phrase from Louis, taken from any period, is enough to remind us of his mastery. Knowledge and understanding of his art enabled him to present a series of variations that he considered to be his definitive solo on a particular theme. And who are we to doubt his wisdom? For that solo emerged from Louis' horn with all the intensity and jazz feeling of which he was capable. Louis was as dedicated to his audiences as they were to him, and he was determined, regardless of climate or conditions, that his public would hear a consistent and entertaining programme. The success of this policy is borne out by listening to live recordings by the All Stars, from all periods and places: *Muskrat Ramble* (Boston, 1947), *My Monday Date* (Pasadena, 1951), *All Of Me* (Milan, Italy, 1955).

In 1954, Louis and the All Stars recorded one of the great jazz albums, 'Louis Armstrong Plays W. C. Handy'. On this, Louis' brilliance surprised even his most dedicated admirers. Some of the material was familiar, but on several tracks he showcased Handy compositions that had been dormant for years, bearing out his colleagues' contention that his gift for interpreting fresh material was super-professional. His use of high notes was as effective as ever. Today, with scientific teaching methods, there are many high-note specialists, but no trumpeter has ever used the upper register to better effect than Louis.

The Fats Waller album was a brilliant follow-up, in which Louis did full justice to one of the greats. No one who had heard Louis' previous recordings of *Ain't Misbehavin'* would think that the genius had left anything unsaid on that sequence, yet on this album he proved that he had more to say. The timing, tone and variations of vibrato that he imparted to *Blue Turning Grey Over You* can be compared to his greatest achievements.

Unlike some veteran jazzmen, Louis had no contempt for his early recordings. In late 1956, he undertook the monumental task of recording his 'Musical Autobiography', again proving that he was supremely capable of revitalizing many of his earlier successes. The sheer quantity of material is amazing, and it is not sacrilegious to say that, in some instances, he improves on the original recordings. Here and there the passing of the years dictated that a key be lowered, but overall the effect is gigantic.

Throughout the All Stars era, Louis regularly took time out to record perennial favourites like *Blueberry Hill* and *La Vie En Rose*, and *Gone Fishin'* was one of his many successful collaborations with Bing Crosby. He also successfully shared record dates with stylists as diverse as

Dave Brubeck and the Dukes of Dixieland. There were several sessions with the Dukes. The group's trumpeter Frank Assunto has a fine command of his instrument, and plays interesting phrases with a good tone; he is, in fact, a very capable jazz trumpeter. On the dates with Louis, however, his part is that of the young student speaker given the task of introducing a world-famous orator. As for the Dukes' rhythm section, it was as united as delegates at a peace conference. Teddy Wilson once said that Louis, more than any other man in jazz, had the ability to pick up a whole group and carry it along with him. The May 1960 session amply proves his point. The Dukes of Dixieland will go into jazz history because of their dates with Louis, for by the very manner of their playing they induced Louis to throw the years aside. Never has the breadth of his tone been so faithfully recorded; even his top G on *Avalon* sounds huge. The thrilling two choruses on *Limehouse Blues* are projected with a spirit reminiscent of the Sunset Café days.

The great style with which Louis entered the '60s is also shown on the records which have Duke Ellington guesting with the All Stars. Louis' chorus on *The Beautiful American* bore testimony to his continued greatness. (The pianist is no slouch either.) His 1961 date with Dave Brubeck produced *Nomad*. Louis sings the exotic lyrics as though he'd known the song all his life, and his middle-register playing of the melody is the epitome of jazz interpretation.

In an age of marathon jazz performances, Louis could still create all the essentials of good jazz within the space of three minutes. He did this on the 1964 recording *It's Been A Long, Long Time*. The vocal is warm and rhythmic, and the concise trumpet solo is full of imagination, poise and presence. There isn't a superfluous note in the whole performance. The 1966 version of *Canal Street Blues* also shows the veteran's powers of eschewing musical irrelevances. Except for a brief clarinet solo by Buster Bailey, the All Stars' arrangement is entirely ensemble. In each successive chorus Louis embellishes the lead with countless subtle variations.

Mack The Knife was a big seller for Louis, but it was *Hello Dolly!* (recorded in late 1963) that took the sounds of Satchmo to millions of new listeners. To hear Louis play that show-tune in person was a perpetual treat; every live rendering had fresh variants. Louis thoroughly deserved the enormous popular success accorded to *Hello Dolly!*, and his *What A Wonderful World* proved that artistry is not an insurmountable obstacle to reaching the top of the Hit Parade.

Shortly before his 70th birthday, he recorded the 'Louis and His Friends' vocal album. Belying his age, he sang, with great ease and assurance, a wide selection of tunes, ranging from Duke Ellington's *Mood Indigo* to The Beatles' *Give Peace A Chance*. His artistry came through on every track, whether in waltz-time on *His Father Wore Long Hair*, or in swing-time for the biographical *Boy From New Orleans*. Eddie Condon, Ornette Coleman, Bobby Hackett, Miles Davis and a host of other jazzmen from all schools attended the recording session to pay homage to him. For Louis, Satchmo, Pops – call him what you will – was the most beloved of all jazzmen. His following was wide and it can only grow with time, for he is the one jazz immortal.

Travellin' *Man*

John Chilton

In May 1919 Louis left New Orleans by train to join Fate Marable's band, who were then preparing to play a summer season aboard Streckfus-line riverboats sailing out of St Louis. During the previous winter Louis had played occasional evening excursions with Marable on boats based in New Orleans. From February until May 1919, Louis also played regular gigs with Kid Ory's band. From June until September each year, Marable's band played excursions out of St Louis; from November until April they were based in New Orleans.

Louis left Fate Marable in September 1921 and returned to New Orleans. He worked in Tom Anderson's Cabaret Club before joining Zutty Singleton's Trio at the Fernandez Club. Louis also did street parade work, occasionally with the Silver Leaf Band and Allen's Brass Band, regularly with Oscar Celestin's Tuxedo Band. In the summer of 1922, he left New Orleans to join King Oliver's Creole Jazz Band (then playing at the Lincoln Gardens, Chicago).

1923 With King Oliver's Creole Jazz Band. Residency at the Lincoln Gardens until late February, then on tour: Illinois, Ohio and Indiana (where Louis made his first recordings – 31 March 1923). Band returned to Chicago and recommenced playing at the Lincoln Gardens.

1924 At the Lincoln Gardens until February, then toured through Ohio, Wisconsin, Michigan and Pennsylvania. Married Lillian Hardin in Chicago 5 February. Band returned to Chicago in May, then resumed touring: Illinois, Indiana, Pennsylvania. Louis left the band in June. Brief lay-off, then worked with Ollie Powers' band at Dreamland, Chicago, before journeying to New York in September to join Fletcher Henderson's Orchestra. With Henderson at the Roseland Ballroom, New York, from 13 October.

1925 With Henderson at the Roseland until 31 May – during this period the band also played many private engagements and theatre dates. Summer tour with Henderson: Connecticut, Maine, Maryland, Massachusetts and Pennsylvania. Resumed residency at the Roseland on 4 October. Early in November, Louis left Fletcher Henderson and

287

returned to Chicago, where he joined his wife's band, 'Lil Armstrong's Dreamland Syncopators'. On 12 November Louis made first of the 'Hot Five' recordings. From December began doubling by also playing engagements with Erskine Tate's Orchestra at the Vendome Theater, Chicago.

1926 Worked with Lil's band at Dreamland, and with Tate at the Vendome. Joined Carroll Dickerson's Orchestra at the Sunset Café in April (and there first met Joe Glaser), continued to double with Erskine Tate. Three-week vacation with Lil in Idlewild, Michigan (August). Continued to work with Dickerson and Tate for the remainder of the year; out of action through illness for part of December.

1927 Continued at Sunset Café with Carroll Dickerson until February, then began leading own big band, 'Louis Armstrong and his Stompers', at the same venue. Continued to double with Erskine Tate until April, from then on doubled with Clarence Jones' Orchestra at the Metropolitan Theater. Louis led at Sunset Café for most of the year; the band also worked at other Chicago venues, including a two-week stint at the Blackhawk in July. Continued to double with Clarence Jones until December. In November Louis, Earl Hines and Zutty Singleton opened their own night-club at the Warwick Hall (featuring Louis Armstrong's Hot Six). The ill-fated venture ended a few weeks later.

1928 In February, Louis again worked with Clarence Jones' Orchestra. In March he rejoined Carroll Dickerson (then at Savoy Ballroom), remained with Dickerson throughout the year, but occasionally worked as a soloist outside Chicago, including a two-day spell in May, fronting drummer Floyd Campbell's band on the *SS St Paul* out of St Louis.

1929 For the first five months of the year Louis and Carroll Dickerson worked regularly at the Savoy Ballroom, Chicago. They also did occasional one-night stands, including Graystone Ballroom, Detroit (January), St Louis (February) and Detroit (March). In March, Louis went to New York to guest for two days with Luis Russell's band; he returned to Chicago and resumed working with Dickerson; he also guested with Dave Peyton's Orchestra at the Regal Theater, Chicago (28 April to 4 May). Louis and Carroll Dickerson remained at the Savoy Ballroom, Chicago, until mid-May (they also played a one-nighter at the Paradise Ballroom, Cincinnati, on 7 May). In the third week of May, Louis and Carroll Dickerson barnstormed their way north. They picked up a few dates in New York, then Louis went to Philadelphia to rehearse with Fletcher Henderson's Orchestra for the Vincent Youmans show 'Great Day'. The reunion with Henderson ended at the rehearsals and Louis returned to New York to front Carroll Dickerson's band for engagements at the Savoy Ballroom (1 and 2 June). Subsequently, the band began a four-month residency at Connie's Inn, New York, on

24 June; when this engagement concluded the Dickerson band disbanded. From June, Louis began doubling by appearing in the show 'Hot Chocolates' accompanied by LeRoy Smith's Orchestra; he also did other theatre work – at the Lafayette (June and October), the Rockland Palace (November) and the Standard Theater, Philadelphia (December).

1930 Louis guested with Luis Russell's band for theatre dates in Washington, D.C., and Baltimore (January), Regal Theater, Chicago (February). In February he began a two-month season at the Coconut Grove, New York, accompanied by the Mills Blue Rhythm Band (then led by drummer William Lynch); the same musicians backed Louis for dates in Detroit, Baltimore, Philadelphia (April), Pittsburgh and Chicago (May), before returning to New York. Louis visited Chicago before moving on to California, where he was featured as a cabaret soloist at Frank Sebastian's Cotton Club in Culver City (from July). During this period, Johnny Collins became Louis' manager.

1931 Louis left California in March and returned to Chicago. In April he began a residency at the Show Boat in Chicago, leading a big band organized for him by trumpeter Zilner Randolph. In mid-May the band left Chicago and toured through Illinois, Kentucky, Ohio and West Virginia before playing a week's residency at the Graystone Ballroom, Detroit (23–29 May). The band played dates in Milwaukee and Minneapolis before commencing a three-month residency at the Surburban Gardens, New Orleans (mid-June). The band left Louisiana in September and played dates in Dallas, Oklahoma City, Houston, Memphis, St Louis, Columbus, Cincinnati, Chicago, Cleveland, Philadelphia, Washington and Baltimore, ending the year at the Lincoln Theater, Philadelphia.

1932 Theatre dates in New Haven, Jersey City, Boston and New York. Louis returned to Chicago in March and disbanded. In April, he again went to California to appear at Sebastian's Cotton Club. Returned to New York (via Chicago) and sailed for Europe aboard the *SS Majestic*, arriving in England on 14 July. Opened at the London Palladium on 18 July, then toured Britain – Glasgow, Nottingham, Liverpool, etc. Returned to New York in November, appeared in 'Connie's Hot Chocolates of 1932' at Lafayette Theater (26 November to 2 December). Accompanied by Chick Webb's band, played Pearl Theater, Philadelphia (3 to 10 December), Lincoln Theater, Philadelphia (17 to 24 December) and Howard Theater, Washington.

1933 After playing in Pittsburgh (14 January) returned to Chicago, where Zilner Randolph organized new accompanying band. Dates in Chicago, Louisville, Indianapolis, Omaha and Chicago, then disbanded. Louis played an eleven-day engagement at the Lincoln Theater, Philadelphia (with the Hardy Brothers' Band), 8–19 July, then left for

Europe. Opened in London at the Holborn Empire on 5 August. Jack Hylton became Louis' temporary manager on 30 September. Louis played engagements in Denmark, Sweden, Norway and Holland before returning to London in December.

1934 Toured Britain until April; moved to Paris for a long vacation before playing concerts there (November); toured Belgium, Switzerland and Italy.

1935 Louis returned to New York in late January; an injunction prevented him from fronting Chick Webb's band for dates at the Apollo Theater. Moved back to Chicago, where persistent lip (and managerial) troubles forced him temporarily to give up trumpet-playing. In the spring, he sang with Duke Ellington's band in Chicago (during a one-nighter), and also at an AFM reception given in his honour. Joe Glaser established as Louis' manager. New big band (directed by Zilner Randolph) formed for debut in Indianapolis (1 July). The band toured the mid-west and the south (including New Orleans), also played Pittsburgh, Detroit, Washington, and Apollo Theater, New York (September) before disbanding. Louis began working with Luis Russell's band (billed as 'Louis Armstrong and his Orchestra'); they began a residency at Connie's Inn on 29 October.

1936 At Connie's Inn until February; record-breaking week at Lincoln Theater, Philadelphia. Week at Apollo Theater (March); to Metropolitan, Boston, for new high figure for Louis and the band ($8,000 per week). Louis has tonsillectomy, resumes with successful theatre tour with band: Pittsburgh, New York (May), Detroit (June), St Louis and Chicago (July), Kansas City (August). Filming on the west coast in August, then Texas, Philadelphia, West Virginia (September), Chicago, Washington, Savannah (October), Chicago, New York, St Louis (November), Youngstown and Akron (December). Christmas vacation in Chicago.

1937 Louis spent a period in Provident Hospital, Chicago, for minor throat surgery (January), then dates in Omaha, Boston (February), Massachusetts and Pennsylvania (March), New York (April). Commenced radio series for Fleischmann's Yeast (9 April). Regal Theater, Chicago and Apollo, New York (May), Connecticut (June), Pittsburgh, Washington (July), Boston, then tour of south (September). Filming in Hollywood (October). Engagements in California (November and December).

1938 Louis and band conclude month's engagement at Cotton Club, Culver City, and play residency at Grand Terrace, Chicago, from 28 January until 9 March. Dates in Indianapolis, Pittsburgh, New York, Cincinnati, before six-week tour of the south, including New Orleans (June until August). Solo filming in Hollywood until 27 September, then joined band for tour of Mississippi, Louisiana, Alabama and

Georgia. Divorced from Lil (they had separated in 1931). Married Alpha Smith in Houston, Texas (October). Engagements in New Orleans, Memphis and Kansas City. Detroit, Chicago and Apollo, New York (December). Louis appeared as guest vocalist at Paul Whiteman's Christmas Eve Concert at Carnegie Hall.

1939 Appeared at Strand Theater, New York (January), then wide-ranging theatre and ballroom tours: Baltimore, Kansas City, Hartford, Buffalo, Olcott, Chicago, Lovejoy, Indianapolis, Atlanta, Madison, St Paul, Wrentham, Madison, Lincoln, Miami, Gadsden, Columbia, Owensburg, Dayton, Cleveland. Played at Golden Gate Ballroom, New York (19 October). Started long residency at Cotton Club, New York (7 October). Acting role as Bottom in the musical 'Swingin' The Dream'; the show opened at the Rockefeller Center Theater on 29 November and folded 16 days later.

1940 Ended Cotton Club residency on 5 April. Theatre work at State-Lake, Chicago (June), Apollo and Paramount, New York (July), before touring Alabama, Georgia, South Carolina and Iowa in August. In Chicago (September), California (October), Mississippi and Florida (November and December). Tenor-saxophonist Joe Garland appointed as Louis' musical director in late 1940; Luis Russell remained with the Orchestra.

1941–3 Coast-to-coast tours continue for Louis and his Orchestra. Engagements in Ontario, Canada (June 1941). Residency at Casa Manana, Culver City (March–April 1942). Louis divorced Alpha in 1942, and in the autumn of that year married his fourth wife Lucille Wilson; their marriage lasted until Louis' death.

1944–5 New big band formed to accompany Louis. Saxophonist Teddy McRae appointed as musical director. Louis starred at Esquire's Metropolitan Opera House concert in January 1944. Extensive touring of theatres, ballrooms and service bases. Residency at Zanzibar, New York (December 1944 to March 1945). Residencies in California (August–September) then continual touring. In January 1945, Louis took time out to appear in New Orleans at the Jazz Foundation Concert.

1946–7 Touring, then residency at the Aquarium, New York (April–May 1946), Apollo, New York, and Regal, Chicago (June), Savoy Ballroom, Chicago (August). To Hollywood for major acting role in the film *New Orleans*. Big band continues, but Louis also featured with Edmond Hall's Sextet at Carnegie Hall, New York, on 8 February 1947. Fronted small pick-up band for New York concerts on 18 February and 17 May. Louis entered hospital for extensive check-up, then played at Apollo, New York, in July. Official debut of the Louis Armstrong All Stars at Billy Berg's Club, Hollywood, on 13 August 1947. Later in the year the All Stars played concerts at the Chicago Civic Opera, the New

York Town Hall and the Symphony Hall, Boston. They ended the year playing a return booking at Billy Berg's Club.

1948–9 At Billy Berg's until 19 January. At the Roxy Theater, New York, prior to flying to France for appearances at the Nice Jazz Festival (February). Returned to tour United States. Carnegie Hall concert on 3 May 1948. Booking at first Los Angeles Dixieland Jubilee (October 1948). In January 1949, played inauguration ball for Governor Adlai Stevenson. Dates in Vancouver, BC (January–February). Dates in Louisiana (27–28 February) prior to Louis being crowned King of the Zulus for New Orleans Mardi Gras. Touring with All Stars included trip to Europe (September–November 1949). Residencies in Las Vegas, Los Angeles, Chicago, Detroit and New York, etc.

1950–5 Despite personnel changes the All Stars went from success to success. Regular film and TV appearances, continual bookings all over the United States and Canada. Toured Hawaii (February 1952) and Europe (September–November 1952). Took part in short-lived concert tour with Benny Goodman (April 1953). Toured Australia and Japan in 1954, Europe in late 1955.

1956–60 Toured Australia and Far East in spring of 1956. In May 1956 Louis returned to play in London, for the first time in 22 years. After May 1956 residency at the Empress Hall, he toured Britain with the All Stars; they then journeyed to Africa. In December 1956, Louis returned to London to make one solo appearance at Royal Festival Hall for the Hungarian Relief concert. Louis featured at the Newport Jazz Festival in 1957 and 1958. Extensive touring with the All Stars, including visit to South America (October 1957). A long European tour was interrupted by Louis' illness in Spoleto, Italy (June 1959). Within weeks, Louis was back in action and in late 1960, undertook a wide-ranging tour of Africa; he ended the year filming in Paris.

1961–7 More and more international demand for Louis and the All Stars. During this six-year period the group played dates in Africa, Australia, New Zealand, Mexico, Iceland, India, Singapore, Korea, Hawaii, Japan, Hong Kong, Formosa, east and west Germany, Czechoslovakia, Romania, Yugoslavia, Hungary, France, Holland, Scandinavia and Great Britain. Brief reunion with Kid Ory and Johnny St Cyr at 1962 'Dixieland at Disneyland' concert. In 1963, Louis played for John F. Kennedy at the Waldorf Astoria in New York. In 1964, Louis achieved enormous success with his recording of *Hello Dolly!* He spent part of March 1964 in the Beth Israel Hospital, New York, but played dates in Las Vegas later that month. In 1965, Louis returned from playing in eastern Europe on 9 April, took six weeks off for extensive dental surgery, then flew to Britain on 25 May for a concert tour. In October 1965, the All Stars played their first engagement in New

Orleans for 12 years – Louis was presented with a 'Key To The City'. House-full notices for All Stars in Montreal, Toronto, Las Vegas, Los Angeles and Atlantic City. From 8 July until 4 September 1966 the group did a summer season at the Jones Beach Marine Theater. Pneumonia put Louis out of action from 23 April until 23 June 1967; a month later he flew to one-nighters in Dublin, Antibes, St Tropez and Majorca.

1968 After engagements in Las Vegas, Los Angeles and Chicago, Louis and the All Stars flew to Italy for the San Remo Festival, returning to the United States on 8 February. After playing in Pennsylvania, Maine, Mexico City and New York, the All Stars appeared at the New Orleans Jazz Fest in June. Louis topped Hit Parades throughout the world with *What A Wonderful World*. Triumphant return to Britain for short season at the Variety Club, Batley, Yorkshire, from 17 June. In early July, Louis and the All Stars did concerts in London; a return to Britain was scheduled for December, but by September Louis was seriously ill in the Beth Israel Hospital in New York.

1969 Louis temporarily released from hospital in January, re-entered in February and remained there until April. By June, he was well enough to sing at a benefit for trumpeter Louis Metcalfe; in August he sang *Hello Dolly!* with Duke Ellington's band while they were appearing at the Rainbow Grill, New York. On 6 June, Louis' long-time manager Joe Glaser died. Louis recommenced recording on 23 October.

1970 Louis guested on many TV shows. In May he sang on the 'Louis And His Friends' LP and in August recorded a vocal 'Country and Western' album. He was the guest of honour at a special concert held at the Shrine Auditorium, Los Angeles, on 3 July. He sang at the 'Salute to Satch' night (10 July) at the Newport Jazz Festival. In September he resumed full schedule by playing and singing with the All Stars for a two-week engagement in Las Vegas. On 29 October he played and sang at a charity concert held in London, England. On 26 December he returned to Las Vegas to play a two-week engagement with the All Stars.

1971 Louis continued to appear on many TV shows; on 10 February he played and sang on the David Frost Show with Bing Crosby. In March, Louis and the All Stars played a two-week engagement at the Empire Room of the Waldorf Astoria in New York. Soon after concluding this engagement, Louis suffered a heart attack and entered the Beth Israel Hospital on 15 March. He was in the intensive care unit until mid-April, but left the hospital on 6 May. On 6 July at 5.30 am he died in his sleep at his home in Corona, New York. Rest In Peace, Louis.

Film List

ALL THE FILMS LISTED WERE MADE IN THE USA UNLESS DETAILED OTHERWISE

1931 *Ex-Flame*
1932 *Rhapsody in Black and Blue*
1932 *I'll Be Glad When You're Dead You Rascal You*
(a Betty Boop cartoon, part live, part animation)
1933 *Copenhagen Kalundborg*   Denmark
1936 *Pennies From Heaven*
1937 *Everyday's a Holiday*
1937 *Artists and Models*
1938 *Doctor Rhythm*
Louis' contribution to this film 'The Trumpet Player's Lament', was omitted from the generally released version.
1938 *Goin' Places*
1942 *Shine: Swingin' On Nothin': Sleepy Time Down South: I'll Be Glad When You're Dead You Rascal You*
('Soundies' – each film lasting four minutes)
1942 *Cabin in the Sky*
1944 *Atlantic City*
1944 *Jam Session*
1944 *Hollywood Canteen*
1945 *Pillow to Post*
1946 *New Orleans*
1948 *A Song is Born*
1949 *La Botta e Riposta*   Italy
1951 *The Strip*
1951 *Here Comes the Groom*
1952 *Glory Alley*
1953 *The Glenn Miller Story*
1956 *High Society*
1957 *Satchmo the Great*   On location
1958 *Jazz on a Summer's Day*
1959 *The Beat Generation*
1959 *Kaerlighedens Melodi (The Formula of Love)*   Denmark

1959	*The Five Pennies*	
1960	*La Paloma*	Germany
1960	*The Night Before the Premiere*	Germany
1960	*Auf Wiedersehen*	Germany
1961	*Paris Blues*	France and USA
1961	*Disneyland After Dark*	
1965	*Where the Boys Meet the Girls*	
1966	*A Man Called Adam*	
1969	*Hello Dolly*	

Index

Ahola, Sylvester, 157
Aitken, Gus, 190
Aldam, Jeff, 178
Alexander, Charlie, 153
Alix, May, 260
Allen, Fletcher, 163
Allen, Henry 'Red', 41, 115, 192, 195, 199, 215, 221, 242, 248, 267, 278
Allen, Walter C., 78
Anderson, Cat, 129
Anderson, Ernie, 25, 26–7, 28, 175, 200–1
Anderson, Gene, 122
Arago, G., 185
Archey, Jimmy, 190, 195, 276
Armstrong, Alpha (Smith), 110, 150, 167, 172, 177–9, 184, 197
Armstrong, Beatrice, 44, 55, 134
Armstrong, Clarence, 110, 122
Armstrong, Daisy (Parker), 58–9, 147
Armstrong, Josephine, 44, 55
Armstrong, Lil (Hardin), 73–4, 76–81, 83–4, 87–94, 98, 100, 101–2, 103, 105, 106–10, 122, 127, 137, 149–51, 157, 179, 188, 197, 235, 236, 256, 257, 258, 259, 260, 262, 263, 268
Armstrong, Lucille (Wilson), 15, 19, 24, 25, 29, 197–8, 204, 217, 222–3, 243, 246
Armstrong, Mayann, 33, 44, 46, 48, 55, 59, 77–8, 134, 227, 232–3
Armstrong, Willie, 44, 232–3
Assunto, Frank, 285
Avakian, George, 262

Babcock, Clarence, 260

Bacon, Louis, 190
Bailey, Buster, 66, 84, 88–9, 90, 95, 98, 220, 242
Bailey, Pearl, 245
Ball, Kenny, 39
Barbarin, Paul, 190, 195, 266, 279
Barcelona, Danny, 220, 243
Barefield, Eddie, 196
Barnet, Richard, 189
Basie, Count, 195
Bechet, Sidney, 35, 40–1, 45, 53, 105, 157, 193, 201, 202, 254–5, 280
Beiderbecke, Bix, 39, 61, 66, 126, 221, 248
Belair, Felix, 31
Berg, Billy, 242
Berigan, Bunny, 158, 191, 242, 248
Bermon, Len, 169
Bernie, Ben, 177
Berton, Vic, 133, 137
Bertrand, Jimmy, 260
Bigard, Barney, 16, 199, 201, 242, 281, 282, 283
Big Nose Sidney, 48
Black Benny, 54, 232
Black, Clarence, 118
Black, George, 160, 162
Blair, Lee, 190
Blesh, Rudi, 74, 81
Bolden, Buddy, 47, 233
Bolton, Happy, 48
Boone, Lester, 153
Bottoms, Bill, 101
Braud, Wellman, 122
Bricktop see Ada Smith
Briggs, Pete, 110, 112, 261

297

Brookins, Tommy, 69, 72, 84
Brooks, Percy Mathison, 48–9, 50, 168
Brown, Jewel, 220
Brown, Lawrence, 127, 131, 269
Browne, Scoville, 174, 189
Brubeck, Dave, 205, 285
Burnet, Bob, 275
Bushkin, Joe, 230
Butterbeans and Susie, 114

Caesar, Irving, 131
Calloway, Blanche, 256
Calloway, Cab, 158, 177
Campbell, Floyd, 118
Canetti, N. J., 185, 186
Capone, Al, 88, 121, 144
Cardew, Phil, 168
Carey, Mutt, 60, 85, 86–7
Carmichael, Hoagy, 267–8, 270
Carpenter, Charles, 149
Carr, Mancy, 122, 263, 264
Carter, Benny, 274
Cary, Dick, 200, 201, 242
Casa Loma Orchestra, 195, 196, 277
Casucci, Leonello, 131
Catlett, Buddy, 220, 243
Catlett, Sid, 16, 195, 200, 201, 242, 279, 281, 283
Cauldwell, Happy, 119
Celestin, Papa, 71
Chambers, Elmer, 251
Charters, Sam, 51, 53
Chittison, Herman, 185, 186
Christian, Buddy, 57, 256
Christian, Lillie Delk, 114, 263, 266
Clark, Hy, 260
Clay, Shirley, 110
Clayton, Buck, 129, 131–2
Clonisch, Gabriele, 196
Cole, Cozy, 242, 283
Coleman, Bill, 95–6, 115–16
Coleman, Ornette, 286
Collins, Johnny, 16, 140, 143, 153, 154, 157, 162, 166, 167–8, 169, 173, 176–7, 179, 180, 181, 183, 188, 238–9
Collins, Lee, 19
Collins, Mary, 152, 154
Condon, Eddie, 286

Cook, Sherman 'Professor', 147, 149, 153, 239
Cooke, Doc, 114
Corb, Morty, 243
Cotton Billy, 159, 166, 168
Cox, Ida, 60
Crane, Lionel, 222, 228
Creathe, Charlie, 121
Creathe, Marge, *see* Singleton, Marge
Crosby, Bing, 39, 196, 284
Crosby, Gary, 196
Crosby, Larry, 196
Curry, Bert, 122

Dankworth, Johnny, 221
Darensbourg, Joe, 242
Davis, Ben, 168, 169, 218
Davis, Bobby, 157
Davis, Leonard, 190
Davis, Lew, 168, 169
Davis, Miles, 286
Davis, Professor Peter, 52, 54, 232
Davison, Wild Bill, 115
Dean, Demas, 253
Delaunay, Charles, 186
Dickenson, Vic, 282
Dickerson, Carroll, 109, 110, 111, 117, 118, 119, 120, 122, 123, 124, 127, 238, 265, 266–7
Dickerson, Joe, 118
D'Ippolito, Vic, 242
Dodds, Warren 'Baby', 16, 19, 61, 62, 64, 80, 88, 261
Dodds, Johnny, 41, 60, 63, 64, 67, 81, 88, 111, 238, 249, 256, 257–8, 260–1, 263
Dorsey, Jimmy, 65, 127, 158, 191, 196, 266, 277
Dorsey, Tommy, 65, 127, 266
Driberg, Tom, 169
DuConge, Peter, 163, 185
Dukes of Dixieland, 196, 285
Dunbar, Rudolph, 162
Dunlap, Dick, 189
Dunlap, Louis, 149
Dunn, Johnny, 18, 108
Dutrey, Honore, 63, 64, 72, 88, 110, 249
Dutrey, Sam, 234

Eckstine, Billy, 40, 207, 225
Edwards, Bettie, 181

Eldridge, Roy, 242, 248, 281
Elizalde, Fred, 50
Elkins, Vernon, 127, 128, 129
Ellington, Duke, 23, 95, 123, 127, 158, 177, 188, 191, 195, 196, 197, 285, 286
Ellis, Seger, 266
Escudero, Ralph, 97

Fant, Eddie, 189
Farley, Max, 157
Fawkes, Wally, 30
Feather, Leonard, 37, 48, 205, 282
Featherstonhaugh, Buddy, 168
Ferguson, Alan, 169
Fern, E. A., 114
Filmer, Vic, 168
Finkelstein, Sidney, 130
Fitzgerald, Ella, 196, 215
Fletcher, Milton, 189
Ford, Fats, 242
Foster, Harry, 162
Foster, Pops, 190, 195, 197, 266
Fox, Barbara Coleman, 198
Fox, Roy, 168
Friendly, Fred, 31
Furness, Slim, 178

Gaines, Charlie, 271
Garland, Joe, 240, 242, 279
Gillespie, Dizzy, 108, 242
Glaser, Joe, 16, 17, 24, 25, 26, 28, 110–11, 117, 156, 188, 189, 199, 200, 202, 211, 215, 216, 221, 237, 240, 244–5
Glenn, Tyree, 220, 243
Goffin, Robert, 45, 65, 77, 102, 143, 145–6, 157, 162–3, 164, 172, 186
Gonella, Bruts, 161, 169, 175–6
Gonella, Nat, 39, 159, 161, 164, 168–9, 175–6, 178, 179, 183, 240
Gonsoulin (Gonzales), Bertha, 74, 75, 78
Goodman, Benny, 23, 195
Gordon, Dexter, 281
Granz, Norman, 205
Green, Benny, 23–4
Green, Charlie, 97, 98, 99, 236, 252–3, 272
Guimaraes, L., 185

Hackett, Bobby, 200, 216, 242, 286
Hadlock, Richard, 94
Haggart, Bob, 200
Halberstam, David, 229
Hall, Edmond, 28, 32, 45, 202, 221, 242, 282, 283
Hall, Henry, 169
Hall, Minor, 282
Hall, Tubby, 110, 144, 153, 269
Hamilton, Jack, 185
Hammond, John, 154, 172, 173, 174
Hampton, Lionel, 127–9, 196, 269
Hardin, Lillian see Armstrong, Lillian
Hardy, Emmett, 19
Hawkins, Coleman, 98, 99, 158, 181–3, 236, 251, 281
Haydon, Geoffrey, 62, 90, 228
Hayes, Harry, 169
Hayman, Joe, 163
Hayton, Lenny, 217
Hemphill, Shelton 'Scad', 195, 242, 278
Henderson, Fletcher, 34, 62, 90, 93, 94–103, 108, 111, 113, 116, 118, 123, 126, 127, 141, 195, 236–7, 249, 250, 251, 254, 256
Hibbler, Al, 223
Higginbotham, J. C., 192, 202, 267, 278
Hill, Alex, 265
Hill, Chippie, 60, 104, 114, 256–7
Hinchcliffe, Edwin, 213
Hines, Earl, 16, 110, 111, 117, 121, 174, 201, 242, 262, 263–6, 268, 283
Hite, Les, 127, 129, 155
Hobson, Homer, 122
Hobson, Wilder, 201
Hodeir, André, 112
Hodes, Art, 118
Hodges, Johnny, 282
Holiday, Billie, 39, 166, 196, 207
Holmes, Charlie, 190, 193, 276
Holzfiend, Frank, 28–9
Howard, Kid, 115
Hucko, Peanuts, 200, 242, 283
Hughes, Spike, 162, 169, 174, 176
Hunt, Pee Wee, 277
Hunter, Alberta, 60, 251

299

Hylton, Jack, 162, 168, 180, 181–2, 183

Immerman, Connie, 124, 155
Ingman, Dan, 49, 163–4, 166–8, 176, 178–9, 183
Iona, Andy, 196
Irvis, Charlie, 256

Jackson, Edgar, 49–50, 169
Jackson, Preston, 56, 65, 66, 71, 72–3, 84, 93, 108, 117–18, 144, 146–7, 152, 153, 154
Jackson, Rudy, 66, 88, 89, 90
Jackson, Tony, 151
Jacobson, Bud, 114
James, Burnett, 84
James, George, 153
Jefferson, Maceo, 163, 185
Johnson, Bill, 64, 88
Johnson, Budd, 174, 272, 274
Johnson, Bunk, 15, 47, 53–4, 55, 63, 74, 242
Johnson, Charlie, 163
Johnson, Keg, 174, 272
Johnson, Lonnie, 263, 266
Jolson, Al, 268
Jones, 'Captain' Joseph, 52, 53, 54, 232
Jones, Clarence, 111
Jones, David, 61, 94, 234
Jones, Isham, 66
Jones, Jonah, 39
Jones, Maggie, 60, 104, 116, 236, 253
Jones, Richard M., 114, 256
Jordan, Louis, 196

Kaminsky, Max, 115, 116, 206, 208, 231, 248
Kapp, Dave, 145
Kaye, Danny, 16
Kelly, Chris, 71
Kemp, Hal, 158
Kempton, Murray, 216
Keppard, Freddie, 16, 18, 47, 85, 107–8, 242
Kitt, Eartha, 205
Kyle, Billy, 220, 242, 283

Lala, Pete, 55, 58, 233
Lang, Eddie, 119, 126
Lang, Iain, 162, 179

Langford, Frances, 196
Lanin, Sam, 95, 256
Larkin, Philip, 231
Laurie, Cy, 29
LaVere, Charles, 275
Lawrence, Charlie, 269
Lee, Peggy, 223
Lesburg, Jack, 243
Levine, Henry, 157
Lewis, George, 41
Lewis, Ted, 158, 177
Lewis, Vic, 29
Lindsey, Joe, 56, 58, 117, 269
Liston, Virginia, 251
Little Mack, 48
Livingston, Fud, 157
Lombardo, Guy, 130, 177, 269
Long, Johnny, 188
Longshaw, Fred, 104, 252
Lyttelton, Humphrey, 29, 30, 34, 39, 201, 218, 229

McCarrie, Prentice, 189
McCarthy, Albert, 192, 206
McCord, Castor, 185
McKendrick, Mike, 139, 153, 239, 240, 272
McKenzie, Red, 157
Macqueen-Pope, W., 169
McRae, Teddy, 240
Madison, Bingie, 190, 193, 276
Madison, Kid Shots, 19
Mangel, Ira, 218, 223
Mann, Freddy, 169
Manone, Wingy, 39, 61
Marable, Fate, 16, 60, 61, 234
Mares, Paul, 65
Marshall, Kaiser, 94, 96–7, 98, 119–20, 236
Martin, Sara, 114
Mason, Billy, 168, 169, 172, 178
Mather, Bill, 172–3
Matranga, Henry, 57, 58, 233
Mellers, Wilfrid, 81, 113
Mendl, R. W., 159
Mercer, Johnny, 215, 216
Meryman, Richard, 62, 100, 197
Mezzrow, Mezz, 126, 132, 152–3, 155, 165, 173–4, 188, 238
Middleton, Velma, 29, 33, 215, 216, 244, 281
Miles, Flora, 110
Miley, Bubber, 242

Miller, Ann, 196
Miller, Paul Eduard, 126
Miller, Punch, 71
Mills Blue Rhythm Band, 124, 195, 268, 271
Mills Brothers, 196, 277
Mills, Irving, 179
Mitchell, George, 106
Mole, Miff, 126
Moran, Bugs, 121
Moret, George, 234
Morgan, Russ, 269
Morgan, Sam, 71
Morton, Jelly Roll, 41, 43, 74, 191, 238, 252
Muranyi, Joe, 220, 243
Murrow, Ed, 31, 32

Nance, Ray, 188
Napoleon, Marty, 220
Nicholas, Albert, 40, 45, 53, 192, 193, 195, 278
Nichols, Red, 126
Nina and Frederick, 196
Nkrumah, Kwame, 33
Noble, Ray, 168
Noone, Jimmie, 57, 188, 263

Oldham, Bill, 189
Oldham, George, 189
Oliver, Joe 'King', 15, 19, 23, 29, 33, 34, 37, 40, 47, 54, 56, 58, 60, 62, 64–91, 93, 94, 95, 103, 104, 107, 112, 113, 114, 141, 150, 152, 194, 197, 228–9, 230, 233, 234–5, 241, 242, 245, 248, 249, 252, 258, 275, 277
Oliver, Stella, 73
Ory, Kid, 58, 60, 62, 85, 108, 114, 199, 215, 216, 234, 237, 256, 257, 258, 260, 261, 262, 263, 282
Ostransky, Leroy, 81
Owen, Sid, 169

Page, Hot Lips, 39, 108, 115
Panassié, Hugues, 48, 81, 104, 186, 240
Parham, Tiny, 188
Parker, Daisy see Armstrong, Daisy
Perez, Emmanuel, 15, 241
Perritt, Harry, 169

Petit, Buddy, 18, 71, 86
Pleasants, Henry, 39
Polo, Danny, 157
Ponce, Henry, 57
Powers, Ollie, 91, 92, 110
Pratt, Alfred, 185
Price, Sammy, 116
Prima, Louis, 39
Primrose, William, 176
Prince, Gene, 189
Pugh, 'Doc', 31

Quealey, Chelsea, 157

Rainey, Ma, 60, 104, 116, 251, 252, 253
Ramsey, Frederic, 68
Randall, Freddy, 29
Randolph, Zilner, 139, 146, 153, 174, 189, 239, 240, 269, 272
Rayes, Benn, 29
Razaf, Andy, 124
Redman, Don, 95, 96, 98, 237, 238, 250, 265
Reinhardt, Django, 186
Rena, Kid, 18, 56, 71
Reuss, Allen, 282
Robbins, Fred, 201
Robertson, Zue, 57
Robeson, Paul, 245
Robinson, Fred, 122, 264
Rockwell, Thomas, 119, 120, 123, 124, 145–6, 154
Rodgers, Jimmie, 268
Rolfe, B. A., 242
Rollini, Adrian, 157
Rollini, Arthur, 157
Rosebery, Arthur, 169
Rushton, Joe, 275
Russell, Luis, 119, 124, 127, 141, 189–95, 198, 240, 241, 266, 267, 275, 276, 278, 279
Rust, Brian, 78
Ryan, Jimmy, 201

St Cyr, Johnny, 61, 256, 257, 263
Sebastian, Frank, 124, 127
Schleman, Hilton, 48
Schonfield, Victor, 115, 130–1
Schuller, Gunther, 81, 192
Scott, Bud, 282
Scott, Howard, 251
Selmer, Henri, 49

Shaw, Artie, 195
Shaw, Arvell, 16, 201, 243, 283
Singleton, Marge (Creathe), 60, 121
Singleton, Zutty, 60–1, 117, 119, 121, 122, 127, 188, 264, 265, 275, 282
Smith, Alpha see Armstrong, Alpha
Smith, Bessie, 34, 60, 104, 116, 141, 236, 251–3
Smith, Clara, 60, 104
Smith, Jabbo, 18, 108
Smith, Joe, 95, 104, 242, 250, 251, 252, 253
Smith, Leroy, 124
Smith, Russell, 123
Smith, Shrod, 189
Smith, Trixie, 60, 104
Snowden, Elmer, 101
Spanier, Muggsy, 65, 106, 115, 250
Spivey, Victoria, 266
Starita, Ray, 169
Stearns, Marshall, 126
Stewart, Rex, 95, 101, 115, 221, 242, 248
Stewart, Sammy, 90, 235
Stone, Lew, 168
Streisand, Barbra, 217, 218
Strong, Jimmy, 122, 264
Sullivan, Joe, 119
Sylvester, Robert, 201

Tate, Erskine, 106, 107, 110, 111, 113, 114, 237, 259
Tate, Jimmy, 106, 237
Tatum, Art, 281
Taylor, Eva, 255
Teagarden, Jack, 16, 39, 61–2, 116, 119, 126, 199–200, 201, 206, 215, 216, 221, 231, 242, 266, 277, 281, 283
Teschmaker, Frank, 65
Thacker, Audrey, 186
Thomas, Hociel, 60, 256
Thomas, James, 189
Thomas, John, 261
Tines, Oliver, 185
Toff, Dave, 166, 169
Törner, Gösta, 25

Trent, Alphonso, 118
Tyree, Henry, 245

Ulanov, Barry, 37, 77, 100

Venuti, Joe, 126, 158
Voce, Steve, 208

Wallace, Sippie, 60, 114, 257
Waller, Fats, 33, 124, 130, 158, 213, 284
Walton, Greely, 190, 276
Walton, William, 176
Waring, Fred, 177
Washington, Buck, 268
Washington, Leon, 189
Washington, Al, 153
Waters, Ethel, 68–9
Watson, Clay, 22, 52
Watts, Grady, 277
Weatherford, Teddy, 259
Webb, Chick, 172, 173–4, 188, 195, 272
Webster, Ben, 123
Welsh, Nolan, 60
West, Mae, 196
Wethington, Crawford, 122
Wettling, George, 65, 66, 200, 220–1, 230
White, Bill, 169
White, Harry, 190
Whiteman, Paul, 177
Williams, Clarence, 34, 103, 236, 250, 254, 255
Williams, Cootie, 39, 242
Williams, Elmer, 272
Williams, Martin, 36, 48, 81
Williams, Spencer, 155
Wilson, Garland, 178, 185
Wilson, Lucille see Armstrong, Lucille
Wilson, Teddy, 174, 272, 273, 285
Winnick, Maurice, 169

Yorke, Peter, 168
Youmans, Vincent, 120
Young, Trummy, 30, 32, 229, 243, 283

Zeno, Henry, 61